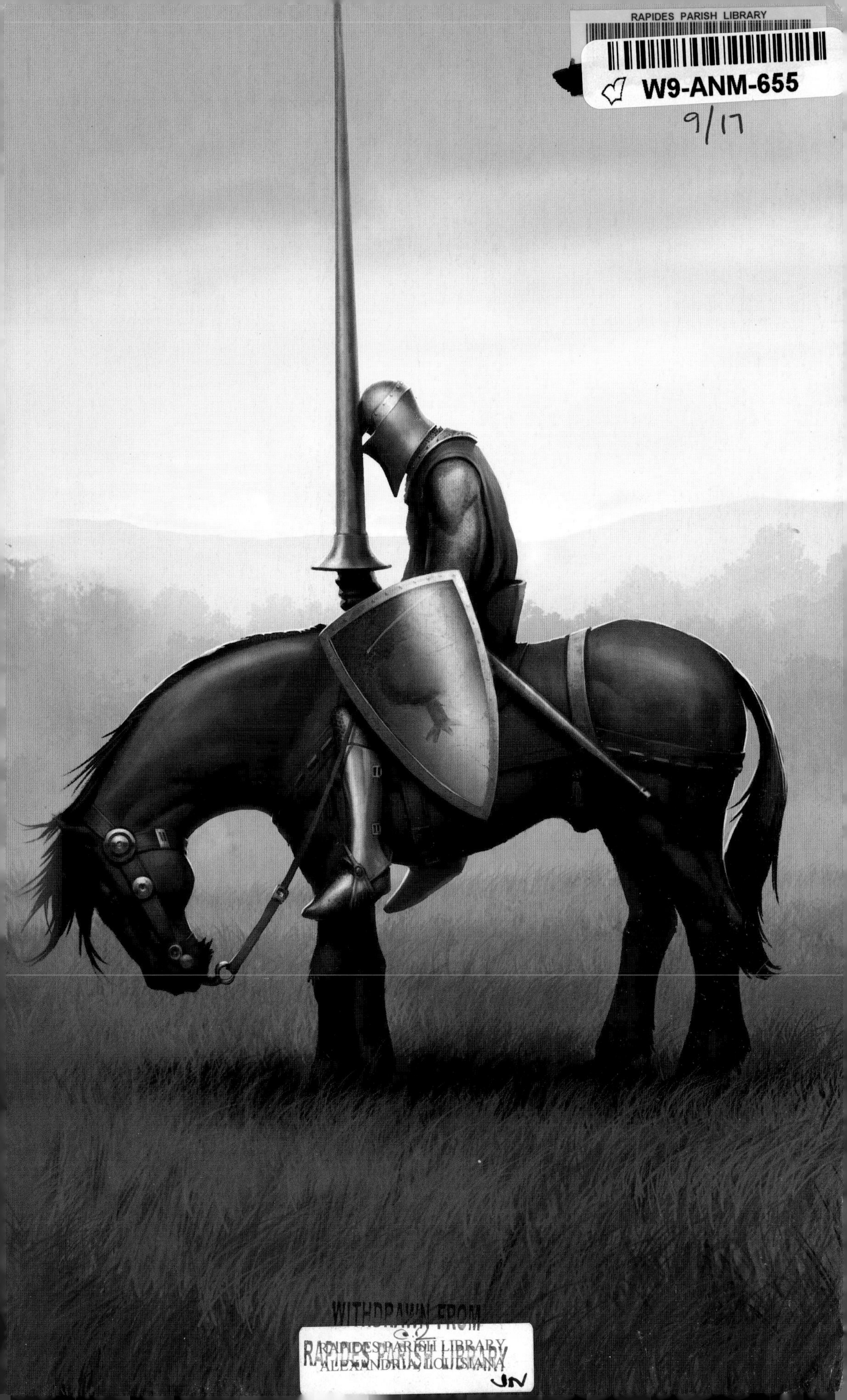

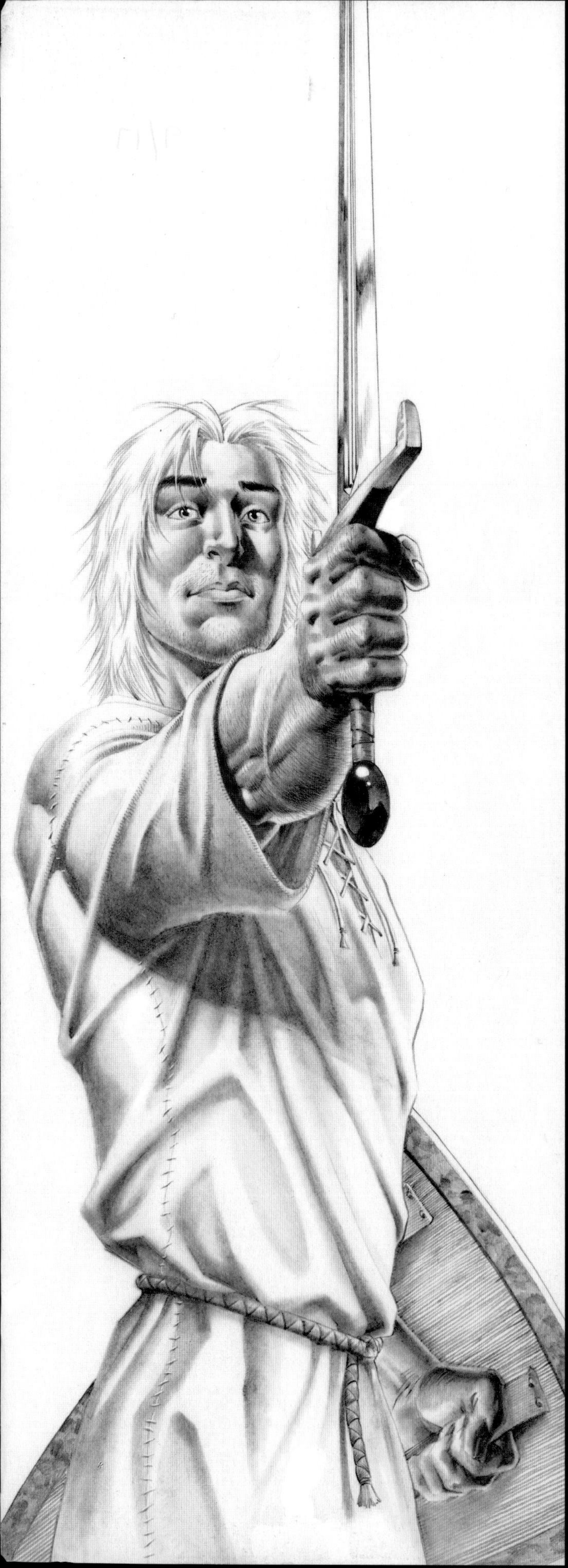

George R. R. Martin's The Hedge Knight
The Graphic Novel

WRITTEN BY
GEORGE R. R. MARTIN

ADAPTATION BY
BEN AVERY

PENCILS BY
MIKE S. MILLER

COLORS BY
MIKE CROWELL

COLORS BY
TEAM KANDORA
TRANSPARENCY DIGITAL

LETTERED BY
BILL TORTOLINI
LITHIUM PRO DESIGN

COVER ART BY
MIKE S. MILLER

COVER COLORED BY
MOHAN SIVAKAMI

EDITED BY
ROBERT SILVERBERG

THEMATIC CONSULTANTS
ELIO M. GARCIA &
LINDA ANTONSSON

JET CITY COMICS EDITION DESIGN BY
DERON BENNETT
ANDWORLD DESIGN

SENIOR PRODUCTION MANAGER
JILL TAPLIN

SENIOR COLLECTION EDITOR
ALEX CARR

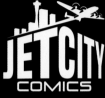

Published by Jet City Comics, Seattle www.apub.com
Library of Congress Catalog Number: 2013914372
ISBN-13: 9781477849101 ISBN-10: 1477849106 EISBN: 9781477899106

ISSUE ONE
COVER A

MIKE S. MILLER

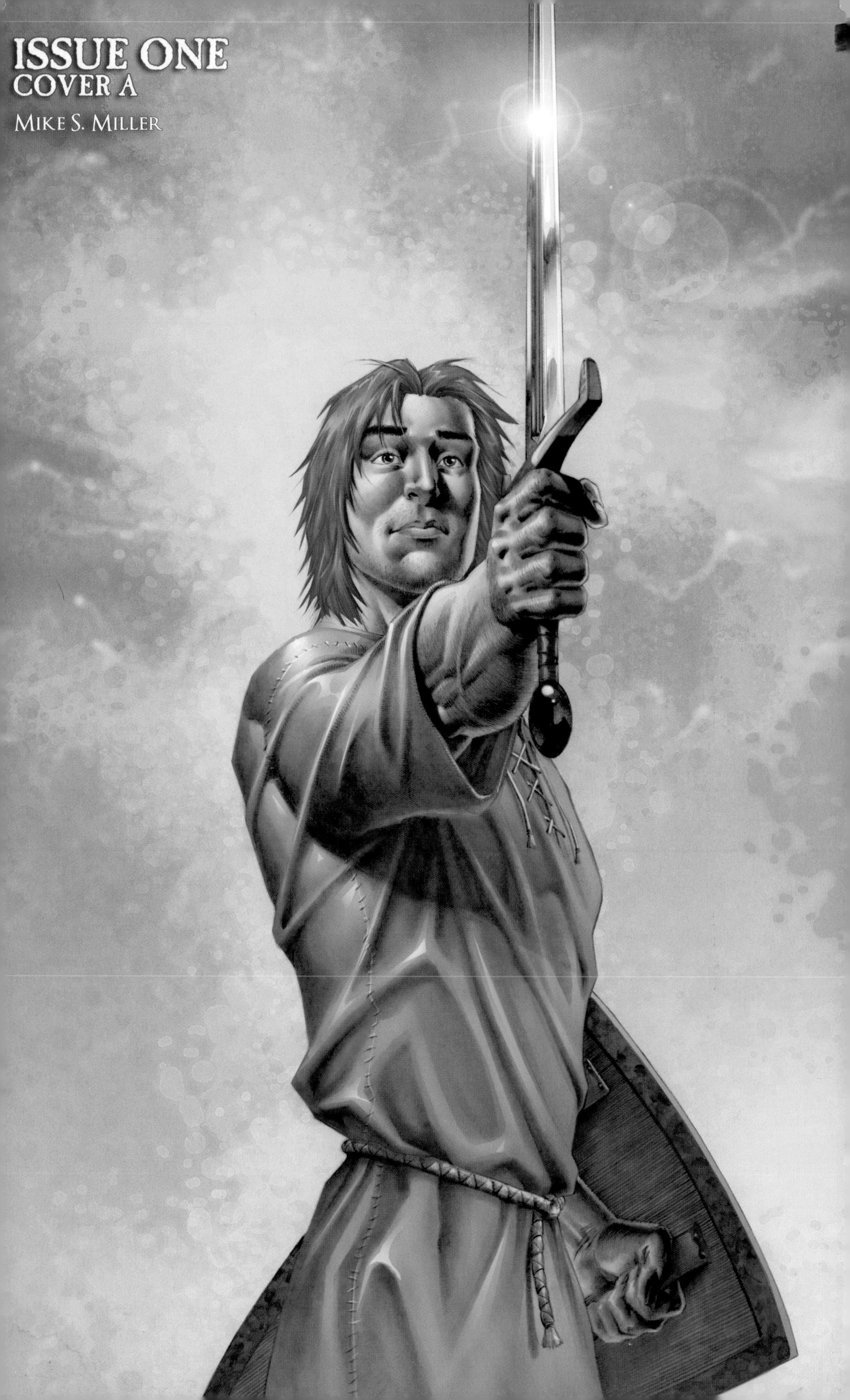

ISSUE ONE
COVER B

MICHAEL KALUTA

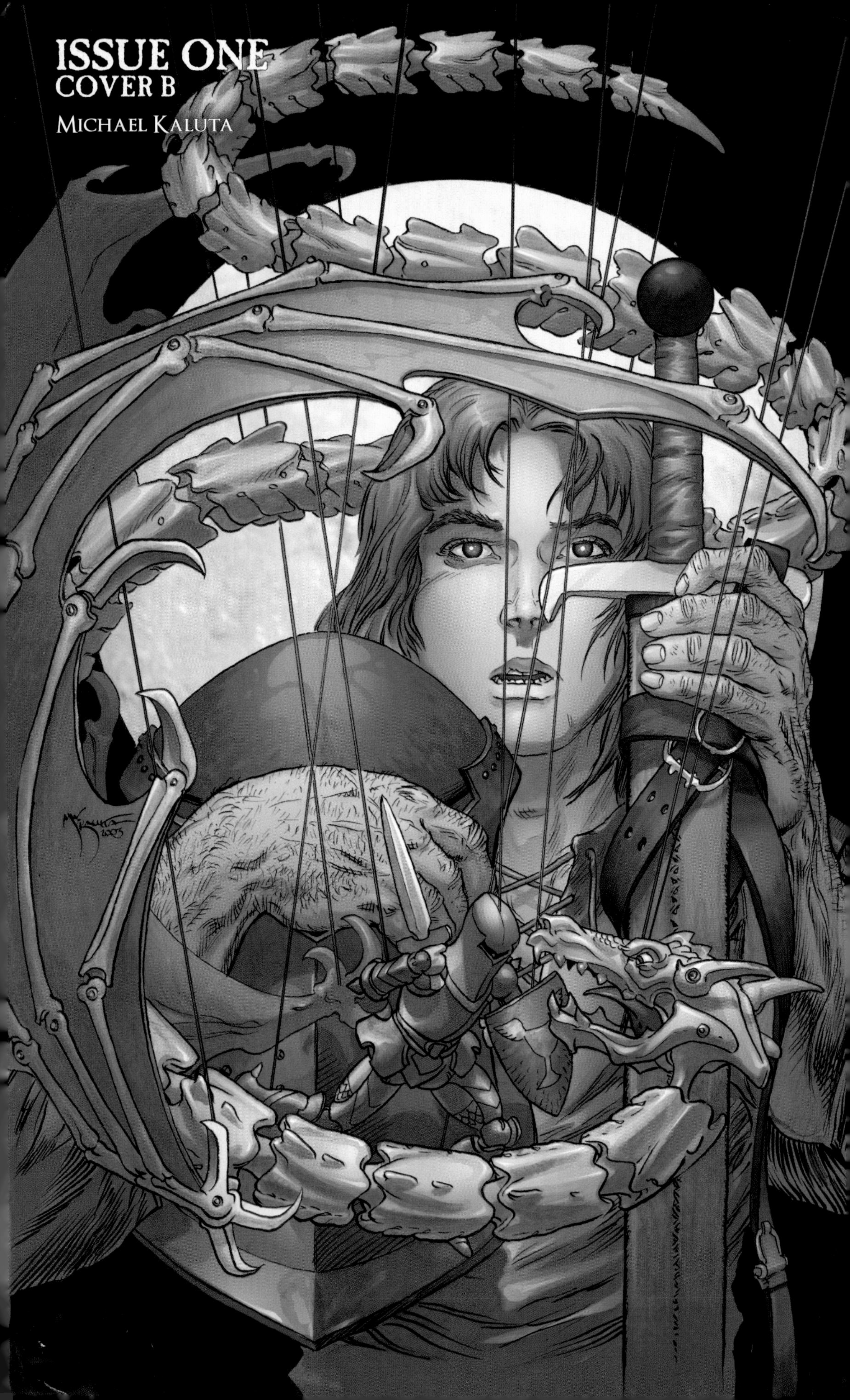

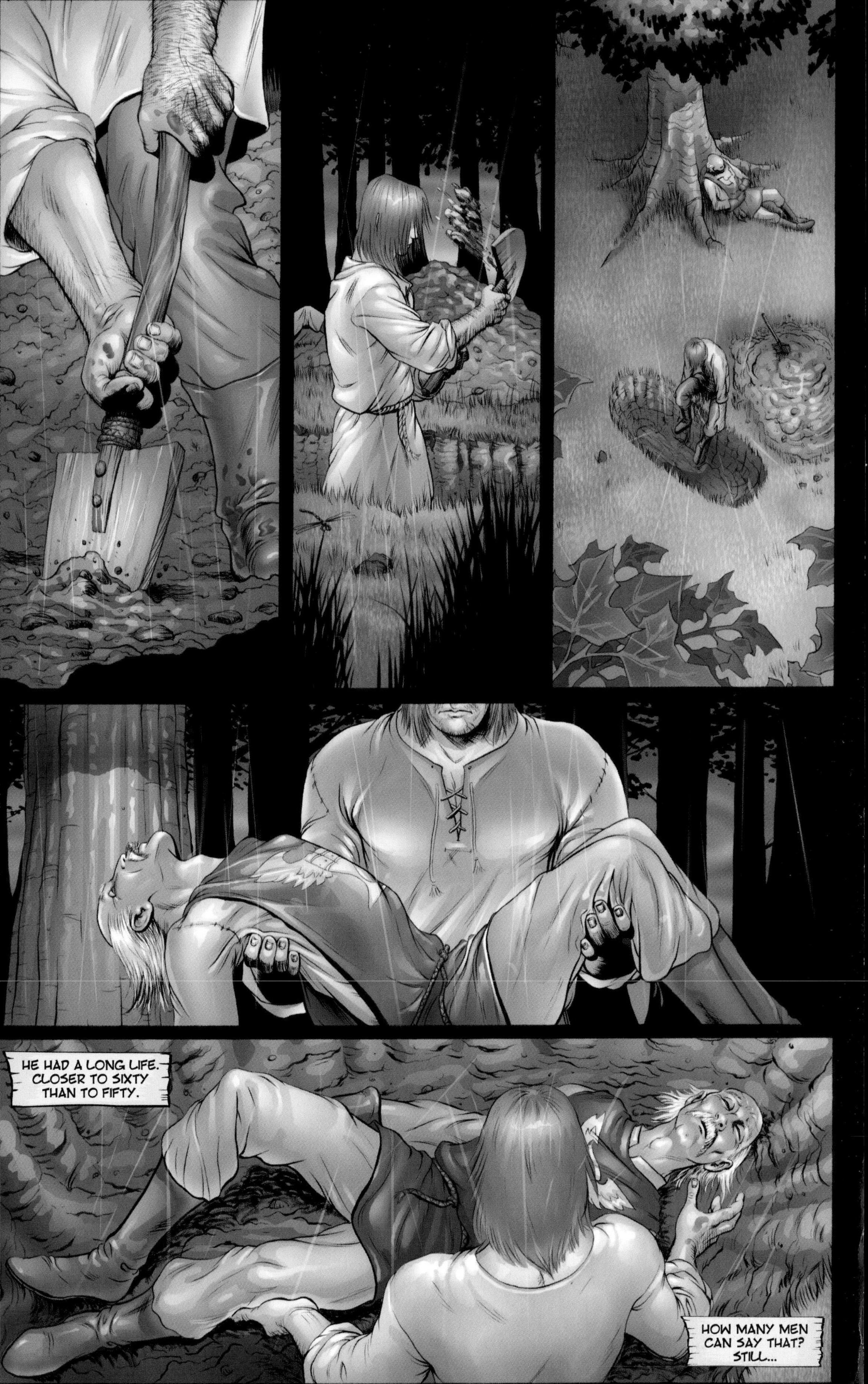
HE HAD A LONG LIFE. CLOSER TO SIXTY THAN TO FIFTY.
HOW MANY MEN CAN SAY THAT? STILL...

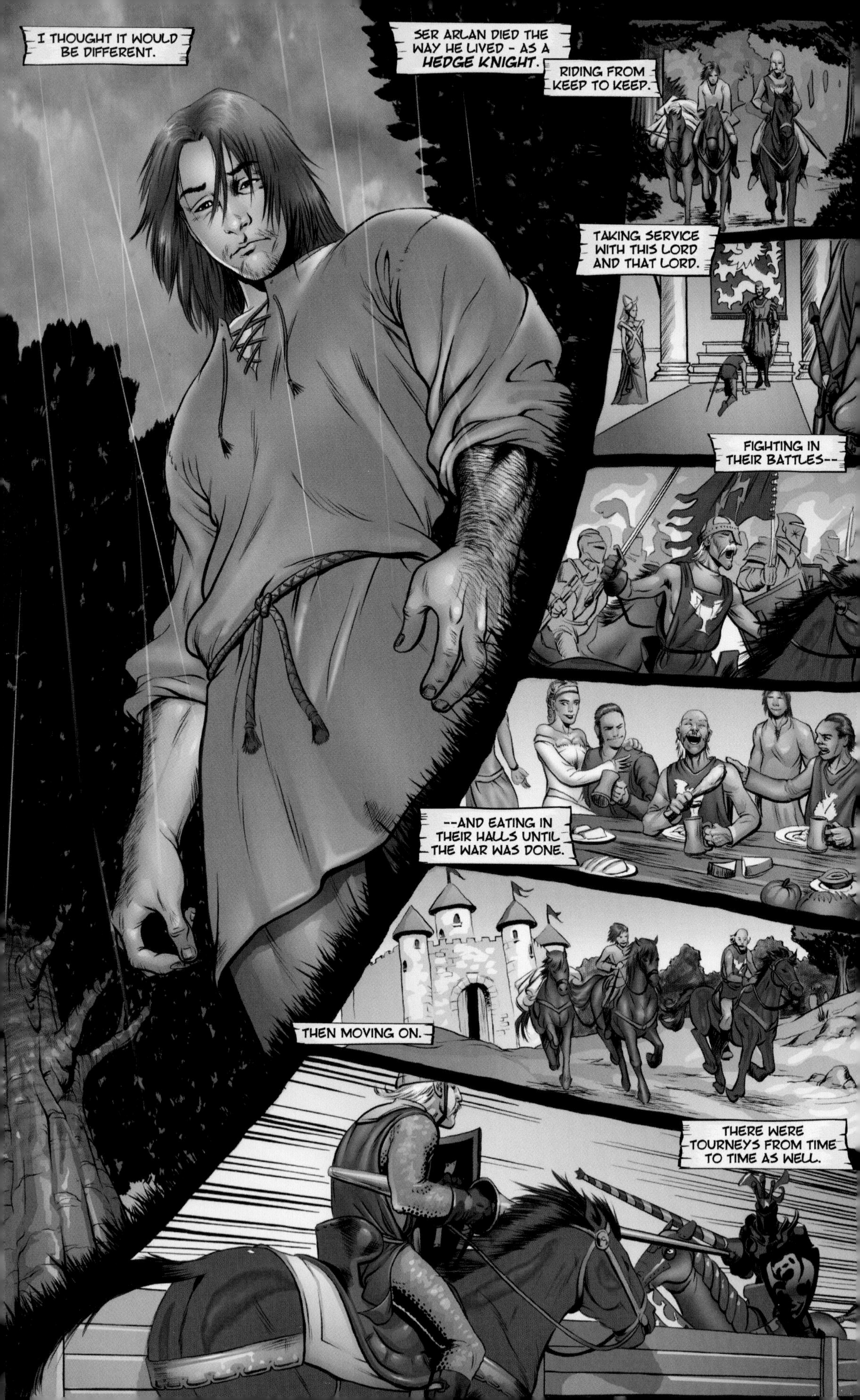
I THOUGHT IT WOULD BE DIFFERENT.
SER ARLAN DIED THE WAY HE LIVED - AS A HEDGE KNIGHT.
RIDING FROM KEEP TO KEEP.
TAKING SERVICE WITH THIS LORD AND THAT LORD.
FIGHTING IN THEIR BATTLES--
--AND EATING IN THEIR HALLS UNTIL THE WAR WAS DONE.
THEN MOVING ON.
THERE WERE TOURNEYS FROM TIME TO TIME AS WELL.

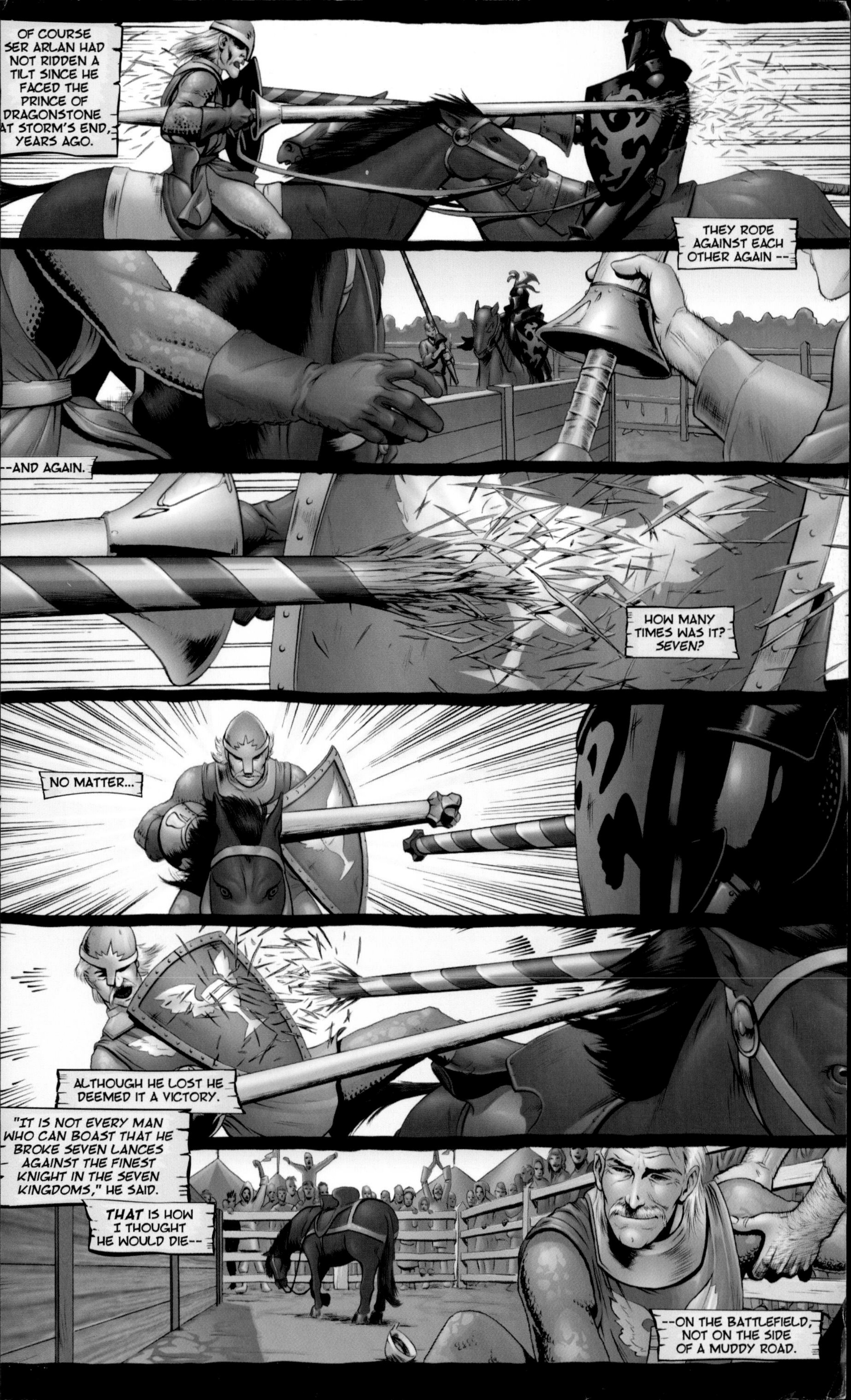

OF COURSE SER ARLAN HAD NOT RIDDEN A TILT SINCE HE FACED THE PRINCE OF DRAGONSTONE AT STORM'S END, YEARS AGO.
THEY RODE AGAINST EACH OTHER AGAIN --
--AND AGAIN.
HOW MANY TIMES WAS IT? SEVEN?
NO MATTER...
ALTHOUGH HE LOST HE DEEMED IT A VICTORY.
"IT IS NOT EVERY MAN WHO CAN BOAST THAT HE BROKE SEVEN LANCES AGAINST THE FINEST KNIGHT IN THE SEVEN KINGDOMS," HE SAID.
THAT IS HOW I THOUGHT HE WOULD DIE--
--ON THE BATTLEFIELD, NOT ON THE SIDE OF A MUDDY ROAD.

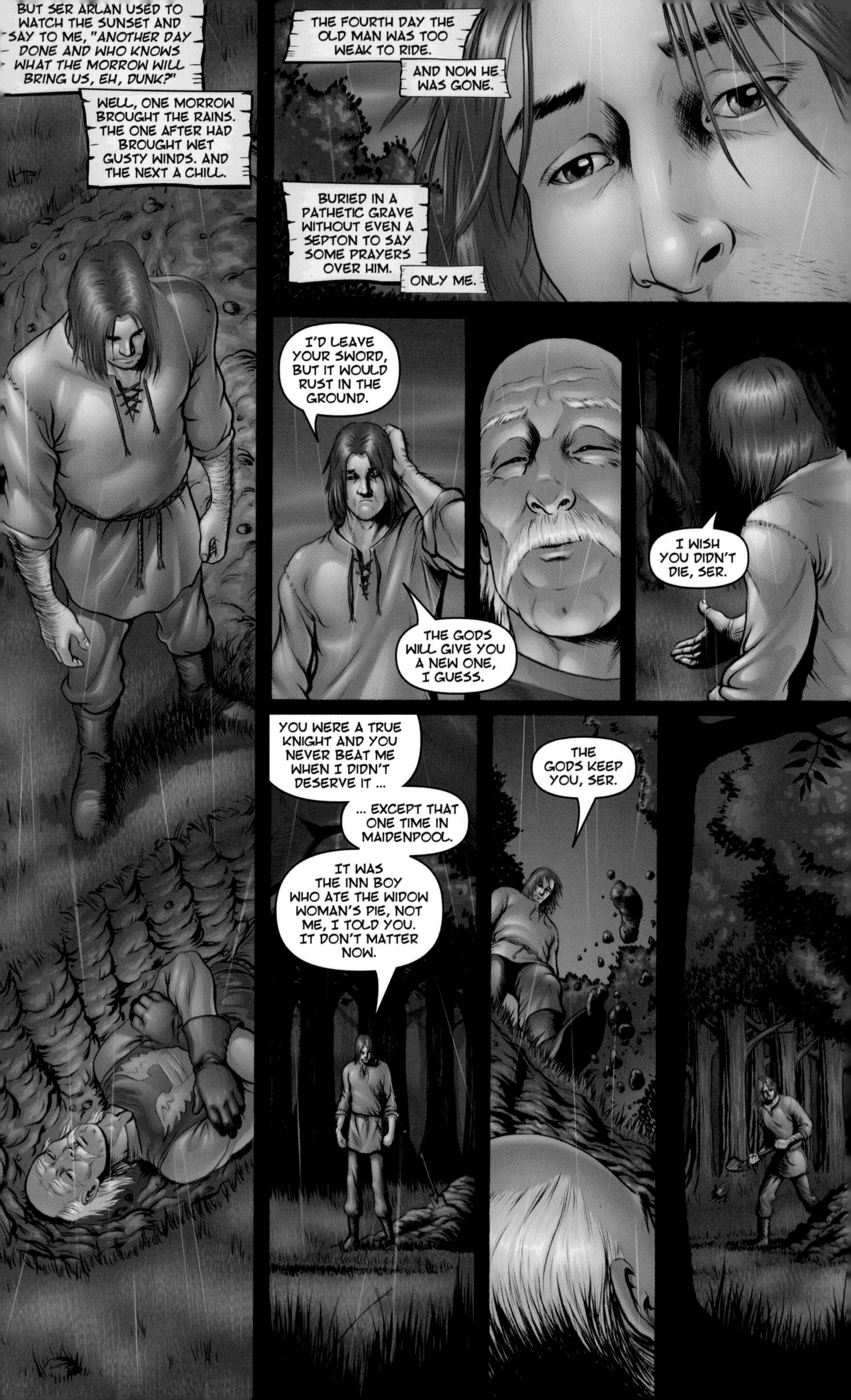
BUT SER ARLAN USED TO WATCH THE SUNSET AND SAY TO ME, "ANOTHER DAY DONE AND WHO KNOWS WHAT THE MORROW WILL BRING US, EH, DUNK?"
WELL, ONE MORROW BROUGHT THE RAINS. THE ONE AFTER HAD BROUGHT WET GUSTY WINDS. AND THE NEXT A CHILL.
THE FOURTH DAY THE OLD MAN WAS TOO WEAK TO RIDE.
AND NOW HE WAS GONE.
BURIED IN A PATHETIC GRAVE WITHOUT EVEN A SEPTON TO SAY SOME PRAYERS OVER HIM.
ONLY ME.
I'D LEAVE YOUR SWORD, BUT IT WOULD RUST IN THE GROUND.
THE GODS WILL GIVE YOU A NEW ONE, I GUESS.
I WISH YOU DIDN'T DIE, SER.
YOU WERE A TRUE KNIGHT AND YOU NEVER BEAT ME WHEN I DIDN'T DESERVE IT ...
... EXCEPT THAT ONE TIME IN MAIDENPOOL.
IT WAS THE INN BOY WHO ATE THE WIDOW WOMAN'S PIE, NOT ME, I TOLD YOU. IT DON'T MATTER NOW.
THE GODS KEEP YOU, SER.

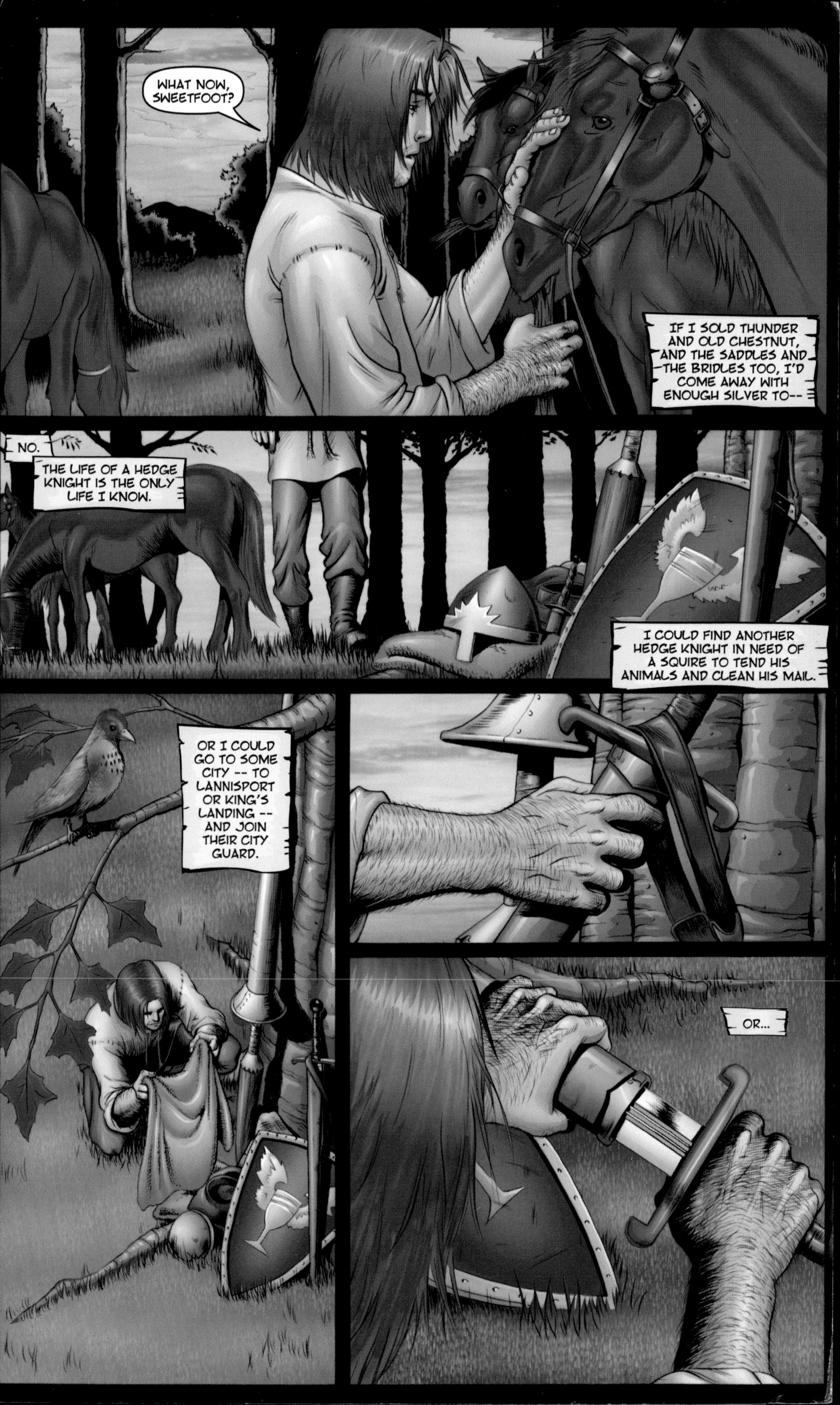
WHAT NOW, SWEETFOOT?
IF I SOLD THUNDER AND OLD CHESTNUT, AND THE SADDLES AND THE BRIDLES TOO, I'D COME AWAY WITH ENOUGH SILVER TO--
NO.
THE LIFE OF A HEDGE KNIGHT IS THE ONLY LIFE I KNOW.
I COULD FIND ANOTHER HEDGE KNIGHT IN NEED OF A SQUIRE TO TEND HIS ANIMALS AND CLEAN HIS MAIL.
OR I COULD GO TO SOME CITY -- TO LANNISPORT OR KING'S LANDING -- AND JOIN THEIR CITY GUARD.
OR...

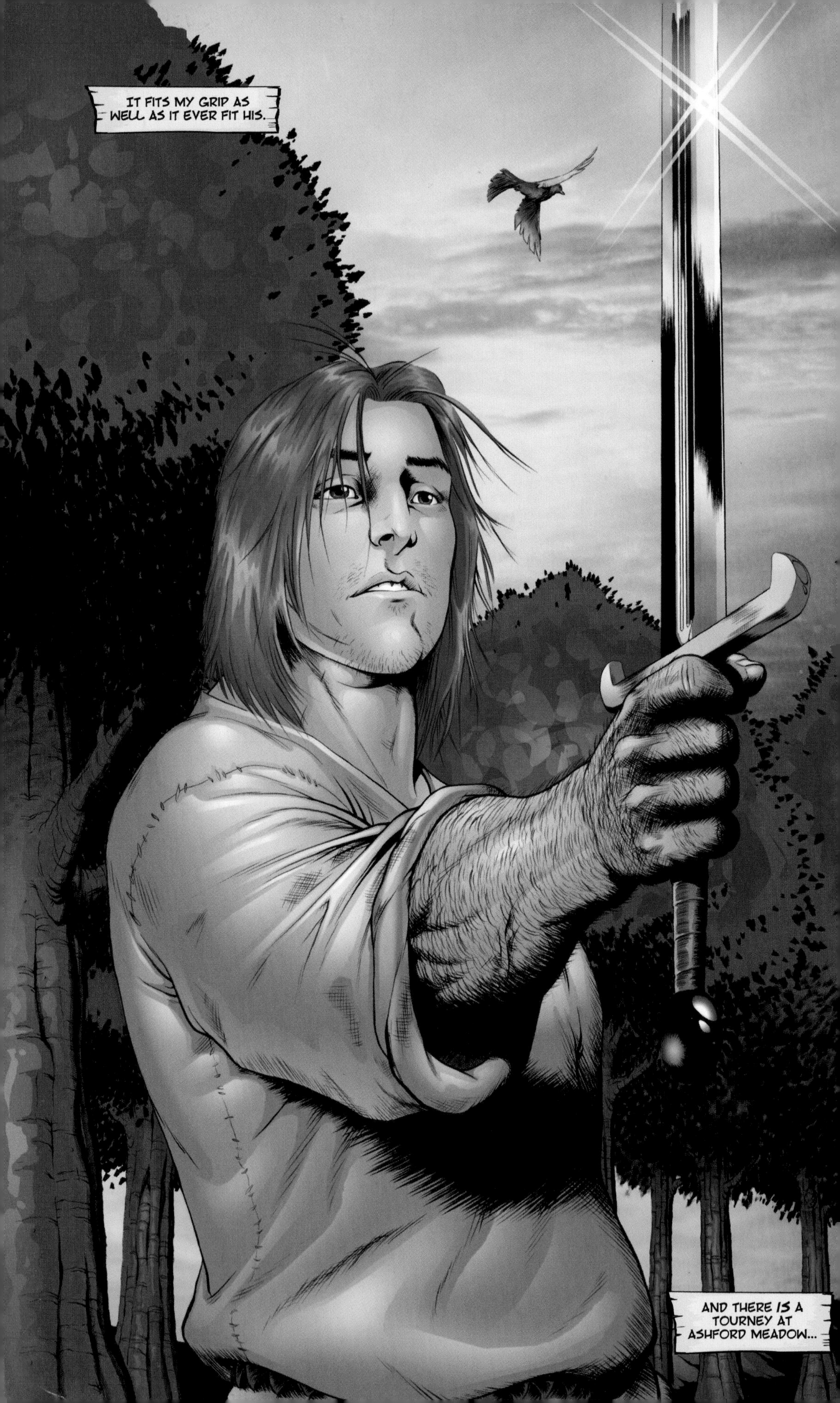
IT FITS MY GRIP AS WELL AS IT EVER FIT HIS.
AND THERE IS A TOURNEY AT ASHFORD MEADOW...

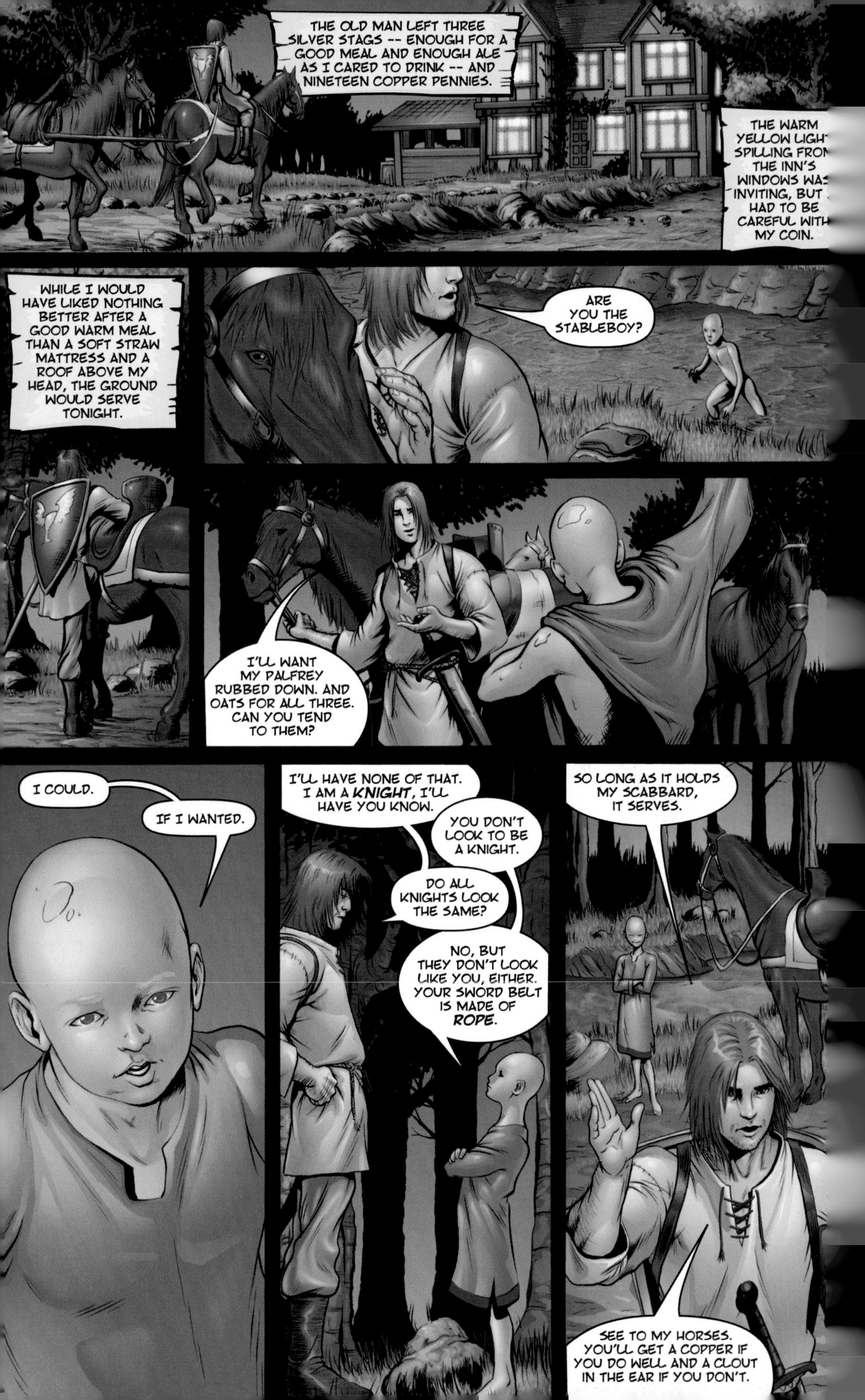

THE OLD MAN LEFT THREE SILVER STAGS -- ENOUGH FOR A GOOD MEAL AND ENOUGH ALE AS I CARED TO DRINK -- AND NINETEEN COPPER PENNIES.
THE WARM YELLOW LIGHT SPILLING FROM THE INN'S WINDOWS WAS INVITING, BUT I HAD TO BE CAREFUL WITH MY COIN.
WHILE I WOULD HAVE LIKED NOTHING BETTER AFTER A GOOD WARM MEAL THAN A SOFT STRAW MATTRESS AND A ROOF ABOVE MY HEAD, THE GROUND WOULD SERVE TONIGHT.
ARE YOU THE STABLEBOY?
I'LL WANT MY PALFREY RUBBED DOWN. AND OATS FOR ALL THREE. CAN YOU TEND TO THEM?
I COULD.
IF I WANTED.
I'LL HAVE NONE OF THAT. I AM A *KNIGHT*, I'LL HAVE YOU KNOW.
YOU DON'T LOOK TO BE A KNIGHT.
DO ALL KNIGHTS LOOK THE SAME?
NO, BUT THEY DON'T LOOK LIKE YOU, EITHER. YOUR SWORD BELT IS MADE OF *ROPE*.
SO LONG AS IT HOLDS MY SCABBARD, IT SERVES.
SEE TO MY HORSES. YOU'LL GET A COPPER IF YOU DO WELL AND A CLOUT IN THE EAR IF YOU DON'T.

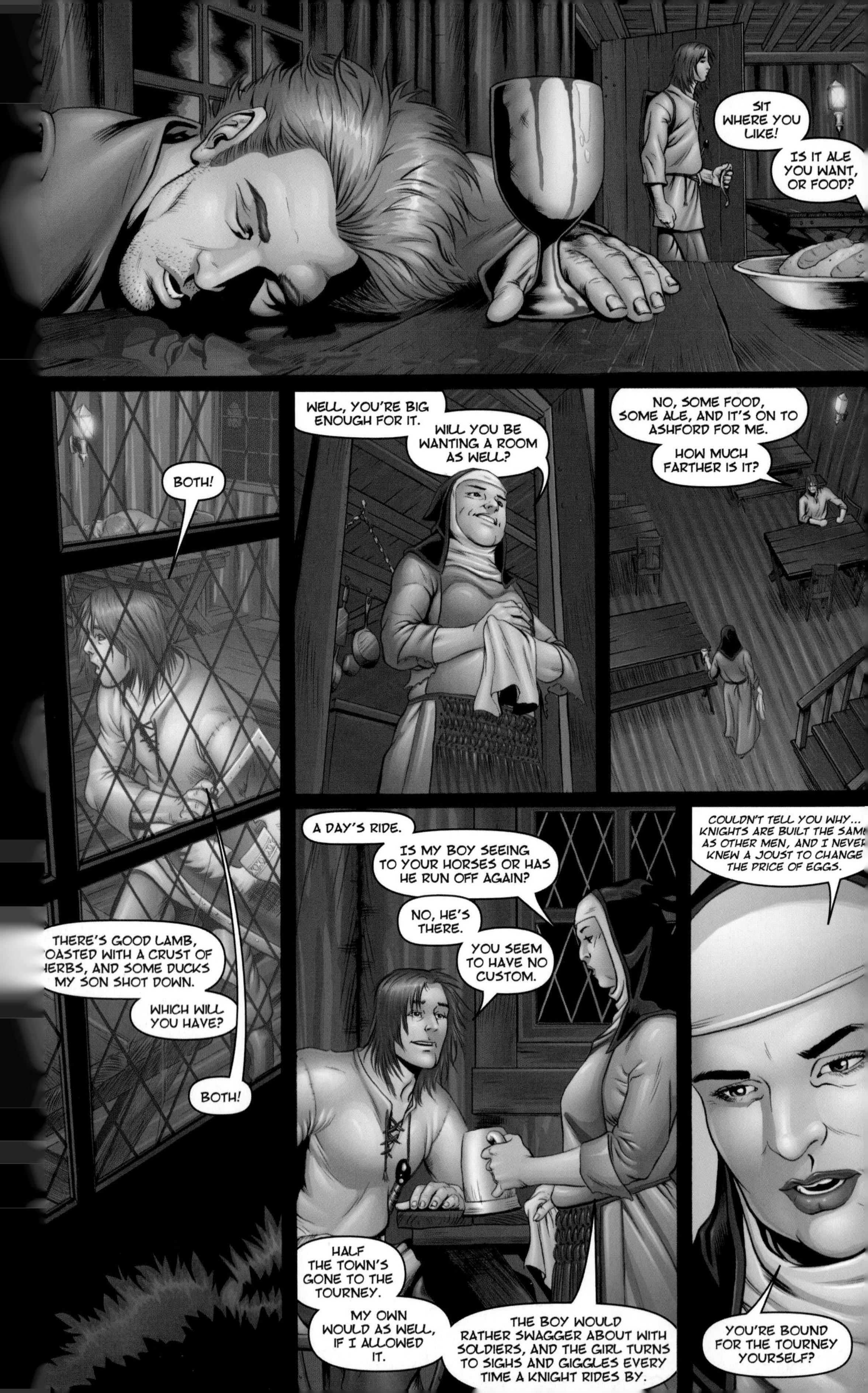
SIT WHERE YOU LIKE!
IS IT ALE YOU WANT, OR FOOD?
BOTH!
WELL, YOU'RE BIG ENOUGH FOR IT.
WILL YOU BE WANTING A ROOM AS WELL?
NO, SOME FOOD, SOME ALE, AND IT'S ON TO ASHFORD FOR ME.
HOW MUCH FARTHER IS IT?
THERE'S GOOD LAMB, ROASTED WITH A CRUST OF HERBS, AND SOME DUCKS MY SON SHOT DOWN.
WHICH WILL YOU HAVE?
BOTH!
A DAY'S RIDE.
IS MY BOY SEEING TO YOUR HORSES OR HAS HE RUN OFF AGAIN?
NO, HE'S THERE.
YOU SEEM TO HAVE NO CUSTOM.
HALF THE TOWN'S GONE TO THE TOURNEY.
MY OWN WOULD AS WELL, IF I ALLOWED IT.
THE BOY WOULD RATHER SWAGGER ABOUT WITH SOLDIERS, AND THE GIRL TURNS TO SIGHS AND GIGGLES EVERY TIME A KNIGHT RIDES BY.
COULDN'T TELL YOU WHY... KNIGHTS ARE BUILT THE SAME AS OTHER MEN, AND I NEVER KNEW A JOUST TO CHANGE THE PRICE OF EGGS.
YOU'RE BOUND FOR THE TOURNEY YOURSELF?

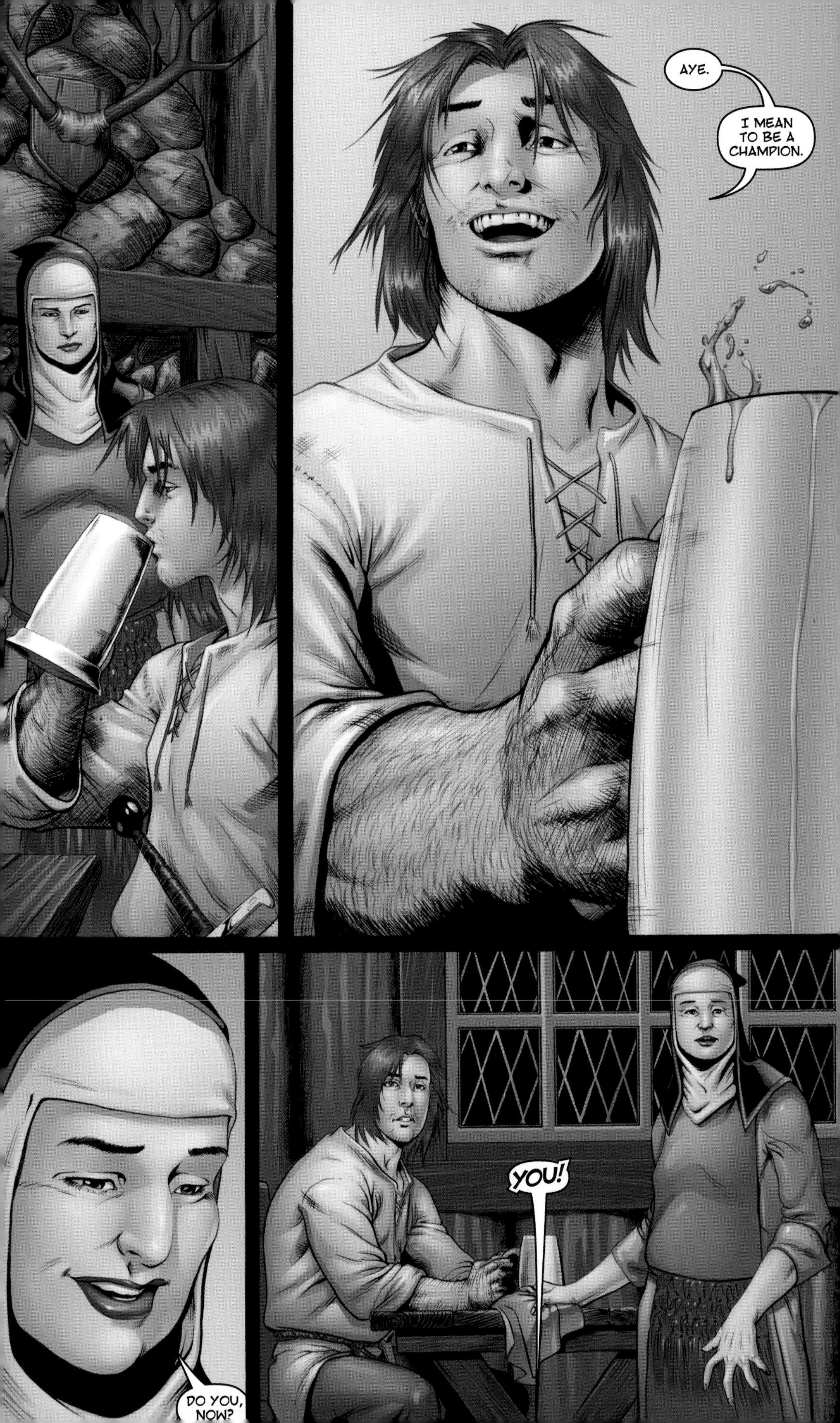
AYE.
I MEAN TO BE A CHAMPION.
DO YOU, NOW?
YOU!

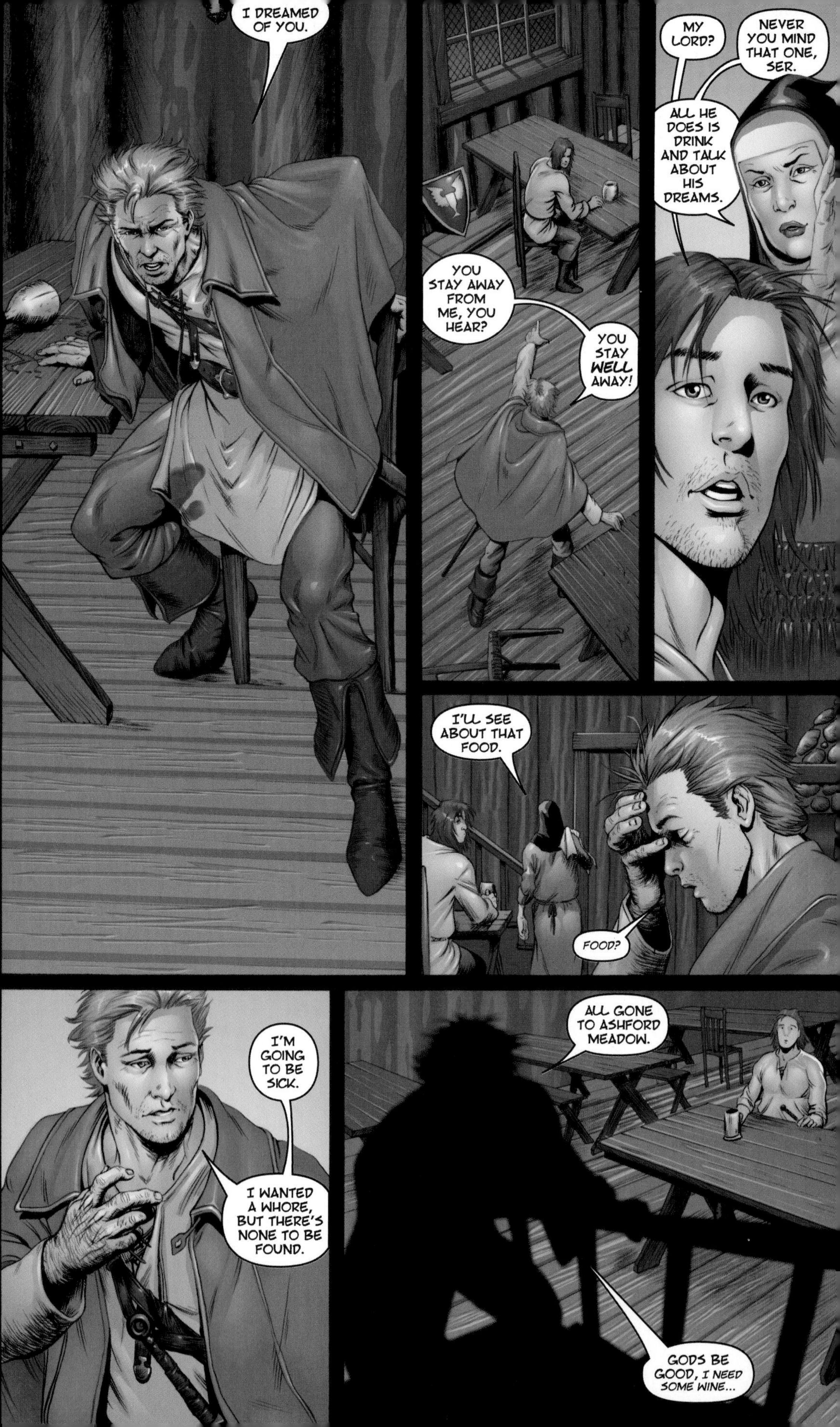
I DREAMED OF YOU.
MY LORD?
NEVER YOU MIND THAT ONE, SER.
ALL HE DOES IS DRINK AND TALK ABOUT HIS DREAMS.
YOU STAY AWAY FROM ME, YOU HEAR?
YOU STAY **WELL** AWAY!
I'LL SEE ABOUT THAT FOOD.
FOOD?
I'M GOING TO BE SICK.
I WANTED A WHORE, BUT THERE'S NONE TO BE FOUND.
ALL GONE TO ASHFORD MEADOW.
GODS BE GOOD, I NEED SOME WINE...

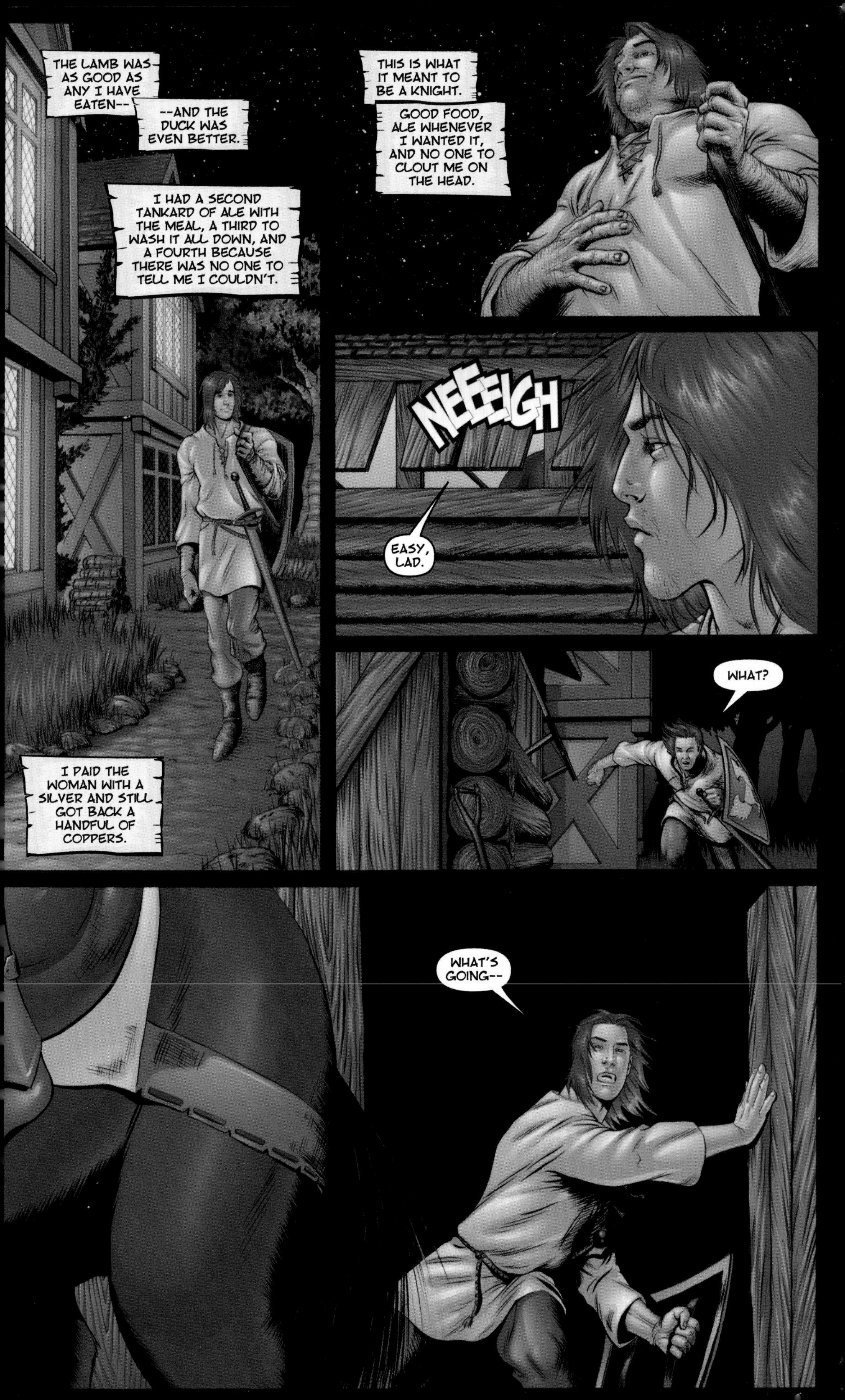
THE LAMB WAS AS GOOD AS ANY I HAVE EATEN--
--AND THE DUCK WAS EVEN BETTER.
I HAD A SECOND TANKARD OF ALE WITH THE MEAL, A THIRD TO WASH IT ALL DOWN, AND A FOURTH BECAUSE THERE WAS NO ONE TO TELL ME I COULDN'T.
I PAID THE WOMAN WITH A SILVER AND STILL GOT BACK A HANDFUL OF COPPERS.
THIS IS WHAT IT MEANT TO BE A KNIGHT.
GOOD FOOD, ALE WHENEVER I WANTED IT, AND NO ONE TO CLOUT ME ON THE HEAD.
NEEEIGH
EASY, LAD.
WHAT?
WHAT'S GOING--

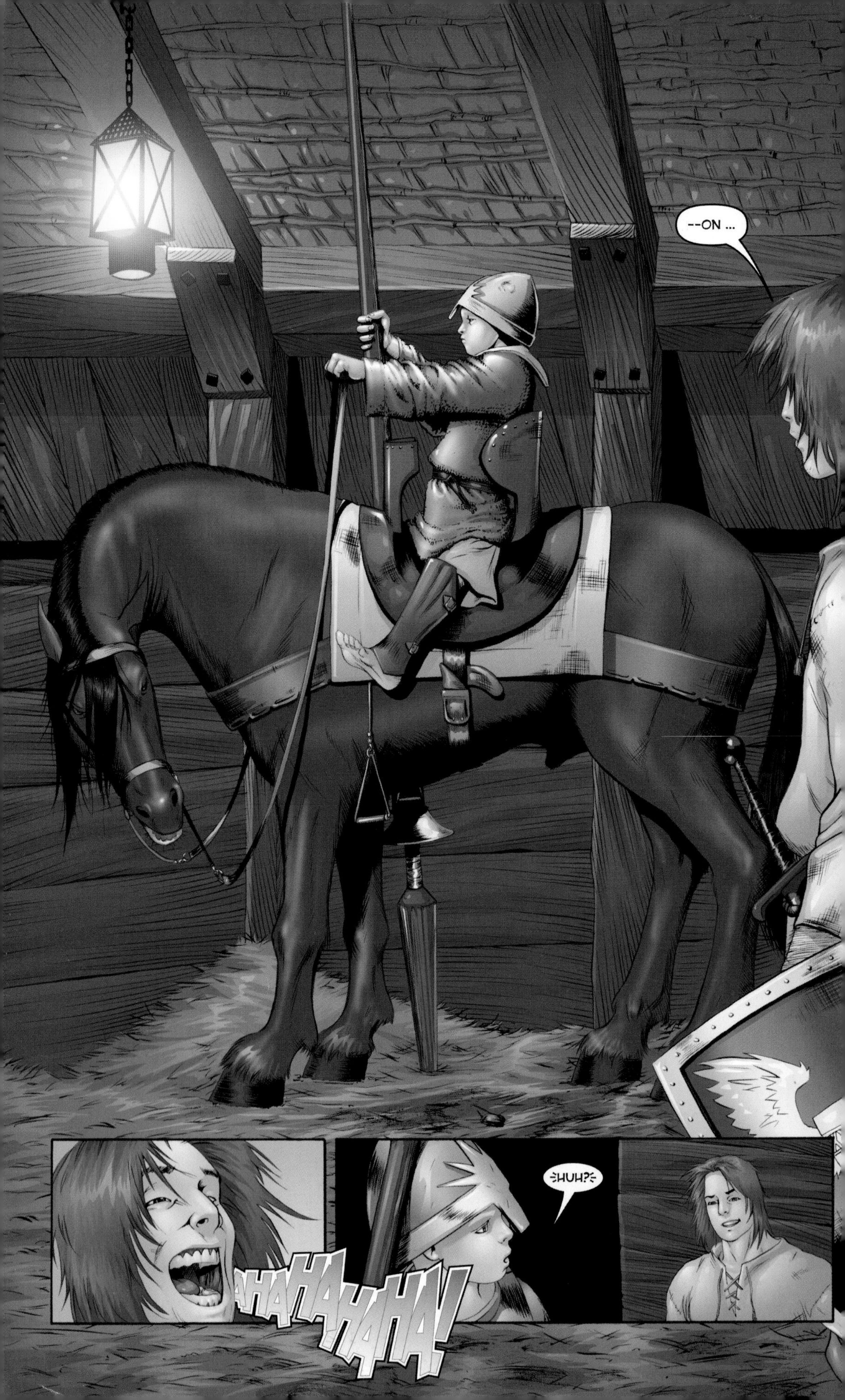
--ON ...
HAHAHAHAHAHA!
HUH?

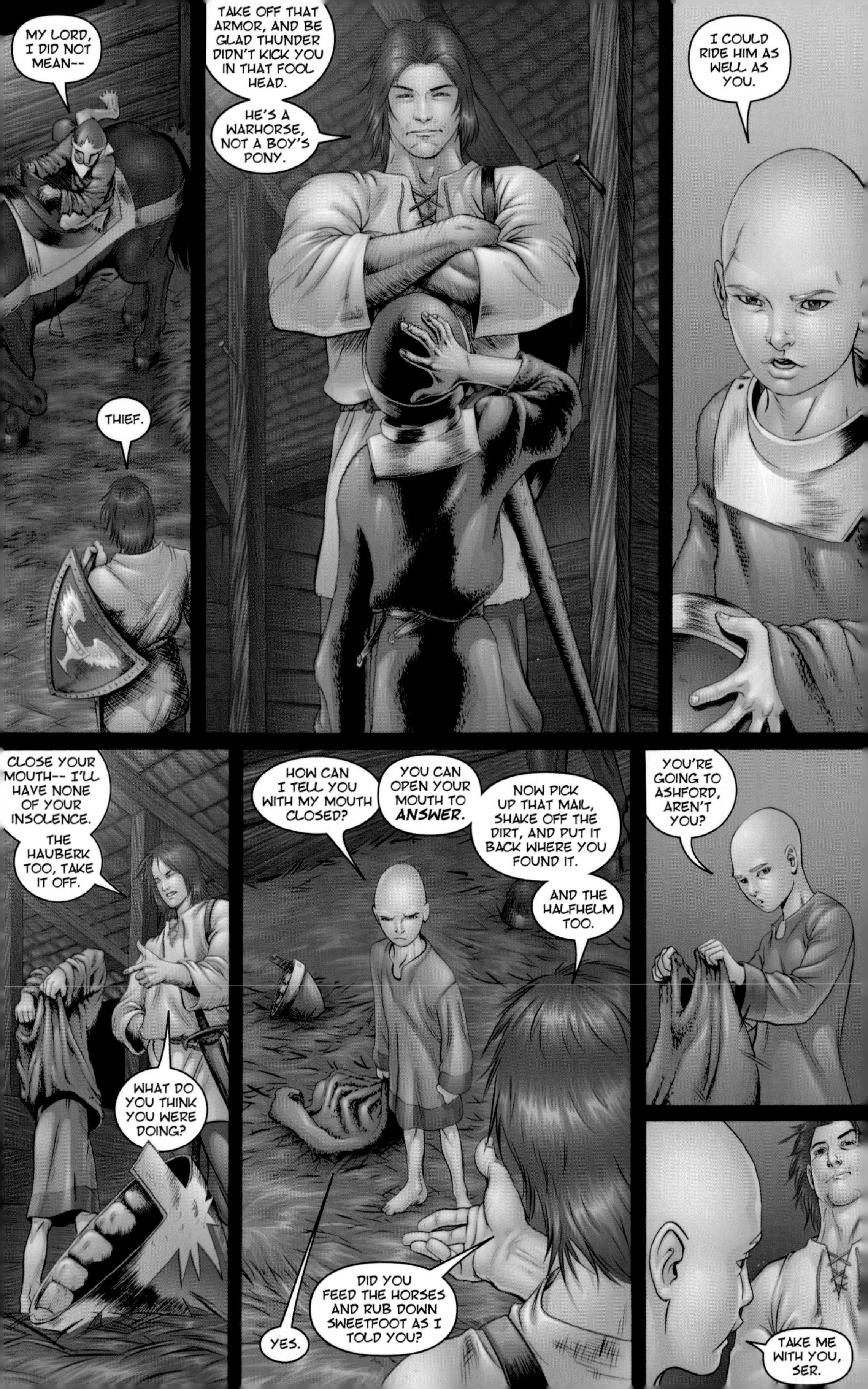
MY LORD, I DID NOT MEAN--
THIEF.
TAKE OFF THAT ARMOR, AND BE GLAD THUNDER DIDN'T KICK YOU IN THAT FOOL HEAD.
HE'S A WARHORSE, NOT A BOY'S PONY.
I COULD RIDE HIM AS WELL AS YOU.
CLOSE YOUR MOUTH-- I'LL HAVE NONE OF YOUR INSOLENCE.
THE HAUBERK TOO, TAKE IT OFF.
WHAT DO YOU THINK YOU WERE DOING?
HOW CAN I TELL YOU WITH MY MOUTH CLOSED?
YOU CAN OPEN YOUR MOUTH TO **ANSWER**.
NOW PICK UP THAT MAIL, SHAKE OFF THE DIRT, AND PUT IT BACK WHERE YOU FOUND IT.
AND THE HALFHELM TOO.
DID YOU FEED THE HORSES AND RUB DOWN SWEETFOOT AS I TOLD YOU?
YES.
YOU'RE GOING TO ASHFORD, AREN'T YOU?
TAKE ME WITH YOU, SER.

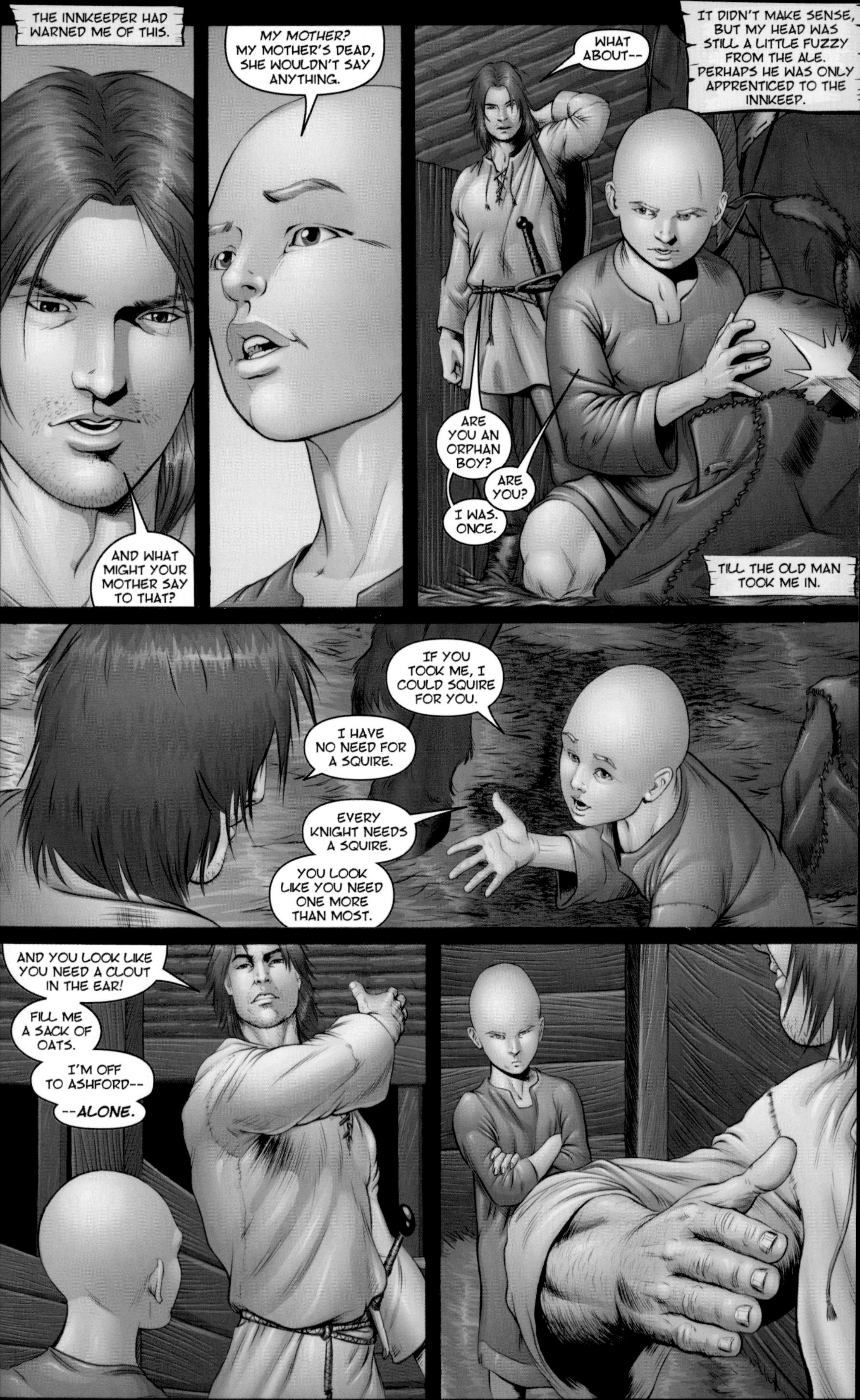
THE INNKEEPER HAD WARNED ME OF THIS.
AND WHAT MIGHT YOUR MOTHER SAY TO THAT?
MY MOTHER? MY MOTHER'S DEAD, SHE WOULDN'T SAY ANYTHING.
WHAT ABOUT--
IT DIDN'T MAKE SENSE, BUT MY HEAD WAS STILL A LITTLE FUZZY FROM THE ALE. PERHAPS HE WAS ONLY APPRENTICED TO THE INNKEEP.
ARE YOU AN ORPHAN BOY?
ARE YOU?
I WAS. ONCE.
TILL THE OLD MAN TOOK ME IN.
IF YOU TOOK ME, I COULD SQUIRE FOR YOU.
I HAVE NO NEED FOR A SQUIRE.
EVERY KNIGHT NEEDS A SQUIRE.
YOU LOOK LIKE YOU NEED ONE MORE THAN MOST.
AND YOU LOOK LIKE YOU NEED A CLOUT IN THE EAR!
FILL ME A SACK OF OATS.
I'M OFF TO ASHFORD--
--ALONE.

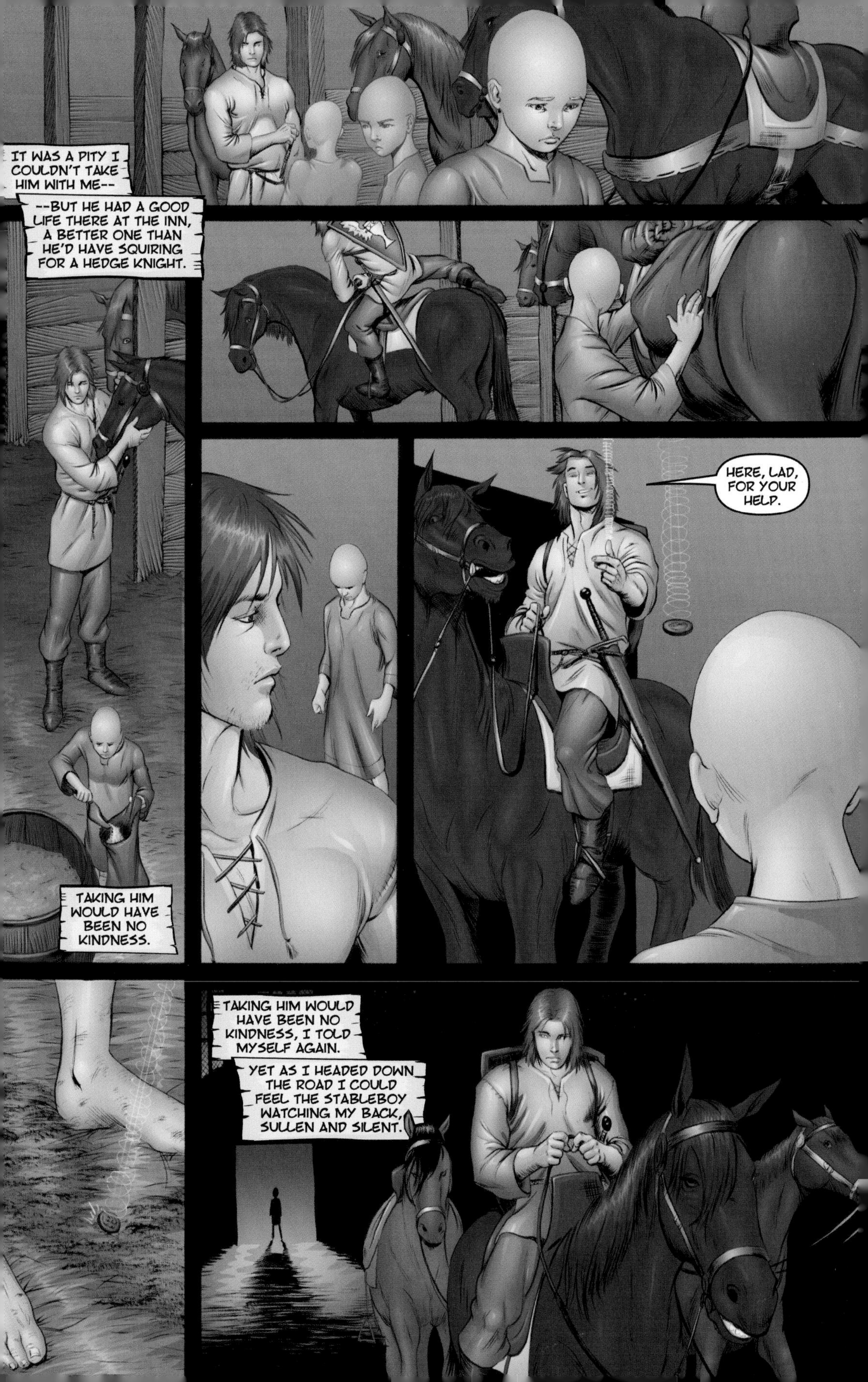
IT WAS A PITY I COULDN'T TAKE HIM WITH ME--
--BUT HE HAD A GOOD LIFE THERE AT THE INN, A BETTER ONE THAN HE'D HAVE SQUIRING FOR A HEDGE KNIGHT.
HERE, LAD, FOR YOUR HELP.
TAKING HIM WOULD HAVE BEEN NO KINDNESS.
TAKING HIM WOULD HAVE BEEN NO KINDNESS, I TOLD MYSELF AGAIN.
YET AS I HEADED DOWN THE ROAD I COULD FEEL THE STABLEBOY WATCHING MY BACK, SULLEN AND SILENT.

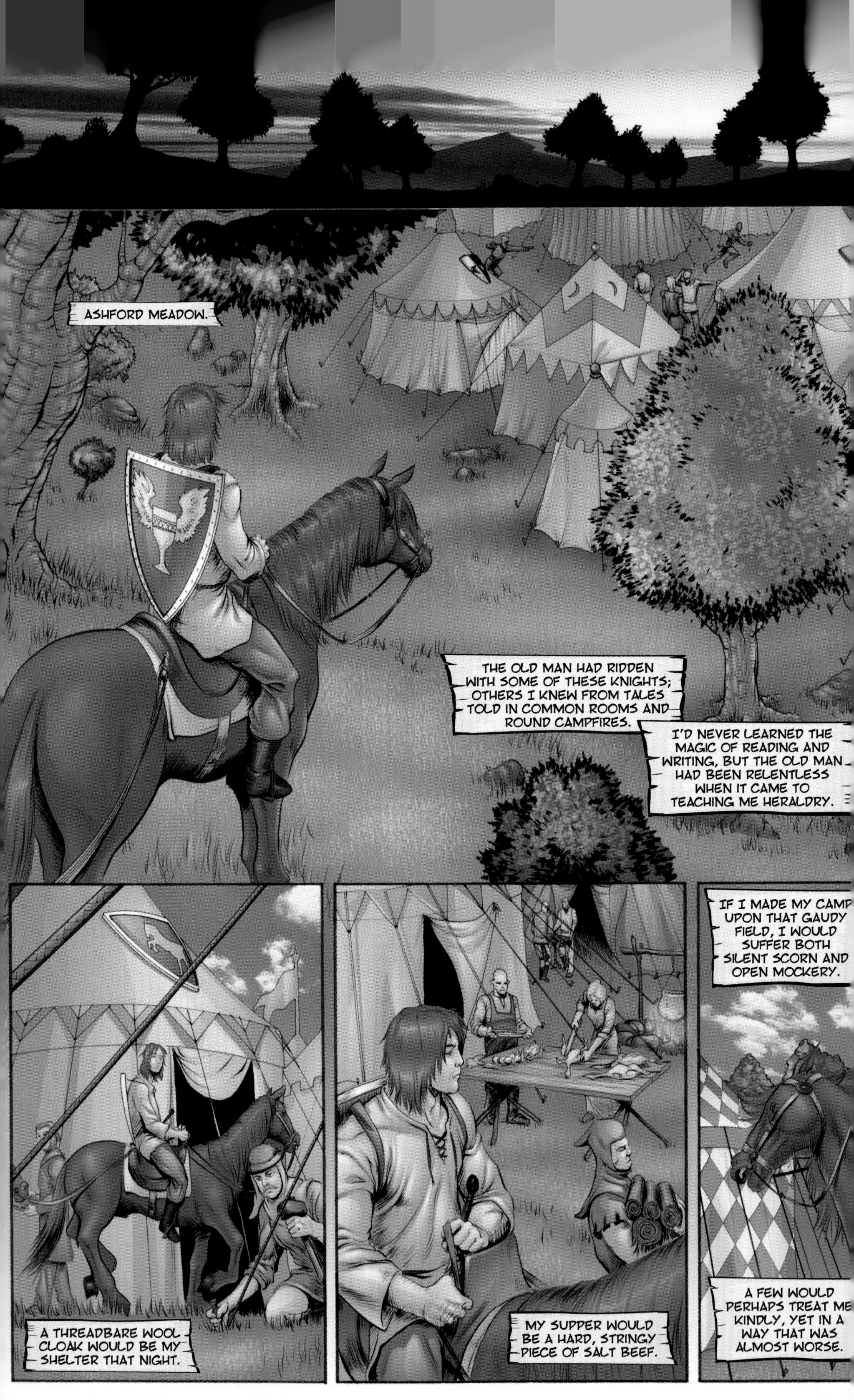
ASHFORD MEADOW.
THE OLD MAN HAD RIDDEN WITH SOME OF THESE KNIGHTS; OTHERS I KNEW FROM TALES TOLD IN COMMON ROOMS AND ROUND CAMPFIRES.
I'D NEVER LEARNED THE MAGIC OF READING AND WRITING, BUT THE OLD MAN HAD BEEN RELENTLESS WHEN IT CAME TO TEACHING ME HERALDRY.
A THREADBARE WOOL CLOAK WOULD BE MY SHELTER THAT NIGHT.
MY SUPPER WOULD BE A HARD, STRINGY PIECE OF SALT BEEF.
IF I MADE MY CAMP UPON THAT GAUDY FIELD, I WOULD SUFFER BOTH SILENT SCORN AND OPEN MOCKERY.
A FEW WOULD PERHAPS TREAT ME KINDLY, YET IN A WAY THAT WAS ALMOST WORSE.

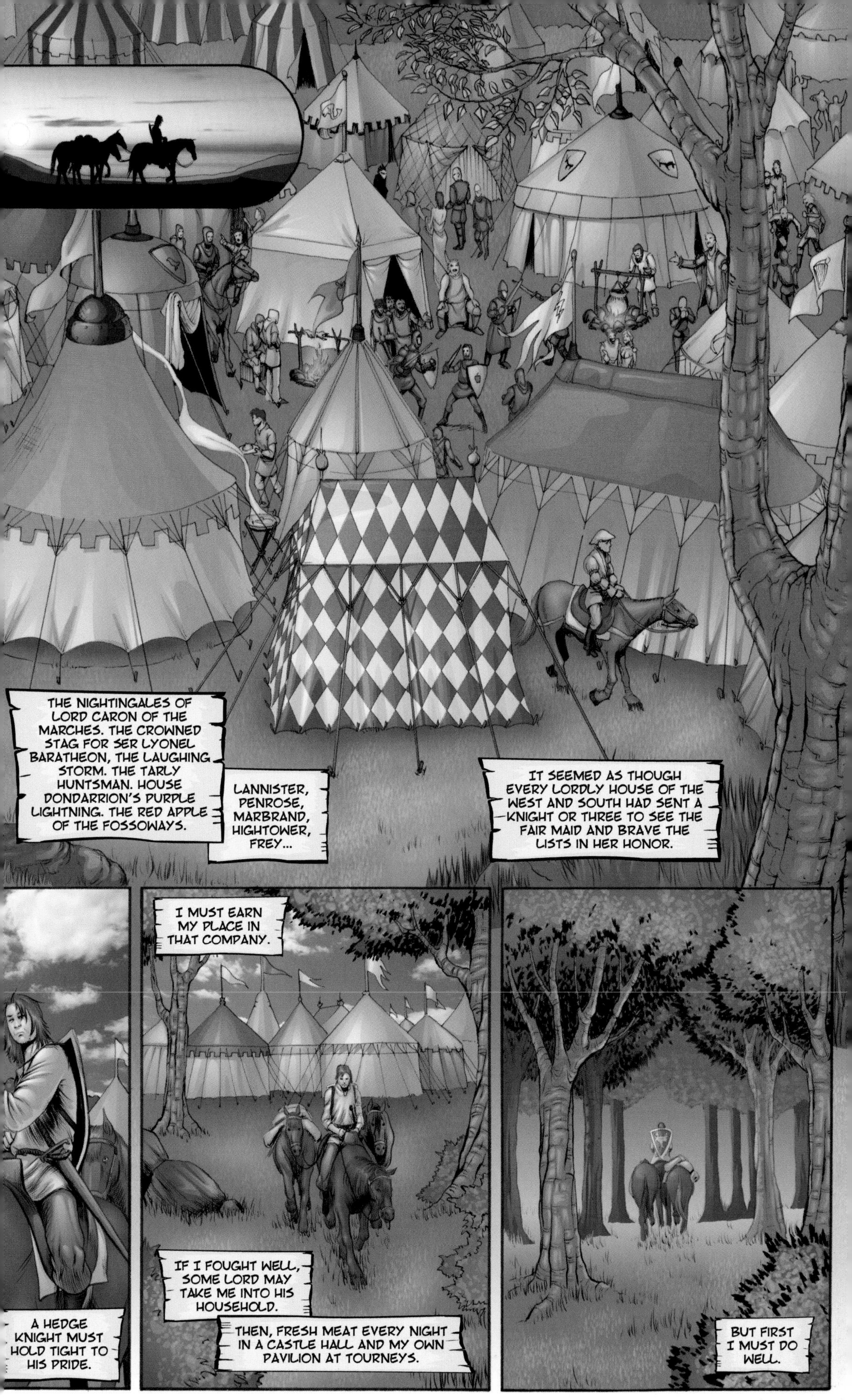
THE NIGHTINGALES OF LORD CARON OF THE MARCHES. THE CROWNED STAG FOR SER LYONEL BARATHEON, THE LAUGHING STORM. THE TARLY HUNTSMAN. HOUSE DONDARRION'S PURPLE LIGHTNING. THE RED APPLE OF THE FOSSOWAYS.
LANNISTER, PENROSE, MARBRAND, HIGHTOWER, FREY...
IT SEEMED AS THOUGH EVERY LORDLY HOUSE OF THE WEST AND SOUTH HAD SENT A KNIGHT OR THREE TO SEE THE FAIR MAID AND BRAVE THE LISTS IN HER HONOR.
A HEDGE KNIGHT MUST HOLD TIGHT TO HIS PRIDE.
I MUST EARN MY PLACE IN THAT COMPANY.
IF I FOUGHT WELL, SOME LORD MAY TAKE ME INTO HIS HOUSEHOLD.
THEN, FRESH MEAT EVERY NIGHT IN A CASTLE HALL AND MY OWN PAVILION AT TOURNEYS.
BUT FIRST I MUST DO WELL.

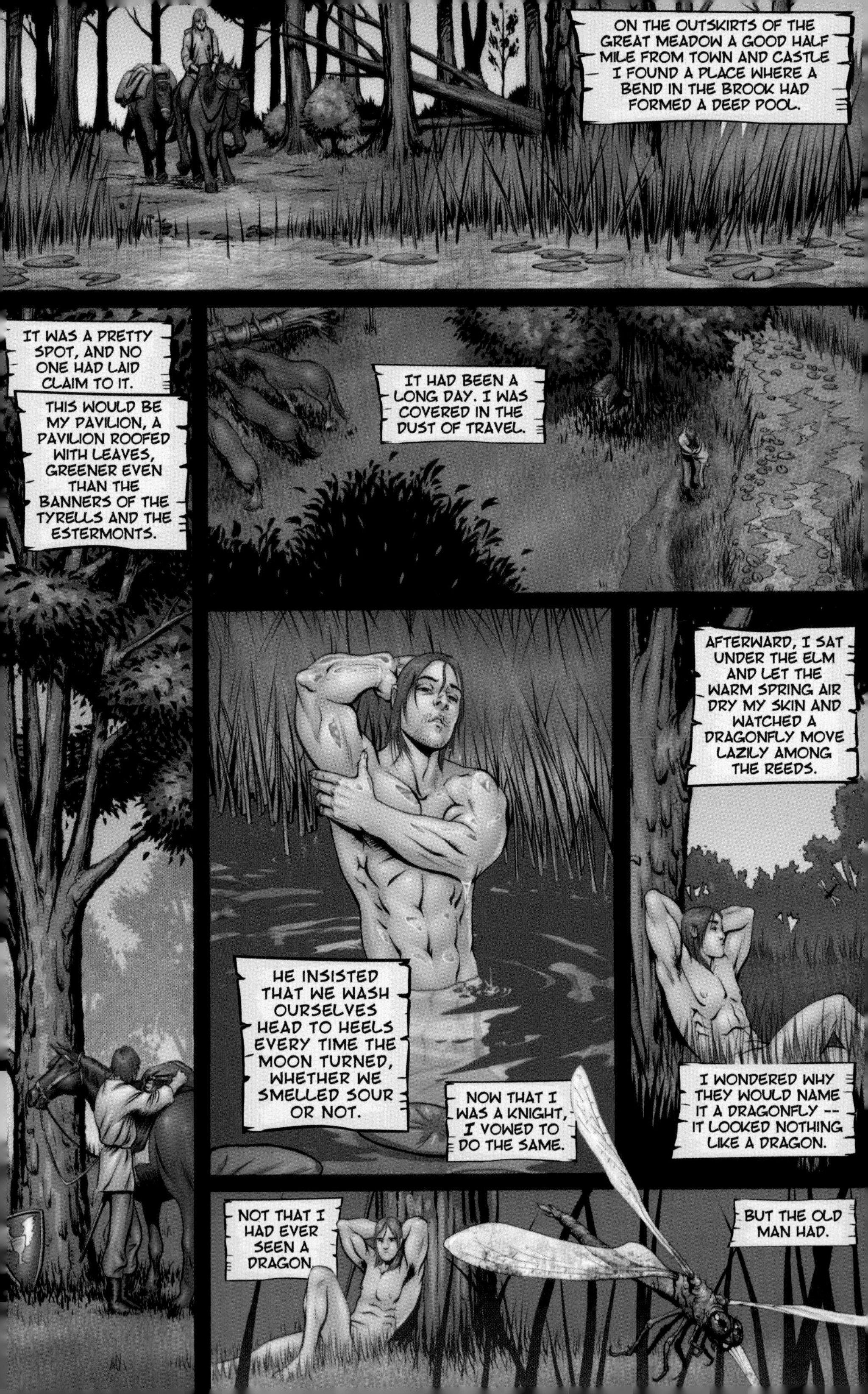

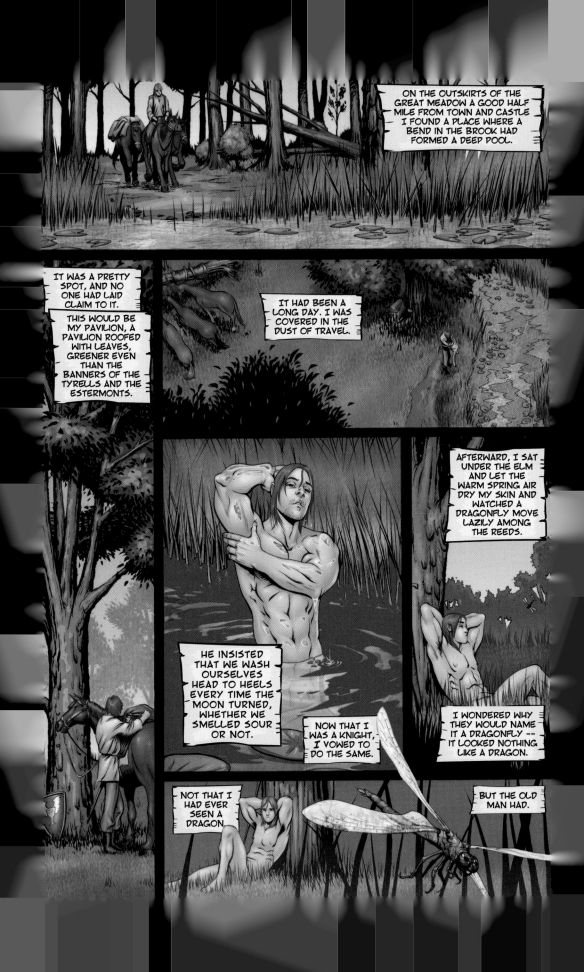

ON THE OUTSKIRTS OF THE GREAT MEADOW A GOOD HALF MILE FROM TOWN AND CASTLE I FOUND A PLACE WHERE A BEND IN THE BROOK HAD FORMED A DEEP POOL.
IT WAS A PRETTY SPOT, AND NO ONE HAD LAID CLAIM TO IT.
THIS WOULD BE MY PAVILION, A PAVILION ROOFED WITH LEAVES, GREENER EVEN THAN THE BANNERS OF THE TYRELLS AND THE ESTERMONTS.
IT HAD BEEN A LONG DAY. I WAS COVERED IN THE DUST OF TRAVEL.
HE INSISTED THAT WE WASH OURSELVES HEAD TO HEELS EVERY TIME THE MOON TURNED, WHETHER WE SMELLED SOUR OR NOT.
NOW THAT I WAS A KNIGHT, *I* VOWED TO DO THE SAME.
AFTERWARD, I SAT UNDER THE ELM AND LET THE WARM SPRING AIR DRY MY SKIN AND WATCHED A DRAGONFLY MOVE LAZILY AMONG THE REEDS.
I WONDERED WHY THEY WOULD NAME IT A DRAGONFLY -- IT LOOKED NOTHING LIKE A DRAGON.
NOT THAT I HAD EVER SEEN A DRAGON.
BUT THE OLD MAN HAD.

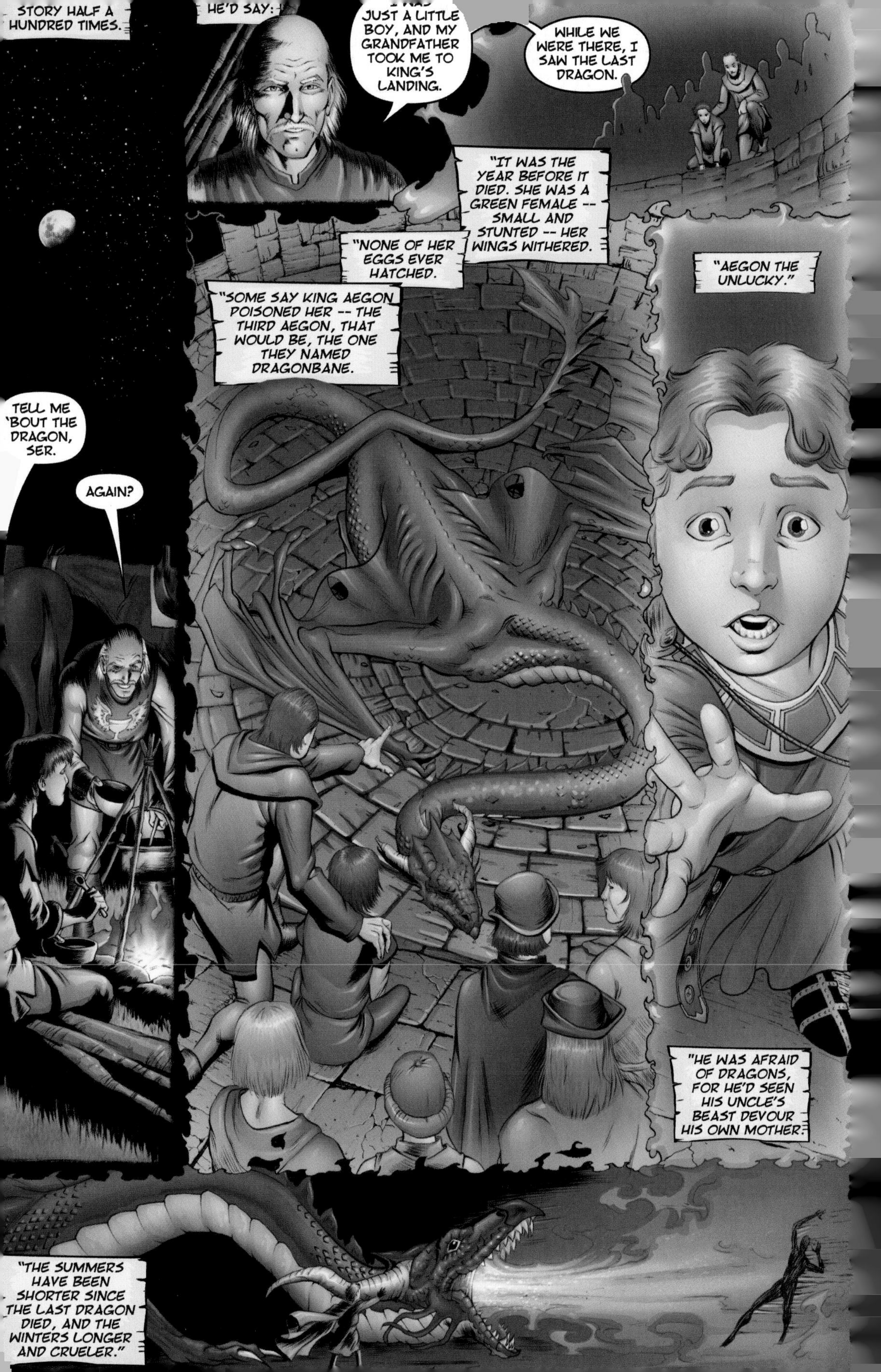
STORY HALF A HUNDRED TIMES.
TELL ME 'BOUT THE DRAGON, SER.
AGAIN?
HE'D SAY:
JUST A LITTLE BOY, AND MY GRANDFATHER TOOK ME TO KING'S LANDING.
WHILE WE WERE THERE, I SAW THE LAST DRAGON.
"IT WAS THE YEAR BEFORE IT DIED. SHE WAS A GREEN FEMALE -- SMALL AND STUNTED -- HER WINGS WITHERED.
"NONE OF HER EGGS EVER HATCHED.
"SOME SAY KING AEGON POISONED HER -- THE THIRD AEGON, THAT WOULD BE, THE ONE THEY NAMED DRAGONBANE.
"AEGON THE UNLUCKY."
"HE WAS AFRAID OF DRAGONS, FOR HE'D SEEN HIS UNCLE'S BEAST DEVOUR HIS OWN MOTHER.
"THE SUMMERS HAVE BEEN SHORTER SINCE THE LAST DRAGON DIED, AND THE WINTERS LONGER AND CRUELER."

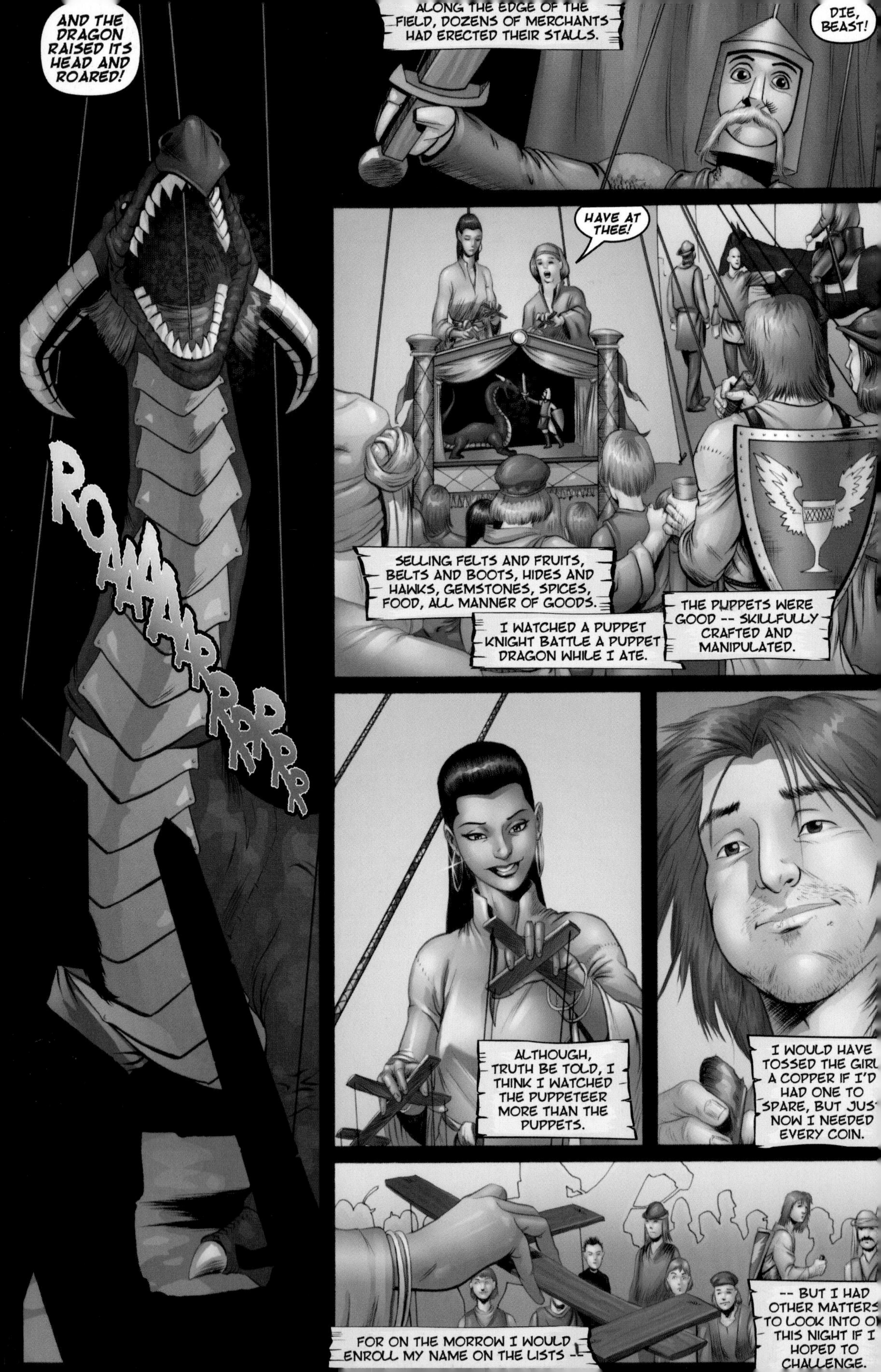

AND THE DRAGON RAISED ITS HEAD AND ROARED!
ROAAAAARRRRRR
ALONG THE EDGE OF THE FIELD, DOZENS OF MERCHANTS HAD ERECTED THEIR STALLS.
DIE, BEAST!
HAVE AT THEE!
SELLING FELTS AND FRUITS, BELTS AND BOOTS, HIDES AND HAWKS, GEMSTONES, SPICES, FOOD, ALL MANNER OF GOODS.
I WATCHED A PUPPET KNIGHT BATTLE A PUPPET DRAGON WHILE I ATE.
THE PUPPETS WERE GOOD -- SKILLFULLY CRAFTED AND MANIPULATED.
ALTHOUGH, TRUTH BE TOLD, I THINK I WATCHED THE PUPPETEER MORE THAN THE PUPPETS.
I WOULD HAVE TOSSED THE GIRL A COPPER IF I'D HAD ONE TO SPARE, BUT JUST NOW I NEEDED EVERY COIN.
FOR ON THE MORROW I WOULD ENROLL MY NAME ON THE LISTS --
-- BUT I HAD OTHER MATTERS TO LOOK INTO ON THIS NIGHT IF I HOPED TO CHALLENGE.

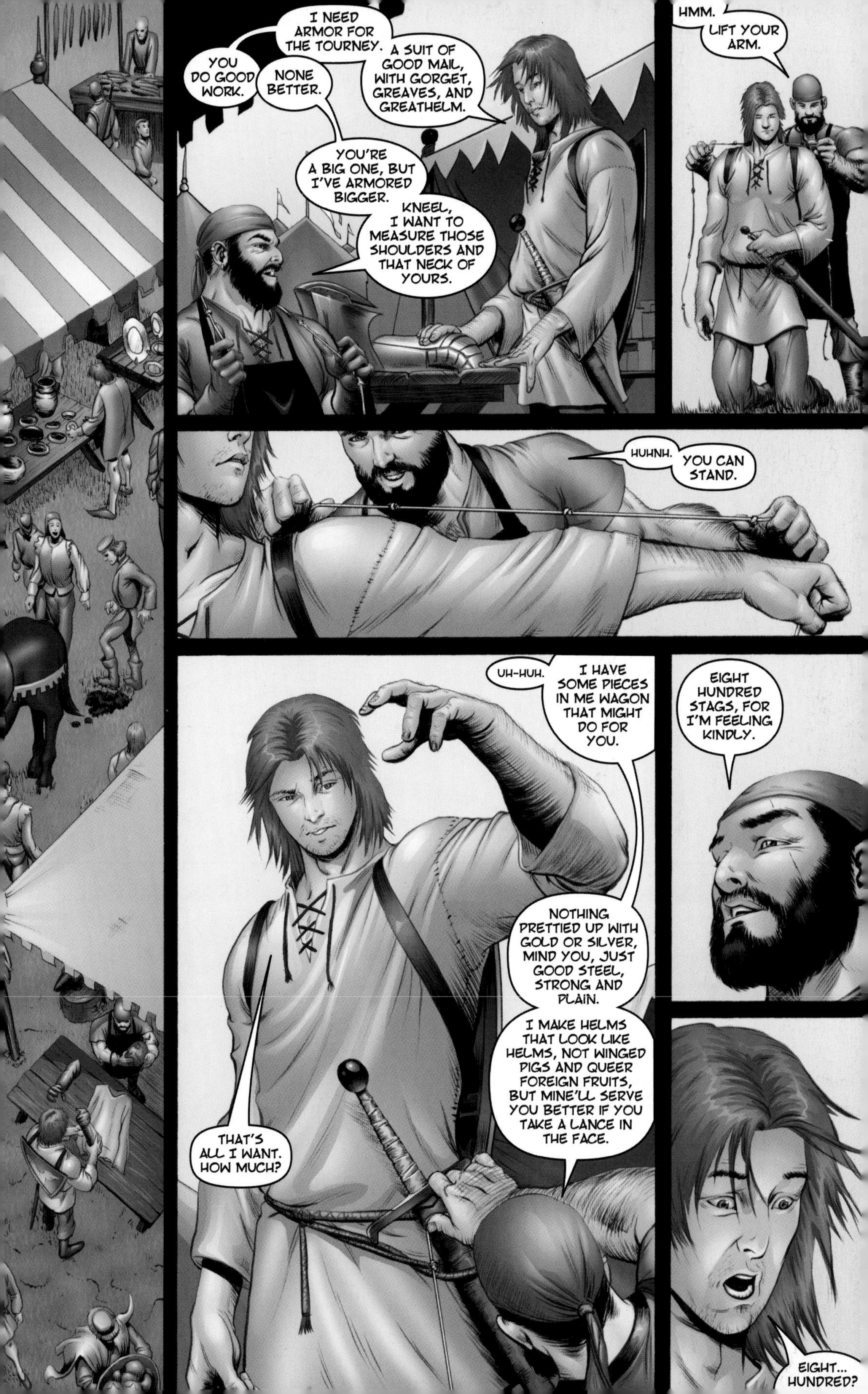
I NEED ARMOR FOR THE TOURNEY.
A SUIT OF GOOD MAIL, WITH GORGET, GREAVES, AND GREATHELM.
YOU DO GOOD WORK.
NONE BETTER.
YOU'RE A BIG ONE, BUT I'VE ARMORED BIGGER.
KNEEL, I WANT TO MEASURE THOSE SHOULDERS AND THAT NECK OF YOURS.
HMM.
LIFT YOUR ARM.
HUHNH.
YOU CAN STAND.
UH-HUH.
I HAVE SOME PIECES IN ME WAGON THAT MIGHT DO FOR YOU.
NOTHING PRETTIED UP WITH GOLD OR SILVER, MIND YOU, JUST GOOD STEEL, STRONG AND PLAIN.
I MAKE HELMS THAT LOOK LIKE HELMS, NOT WINGED PIGS AND QUEER FOREIGN FRUITS, BUT MINE'LL SERVE YOU BETTER IF YOU TAKE A LANCE IN THE FACE.
THAT'S ALL I WANT. HOW MUCH?
EIGHT HUNDRED STAGS, FOR I'M FEELING KINDLY.
EIGHT... HUNDRED?

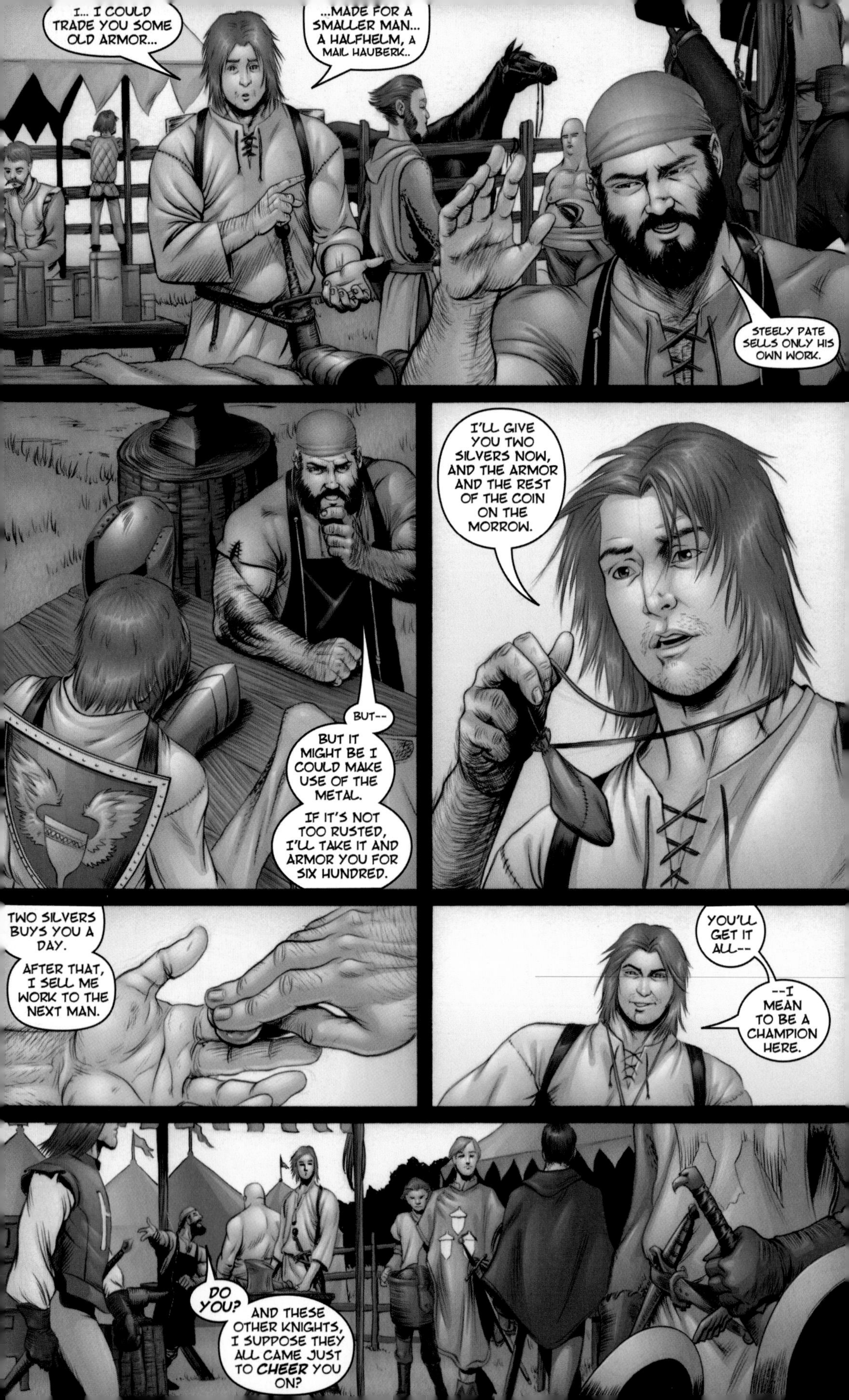
I... I COULD TRADE YOU SOME OLD ARMOR...
...MADE FOR A SMALLER MAN... A HALFHELM, A MAIL HAUBERK..
STEELY PATE SELLS ONLY HIS OWN WORK.
BUT--
BUT IT MIGHT BE I COULD MAKE USE OF THE METAL.
IF IT'S NOT TOO RUSTED, I'LL TAKE IT AND ARMOR YOU FOR SIX HUNDRED.
I'LL GIVE YOU TWO SILVERS NOW, AND THE ARMOR AND THE REST OF THE COIN ON THE MORROW.
TWO SILVERS BUYS YOU A DAY.
AFTER THAT, I SELL ME WORK TO THE NEXT MAN.
YOU'LL GET IT ALL--
--I MEAN TO BE A CHAMPION HERE.
DO YOU?
AND THESE OTHER KNIGHTS, I SUPPOSE THEY ALL CAME JUST TO CHEER YOU ON?

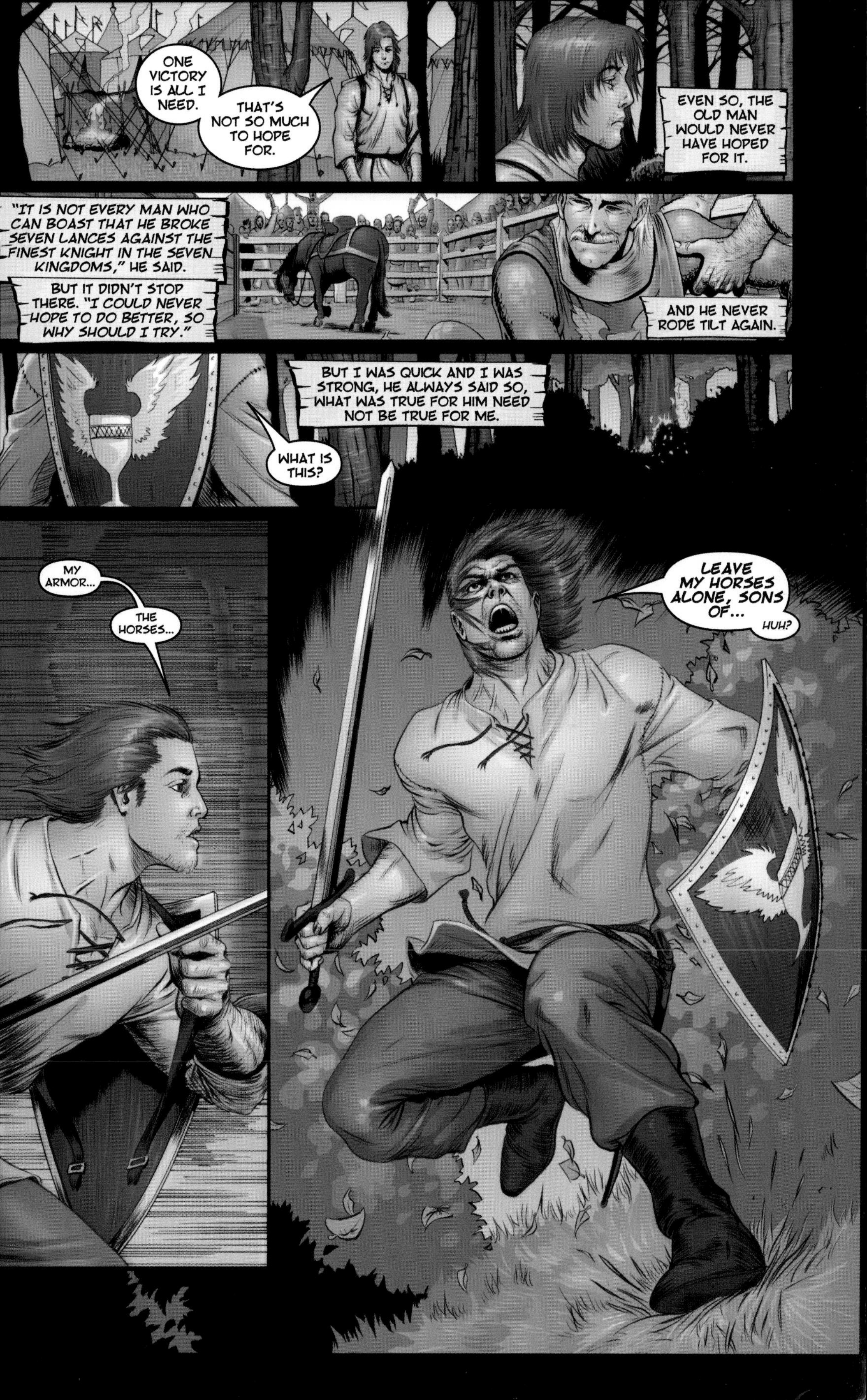

ONE VICTORY IS ALL I NEED.
THAT'S NOT SO MUCH TO HOPE FOR.
EVEN SO, THE OLD MAN WOULD NEVER HAVE HOPED FOR IT.
"IT IS NOT EVERY MAN WHO CAN BOAST THAT HE BROKE SEVEN LANCES AGAINST THE FINEST KNIGHT IN THE SEVEN KINGDOMS," HE SAID.
BUT IT DIDN'T STOP THERE. "I COULD NEVER HOPE TO DO BETTER, SO WHY SHOULD I TRY."
AND HE NEVER RODE TILT AGAIN.
BUT I WAS QUICK AND I WAS STRONG, HE ALWAYS SAID SO, WHAT WAS TRUE FOR HIM NEED NOT BE TRUE FOR ME.
WHAT IS THIS?
MY ARMOR...
THE HORSES...
LEAVE MY HORSES ALONE, SONS OF...
HUH?

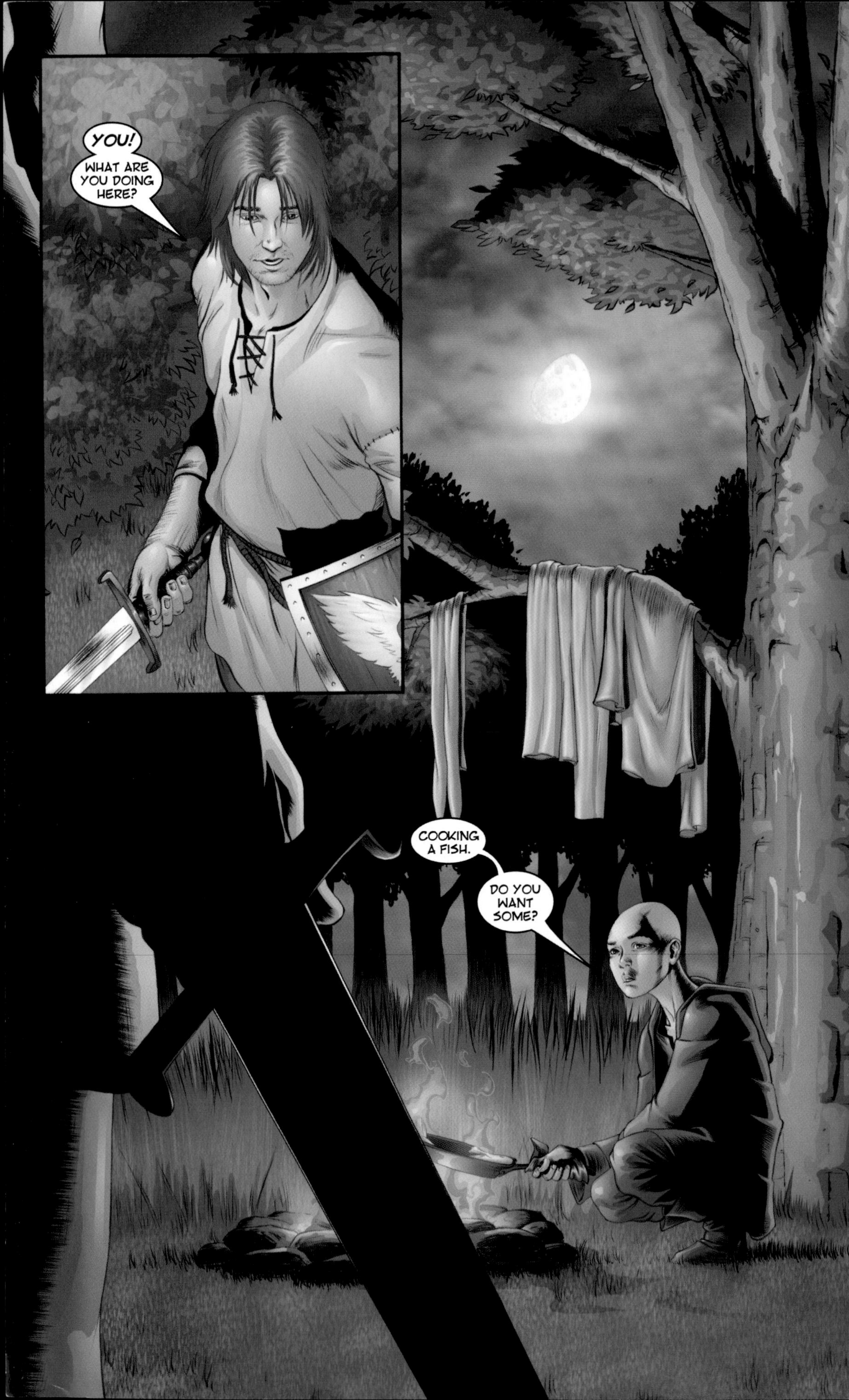
YOU!
WHAT ARE YOU DOING HERE?
COOKING A FISH.
DO YOU WANT SOME?

ISSUE TWO
COVER A

MIKE S. MILLER

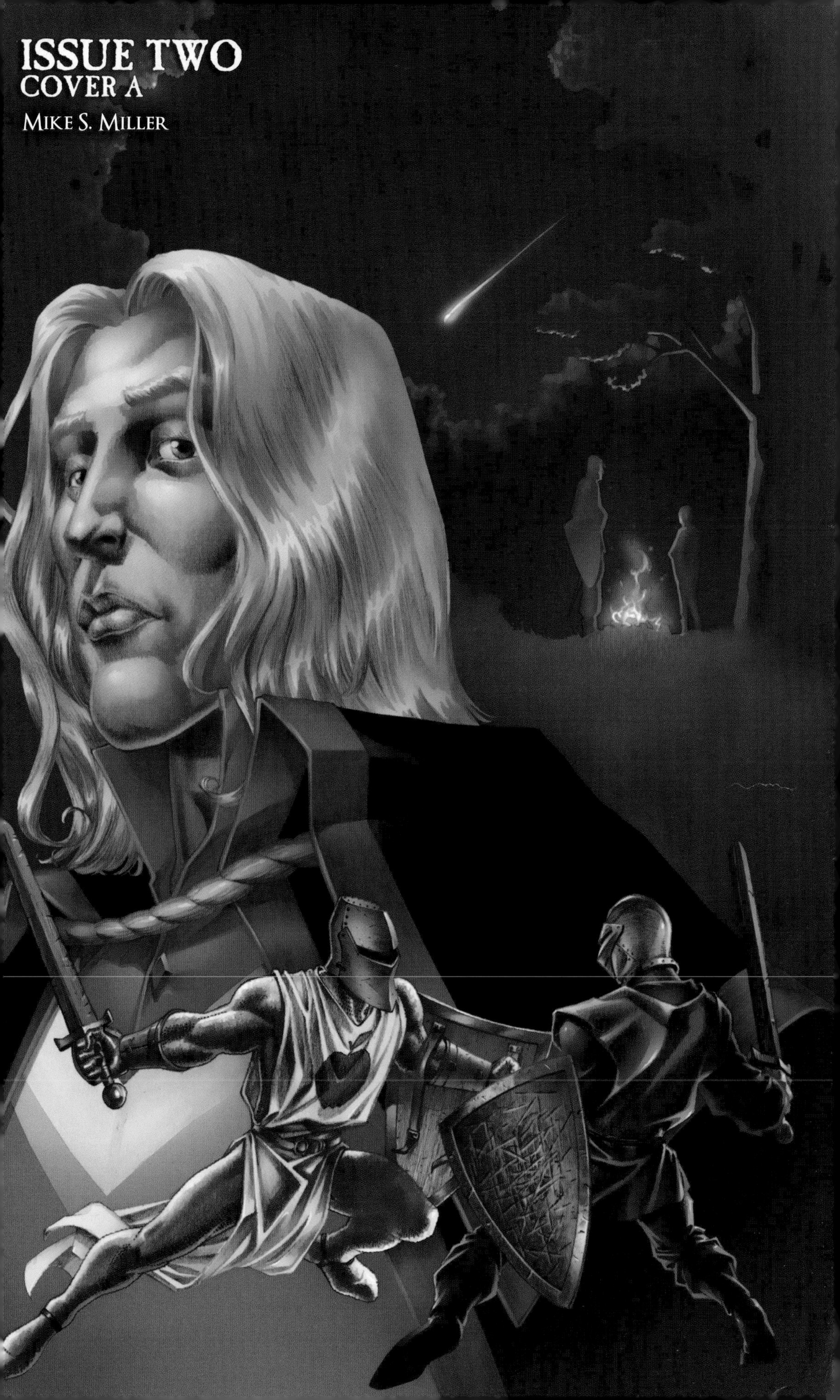

ISSUE TWO
COVER B

BORIS VALLEJO AND JULIE BELL

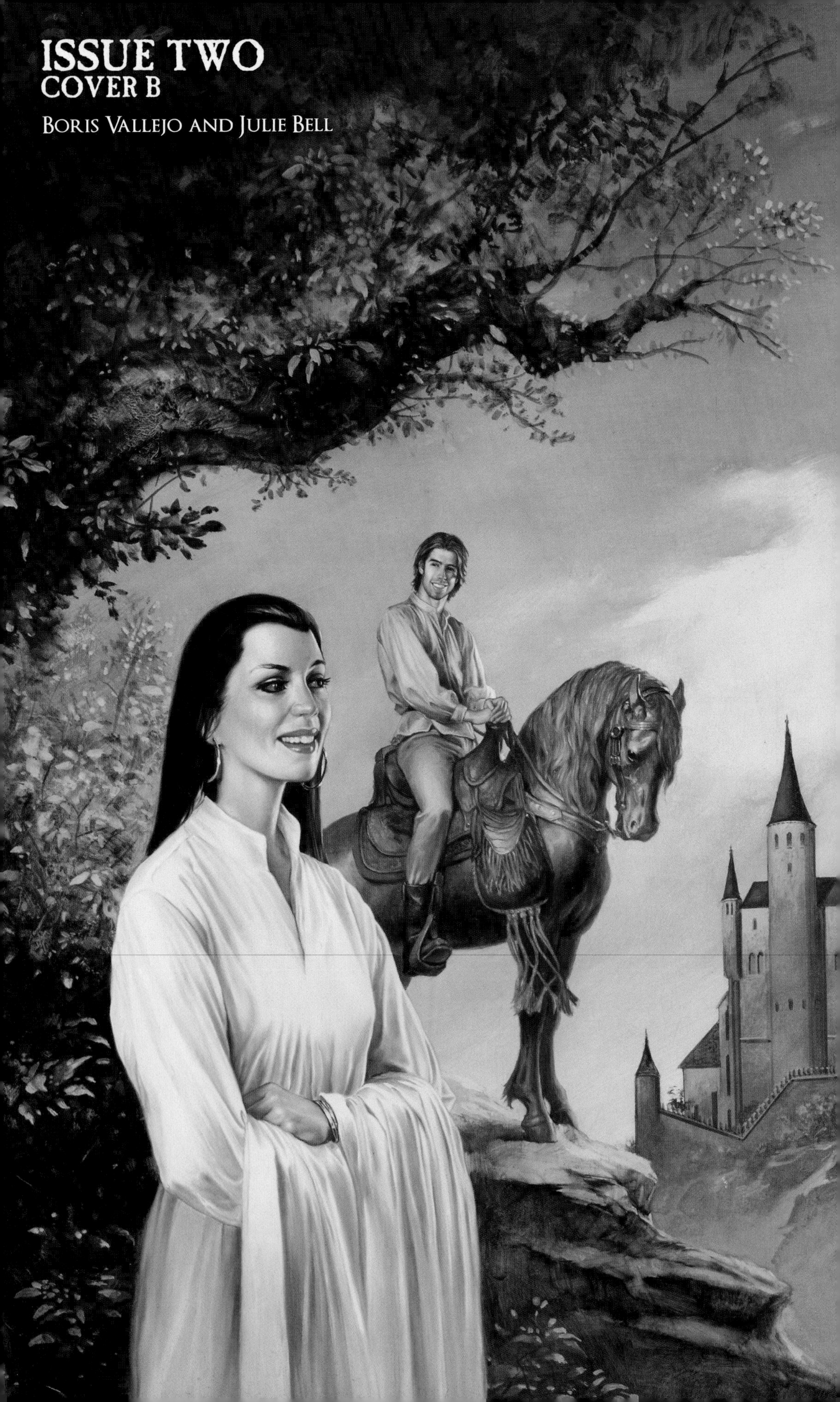

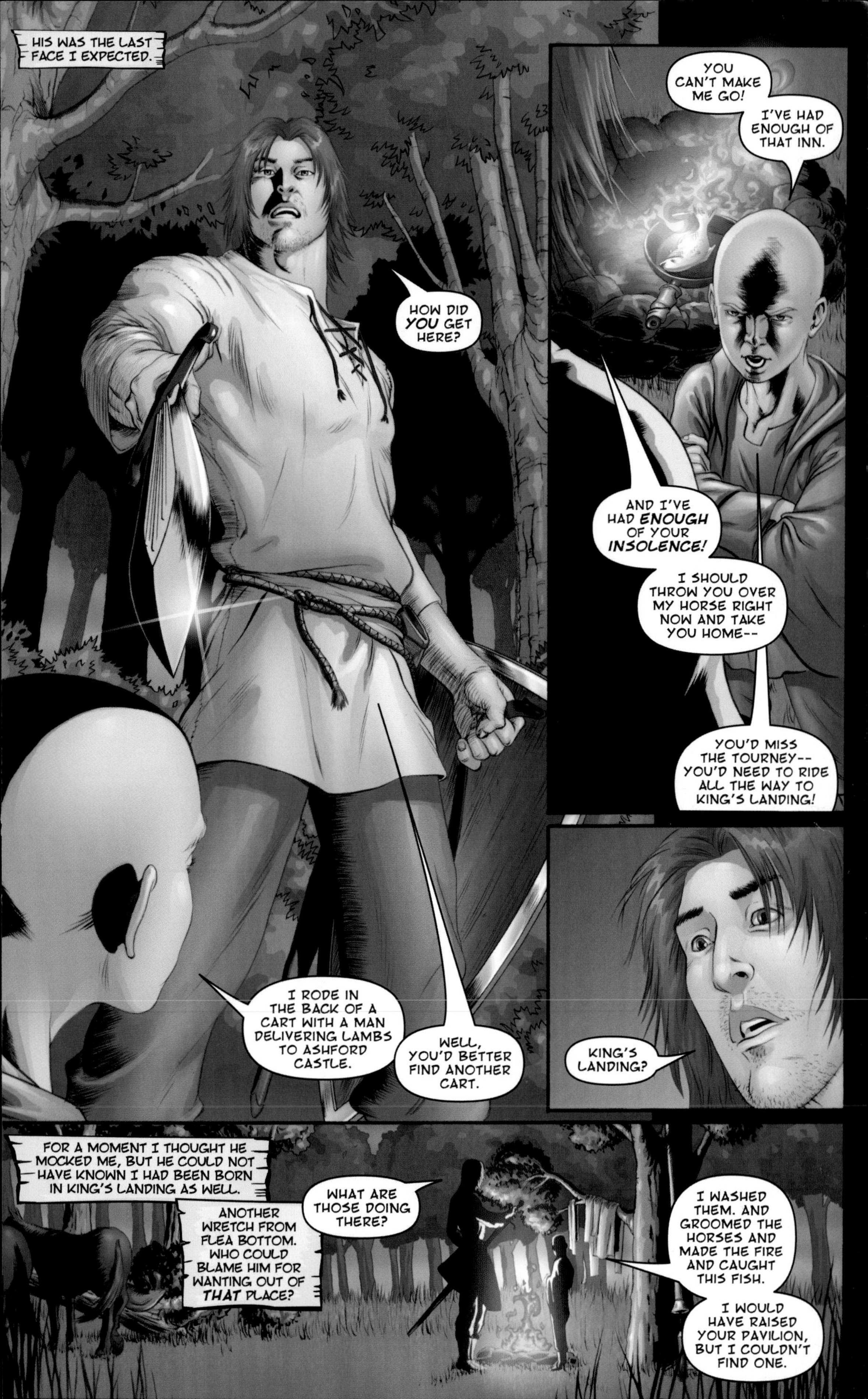
HIS WAS THE LAST FACE I EXPECTED.
HOW DID YOU GET HERE?
I RODE IN THE BACK OF A CART WITH A MAN DELIVERING LAMBS TO ASHFORD CASTLE.
WELL, YOU'D BETTER FIND ANOTHER CART.
YOU CAN'T MAKE ME GO!
I'VE HAD ENOUGH OF THAT INN.
AND I'VE HAD ENOUGH OF YOUR INSOLENCE!
I SHOULD THROW YOU OVER MY HORSE RIGHT NOW AND TAKE YOU HOME--
YOU'D MISS THE TOURNEY-- YOU'D NEED TO RIDE ALL THE WAY TO KING'S LANDING!
KING'S LANDING?
FOR A MOMENT I THOUGHT HE MOCKED ME, BUT HE COULD NOT HAVE KNOWN I HAD BEEN BORN IN KING'S LANDING AS WELL.
ANOTHER WRETCH FROM FLEA BOTTOM. WHO COULD BLAME HIM FOR WANTING OUT OF THAT PLACE?
WHAT ARE THOSE DOING THERE?
I WASHED THEM. AND GROOMED THE HORSES AND MADE THE FIRE AND CAUGHT THIS FISH.
I WOULD HAVE RAISED YOUR PAVILION, BUT I COULDN'T FIND ONE.

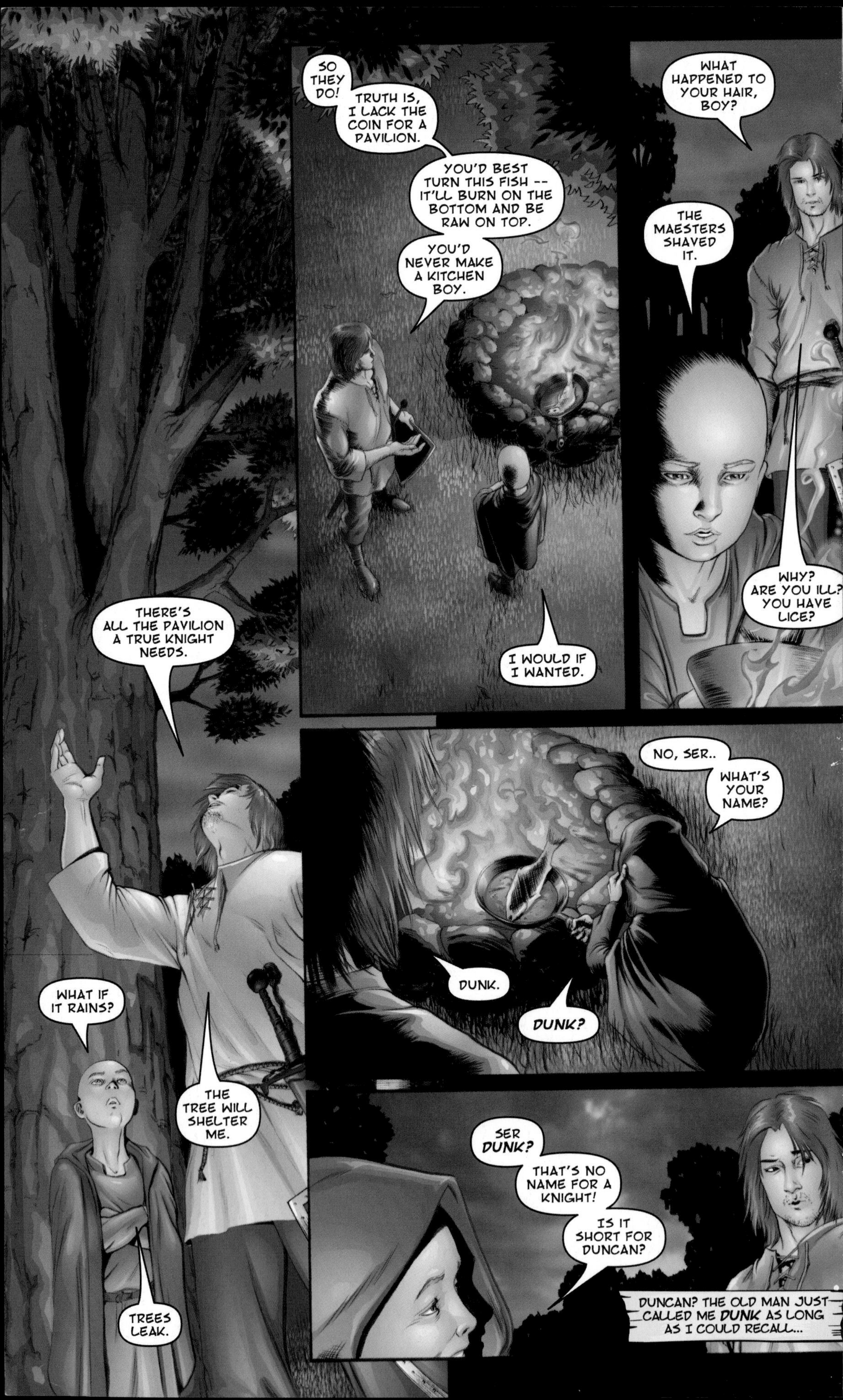

SO THEY DO!
TRUTH IS, I LACK THE COIN FOR A PAVILION.
YOU'D BEST TURN THIS FISH -- IT'LL BURN ON THE BOTTOM AND BE RAW ON TOP.
YOU'D NEVER MAKE A KITCHEN BOY.
I WOULD IF I WANTED.
WHAT HAPPENED TO YOUR HAIR, BOY?
THE MAESTERS SHAVED IT.
WHY? ARE YOU ILL? YOU HAVE LICE?
THERE'S ALL THE PAVILION A TRUE KNIGHT NEEDS.
WHAT IF IT RAINS?
THE TREE WILL SHELTER ME.
TREES LEAK.
NO, SER..
WHAT'S YOUR NAME?
DUNK.
DUNK?
SER DUNK?
THAT'S NO NAME FOR A KNIGHT!
IS IT SHORT FOR DUNCAN?
DUNCAN? THE OLD MAN JUST CALLED ME DUNK AS LONG AS I COULD RECALL...

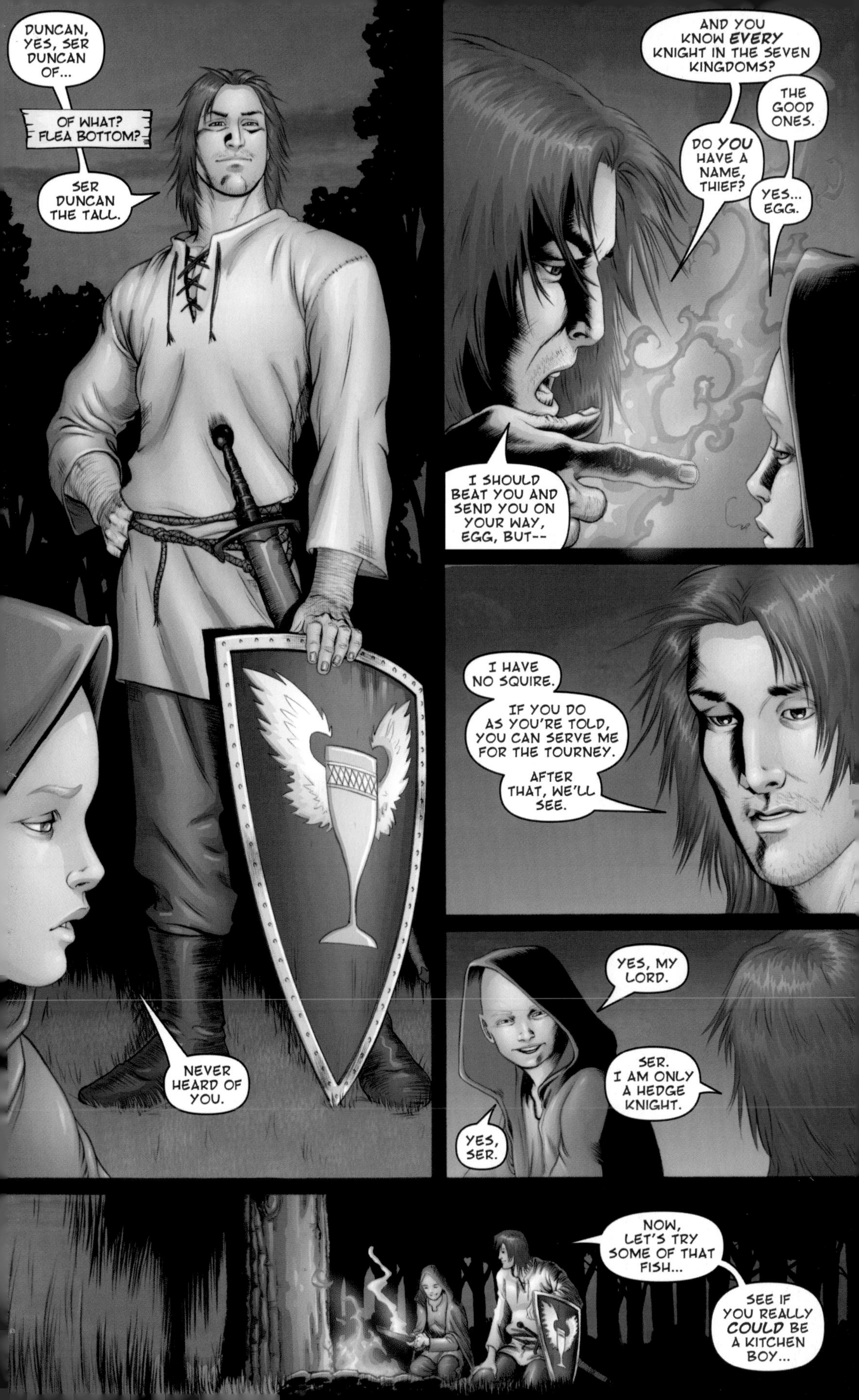
DUNCAN, YES, SER DUNCAN OF...
OF WHAT? FLEA BOTTOM?
SER DUNCAN THE TALL.
NEVER HEARD OF YOU.
AND YOU KNOW EVERY KNIGHT IN THE SEVEN KINGDOMS?
THE GOOD ONES.
DO YOU HAVE A NAME, THIEF?
YES... EGG.
I SHOULD BEAT YOU AND SEND YOU ON YOUR WAY, EGG, BUT--
I HAVE NO SQUIRE.
IF YOU DO AS YOU'RE TOLD, YOU CAN SERVE ME FOR THE TOURNEY.
AFTER THAT, WE'LL SEE.
YES, MY LORD.
SER. I AM ONLY A HEDGE KNIGHT.
YES, SER.
NOW, LET'S TRY SOME OF THAT FISH...
SEE IF YOU REALLY COULD BE A KITCHEN BOY...

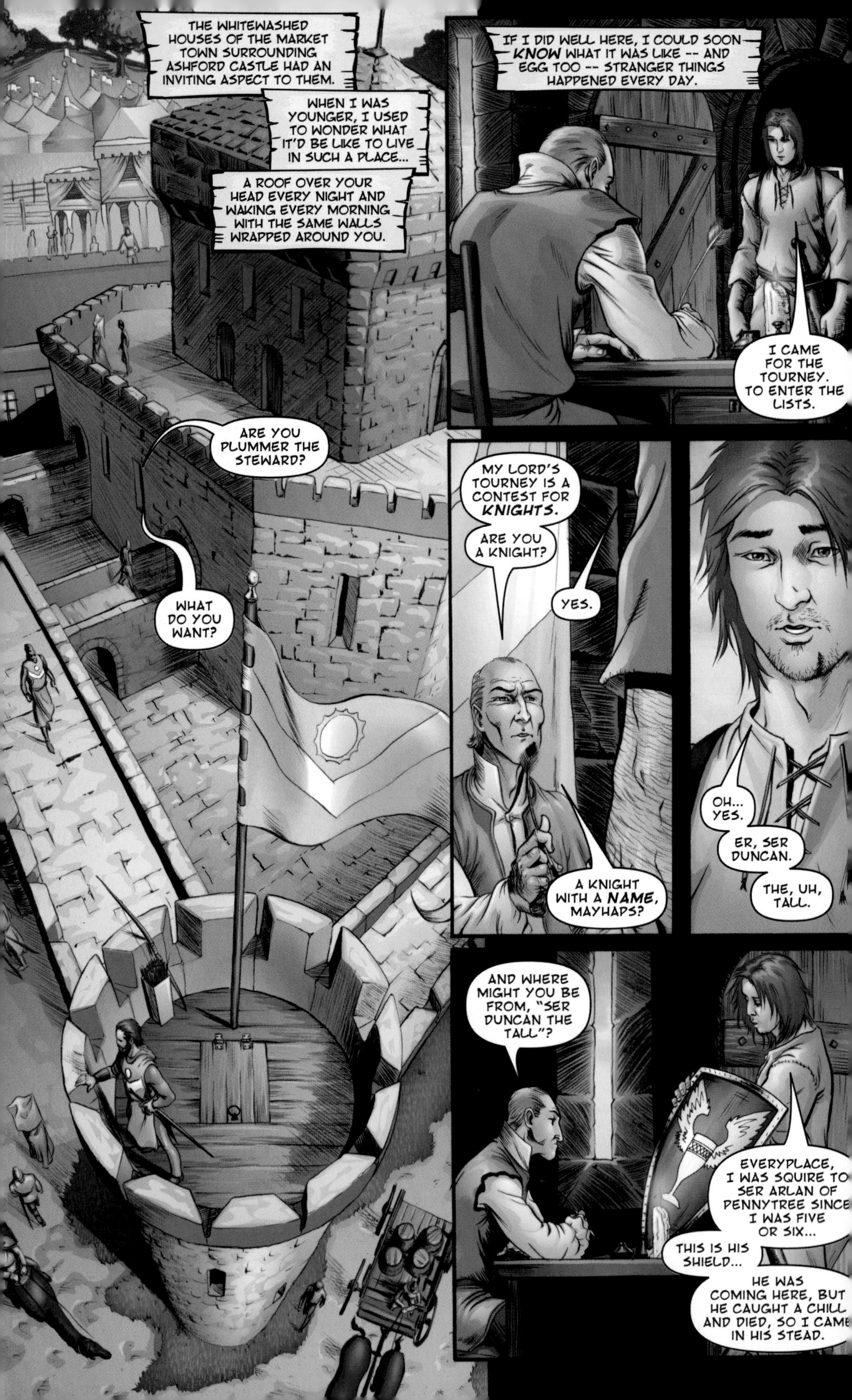
THE WHITEWASHED HOUSES OF THE MARKET TOWN SURROUNDING ASHFORD CASTLE HAD AN INVITING ASPECT TO THEM.
WHEN I WAS YOUNGER, I USED TO WONDER WHAT IT'D BE LIKE TO LIVE IN SUCH A PLACE...
A ROOF OVER YOUR HEAD EVERY NIGHT AND WAKING EVERY MORNING WITH THE SAME WALLS WRAPPED AROUND YOU.
ARE YOU PLUMMER THE STEWARD?
WHAT DO YOU WANT?
IF I DID WELL HERE, I COULD SOON KNOW WHAT IT WAS LIKE -- AND EGG TOO -- STRANGER THINGS HAPPENED EVERY DAY.
I CAME FOR THE TOURNEY. TO ENTER THE LISTS.
MY LORD'S TOURNEY IS A CONTEST FOR KNIGHTS.
ARE YOU A KNIGHT?
YES.
A KNIGHT WITH A NAME, MAYHAPS?
OH... YES.
ER, SER DUNCAN.
THE, UH, TALL.
AND WHERE MIGHT YOU BE FROM, "SER DUNCAN THE TALL"?
EVERYPLACE, I WAS SQUIRE TO SER ARLAN OF PENNYTREE SINCE I WAS FIVE OR SIX...
THIS IS HIS SHIELD...
HE WAS COMING HERE, BUT HE CAUGHT A CHILL AND DIED, SO I CAME IN HIS STEAD.

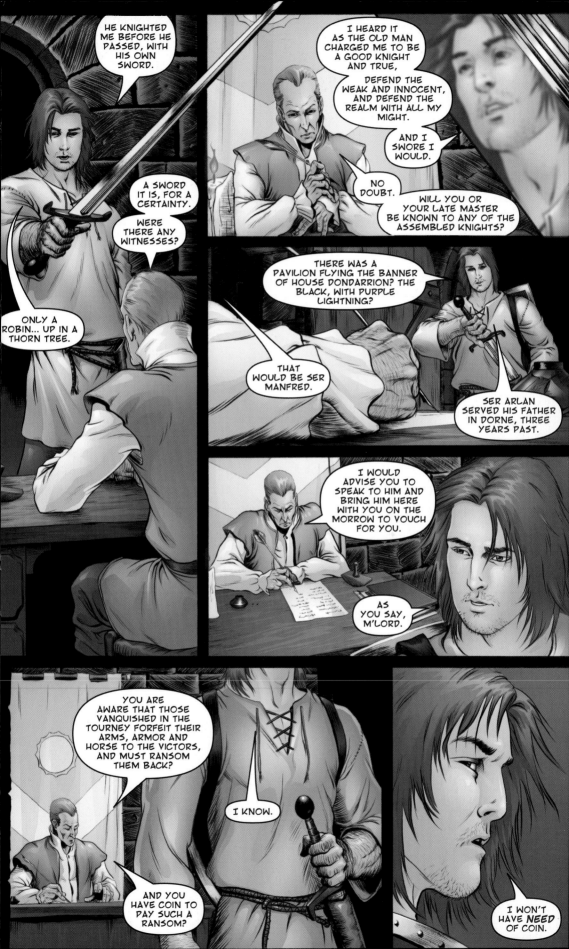

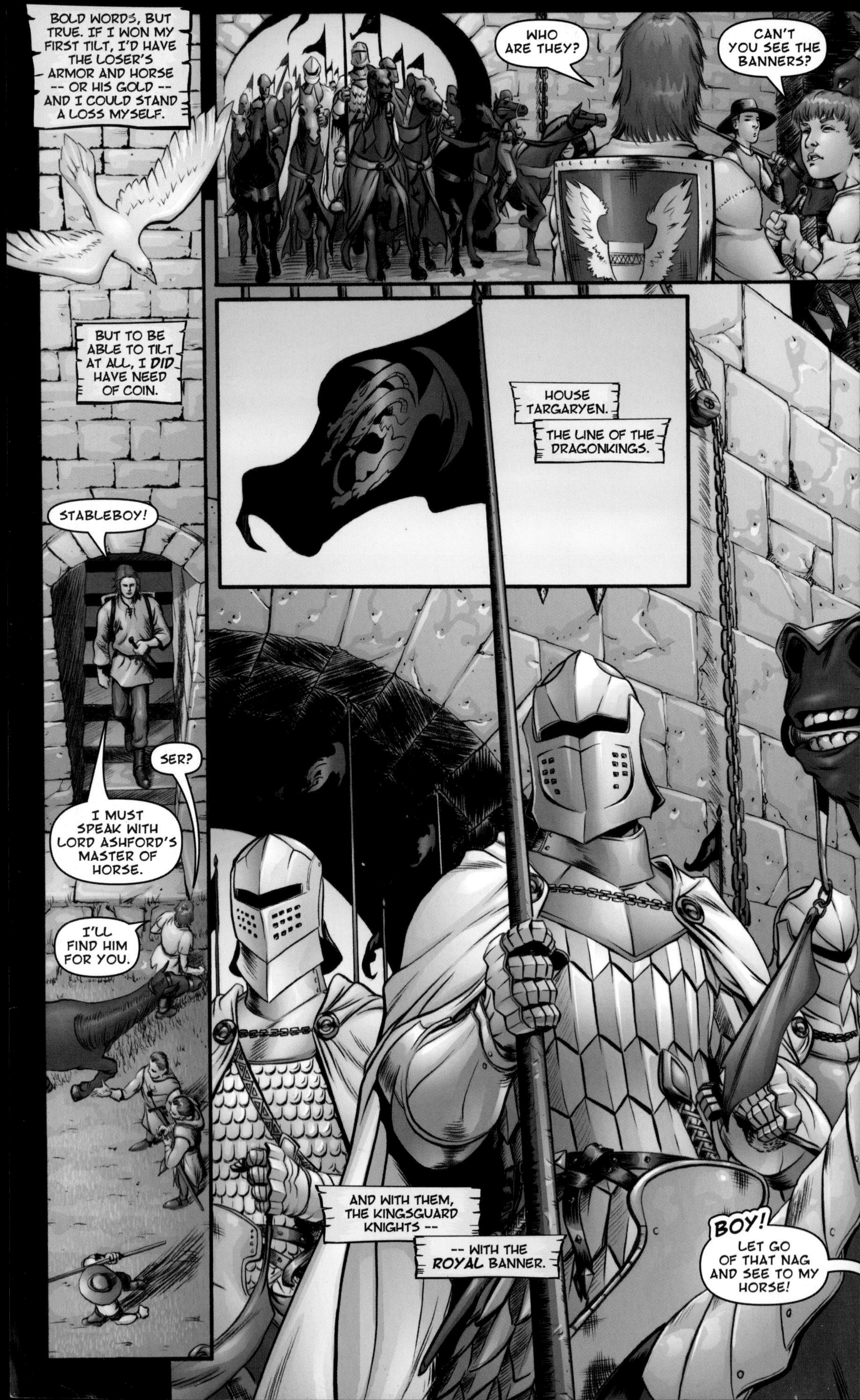
BOLD WORDS, BUT TRUE. IF I WON MY FIRST TILT, I'D HAVE THE LOSER'S ARMOR AND HORSE -- OR HIS GOLD -- AND I COULD STAND A LOSS MYSELF.
WHO ARE THEY?
CAN'T YOU SEE THE BANNERS?
BUT TO BE ABLE TO TILT AT ALL, I DID HAVE NEED OF COIN.
HOUSE TARGARYEN.
THE LINE OF THE DRAGONKINGS.
STABLEBOY!
SER?
I MUST SPEAK WITH LORD ASHFORD'S MASTER OF HORSE.
I'LL FIND HIM FOR YOU.
AND WITH THEM, THE KINGSGUARD KNIGHTS --
-- WITH THE ROYAL BANNER.
BOY!
LET GO OF THAT NAG AND SEE TO MY HORSE!

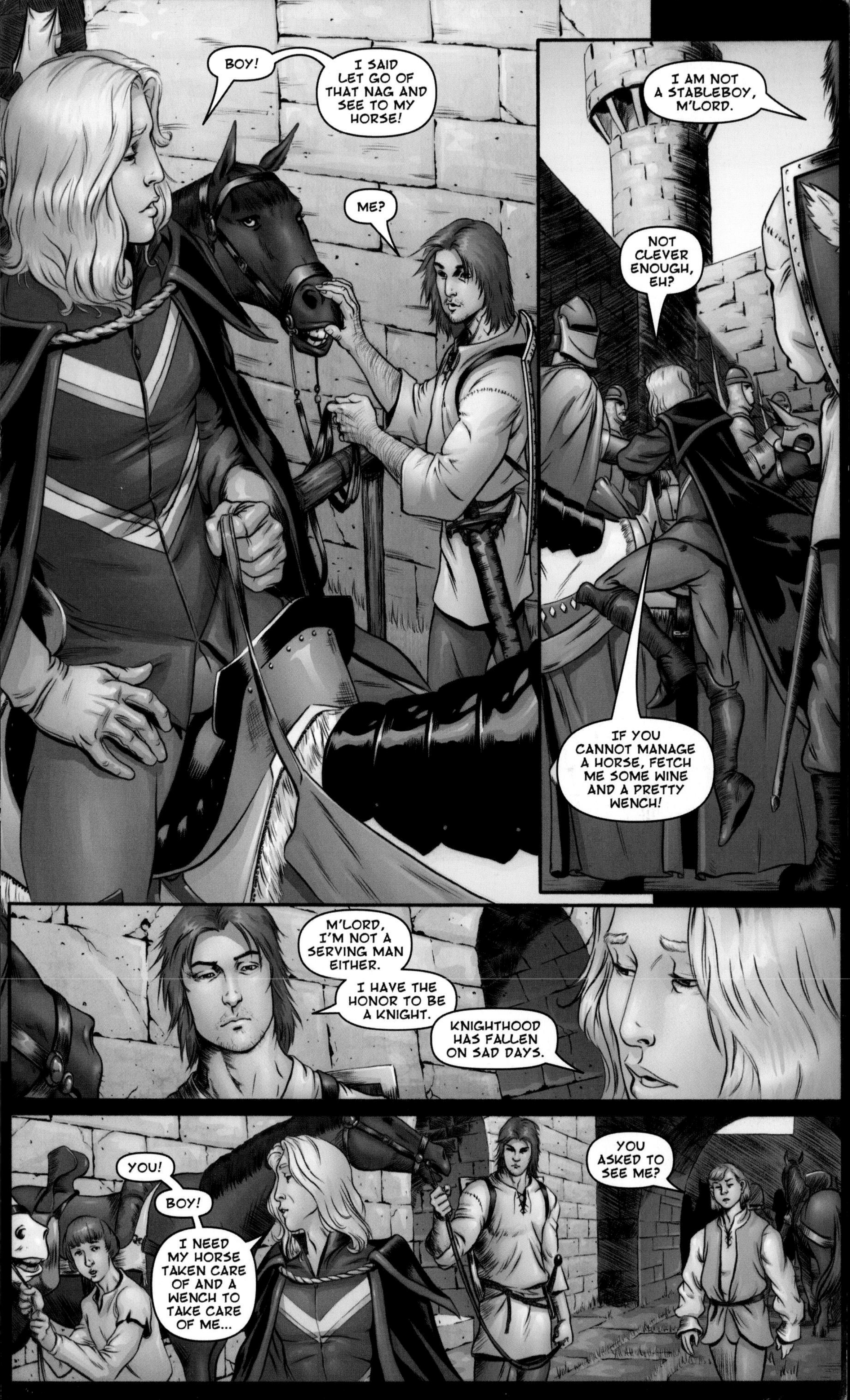
BOY!
I SAID LET GO OF THAT NAG AND SEE TO MY HORSE!
ME?
I AM NOT A STABLEBOY, M'LORD.
NOT CLEVER ENOUGH, EH?
IF YOU CANNOT MANAGE A HORSE, FETCH ME SOME WINE AND A PRETTY WENCH!
M'LORD, I'M NOT A SERVING MAN EITHER.
I HAVE THE HONOR TO BE A KNIGHT.
KNIGHTHOOD HAS FALLEN ON SAD DAYS.
YOU!
BOY!
I NEED MY HORSE TAKEN CARE OF AND A WENCH TO TAKE CARE OF ME...
YOU ASKED TO SEE ME?

WHAT CAN I DO FOR YE?

THIS IS SWEETFOOT.

THE OLD MAN ALWAYS SAID THAT A KNIGHT SHOULD NEVER LOVE A HORSE, SINCE MORE THAN A FEW WERE LIKE TO DIE UNDER HIM.

AH, A FINE LOOKING BEAST! STRONG FLANKS. PROUD GAIT.

AND HOW MUCH WOULD YOU GIVE ME FOR HER?

WELL, OF COURSE, SHE'S NOT PERFECT.

THREE HUNDRED! MORE LIKE THREE THOUSAND!

BOWED LEGS AND BACK. SEEMS TO BE LOSING HAIR. HURRM. FLEAS.

HUHNH... THREE HUNDRED SILVERS.

SER, PLEASE, NOT EVEN IN HER PRIME... FIVE HUNDRED.

TWO THOUSAND.

PERHAPS THERE ARE OTHER STABLEMEN ABOUT WHO ARE AS STUPID AS YOU SEEM TO THINK I AM -- GO TO THEM.

VERY WELL.

AND AN APPLE, TOO!

ONE THOUSAND?

SEVEN HUNDRED AND FIFTY. FINAL OFFER.

SWEETFOOT HAD BORNE SER ARLAN TIRELESSLY OVER THOUSANDS OF MILES, ALL UP AND DOWN THE SEVEN KINGDOMS.

THE EXTRA'S FOR HER.

SEE THAT SHE HAS SOME OATS TONIGHT.

BUT THE OLD MAN NEVER HEEDED HIS OWN COUNSEL ABOUT HIS HORSES.

WHY SHOULD I?

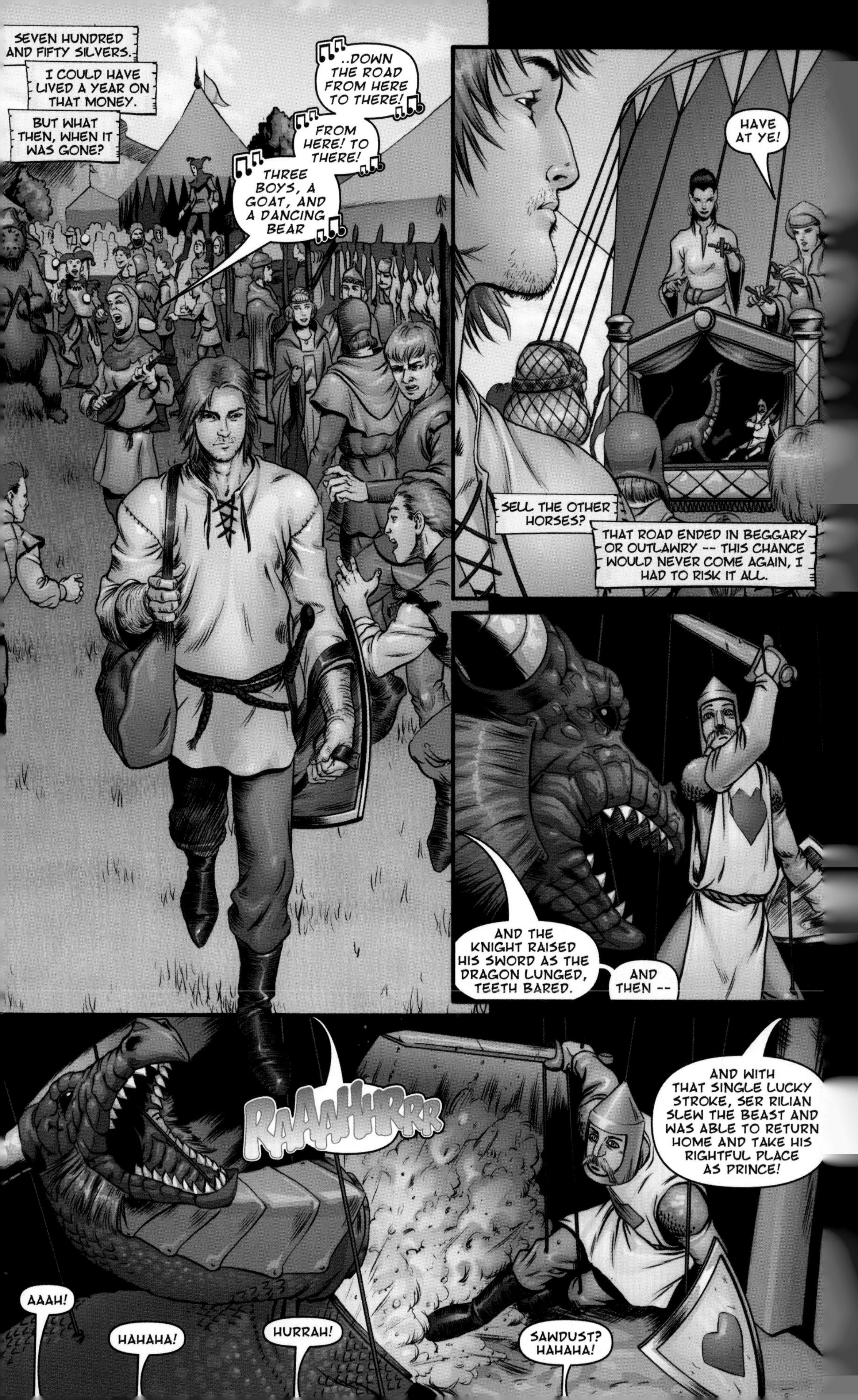
SEVEN HUNDRED AND FIFTY SILVERS.
I COULD HAVE LIVED A YEAR ON THAT MONEY.
BUT WHAT THEN, WHEN IT WAS GONE?
..DOWN THE ROAD FROM HERE TO THERE!
FROM HERE! TO THERE!
THREE BOYS, A GOAT, AND A DANCING BEAR
HAVE AT YE!
SELL THE OTHER HORSES?
THAT ROAD ENDED IN BEGGARY OR OUTLAWRY -- THIS CHANCE WOULD NEVER COME AGAIN, I HAD TO RISK IT ALL.
AND THE KNIGHT RAISED HIS SWORD AS THE DRAGON LUNGED, TEETH BARED.
AND THEN --
RAAAHHRRR
AND WITH THAT SINGLE LUCKY STROKE, SER RILIAN SLEW THE BEAST AND WAS ABLE TO RETURN HOME AND TAKE HIS RIGHTFUL PLACE AS PRINCE!
AAAH!
HAHAHA!
HURRAH!
SAWDUST? HAHAHA!

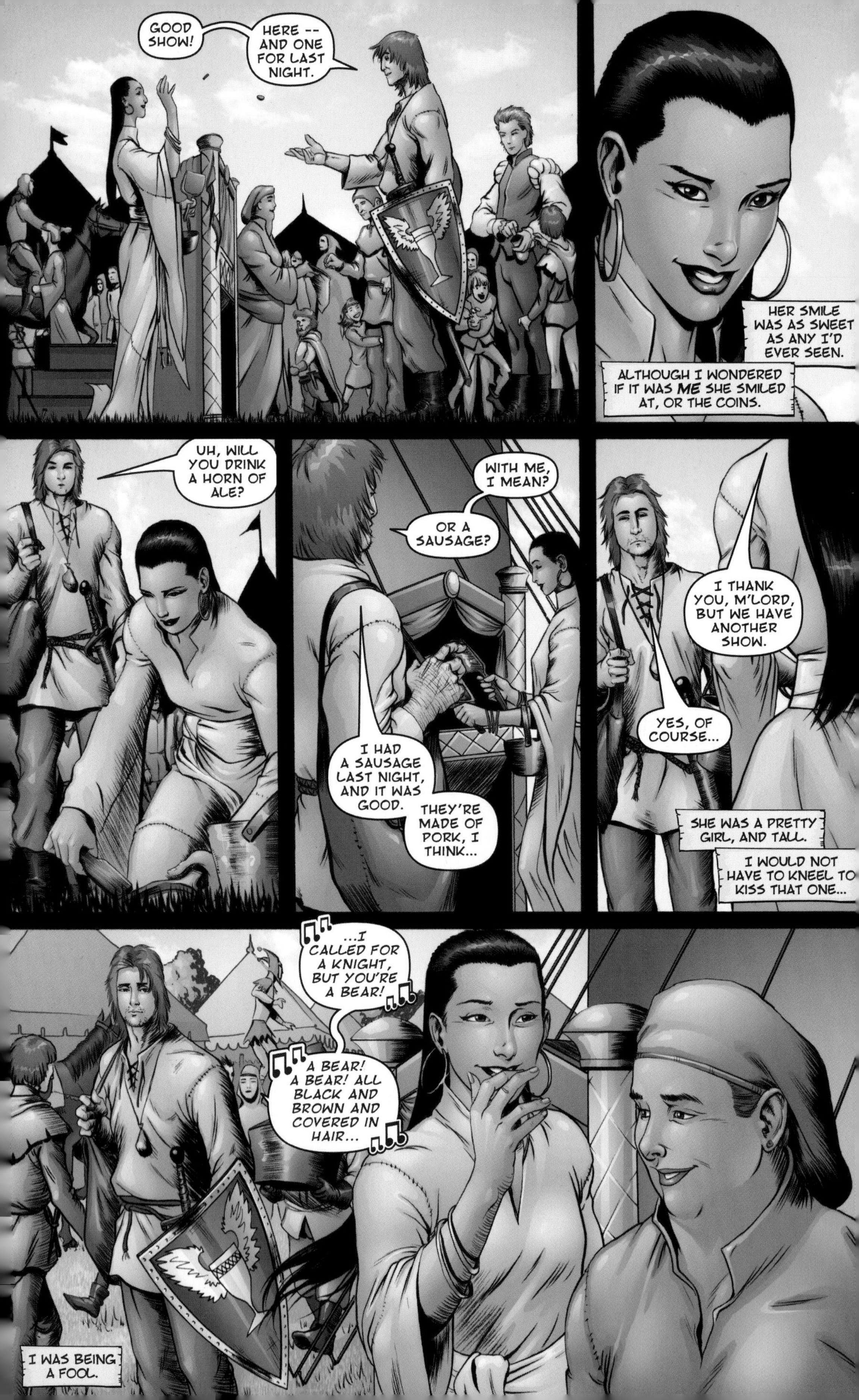
GOOD SHOW!
HERE -- AND ONE FOR LAST NIGHT.
HER SMILE WAS AS SWEET AS ANY I'D EVER SEEN.
ALTHOUGH I WONDERED IF IT WAS ME SHE SMILED AT, OR THE COINS.
UH, WILL YOU DRINK A HORN OF ALE?
WITH ME, I MEAN?
OR A SAUSAGE?
I HAD A SAUSAGE LAST NIGHT, AND IT WAS GOOD.
THEY'RE MADE OF PORK, I THINK...
I THANK YOU, M'LORD, BUT WE HAVE ANOTHER SHOW.
YES, OF COURSE...
SHE WAS A PRETTY GIRL, AND TALL.
I WOULD NOT HAVE TO KNEEL TO KISS THAT ONE...
...I CALLED FOR A KNIGHT, BUT YOU'RE A BEAR!
A BEAR! A BEAR! ALL BLACK AND BROWN AND COVERED IN HAIR...
I WAS BEING A FOOL.

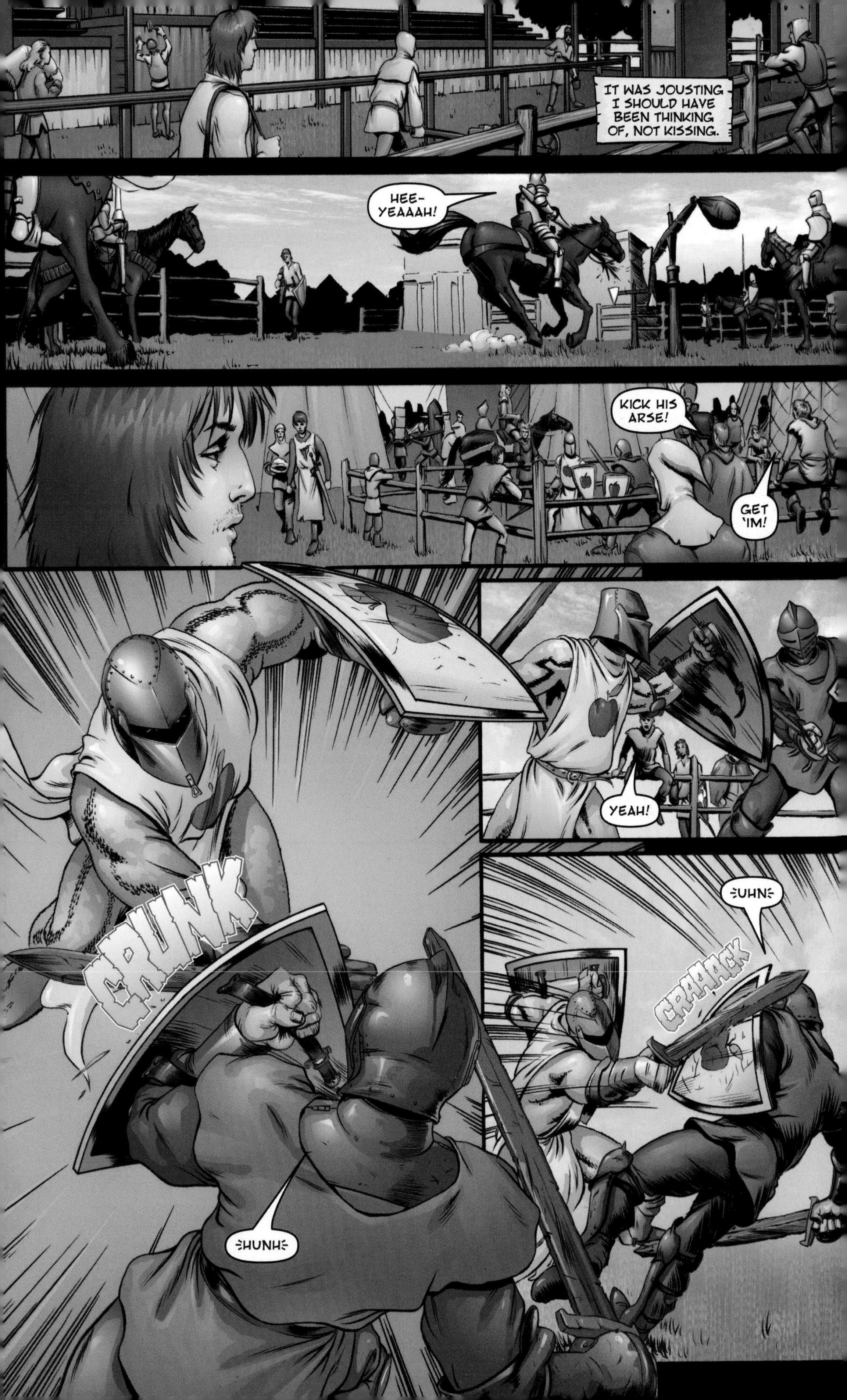
IT WAS JOUSTING I SHOULD HAVE BEEN THINKING OF, NOT KISSING.
HEE-YEAAAH!
KICK HIS ARSE!
GET 'IM!
YEAH!
CRUNK
HUNH
UHN
CRAAACK

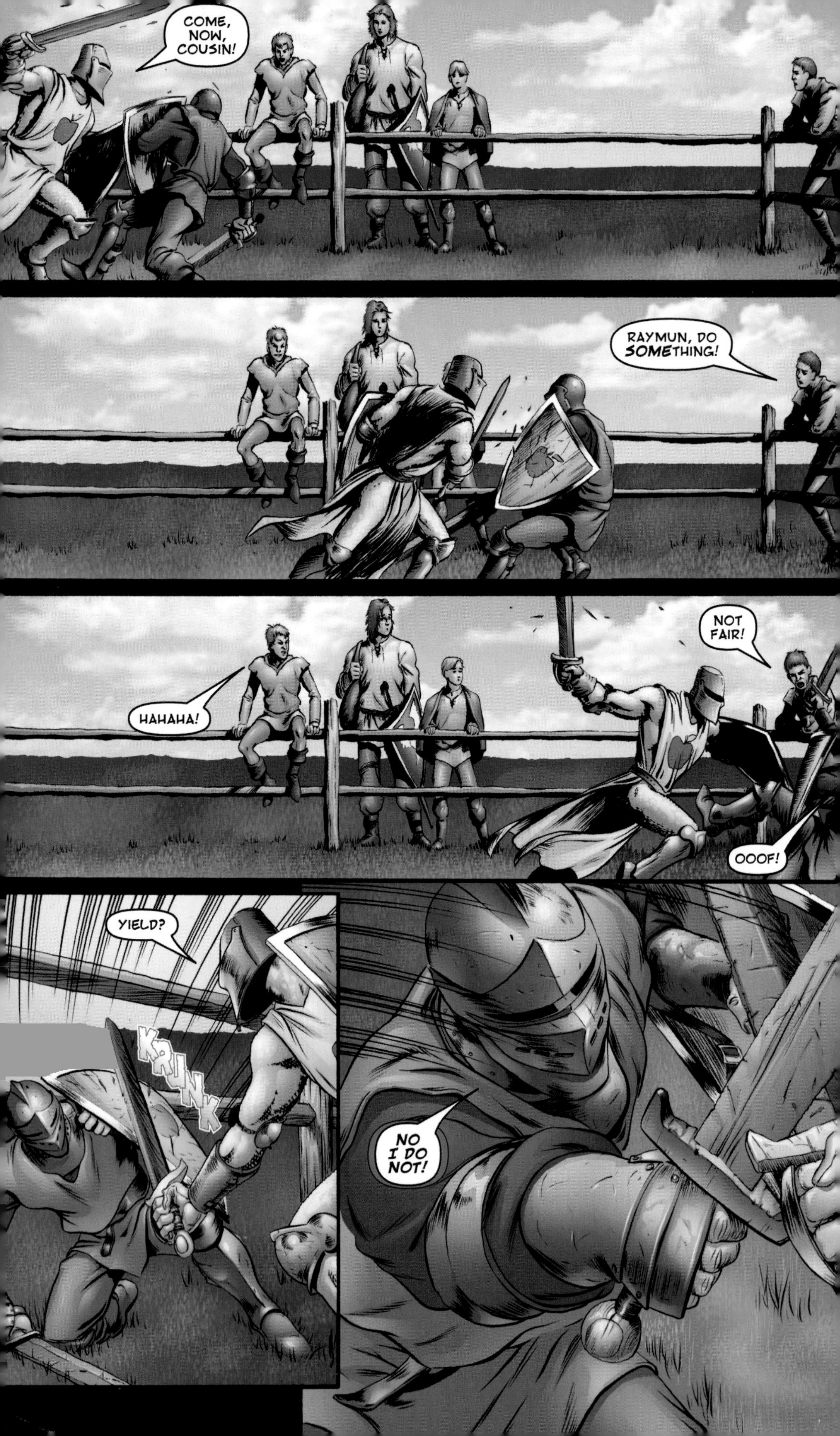
COME, NOW, COUSIN!
RAYMUN, DO SOMETHING!
HAHAHA!
NOT FAIR!
OOOF!
YIELD?
KRUNK
NO I DO NOT!

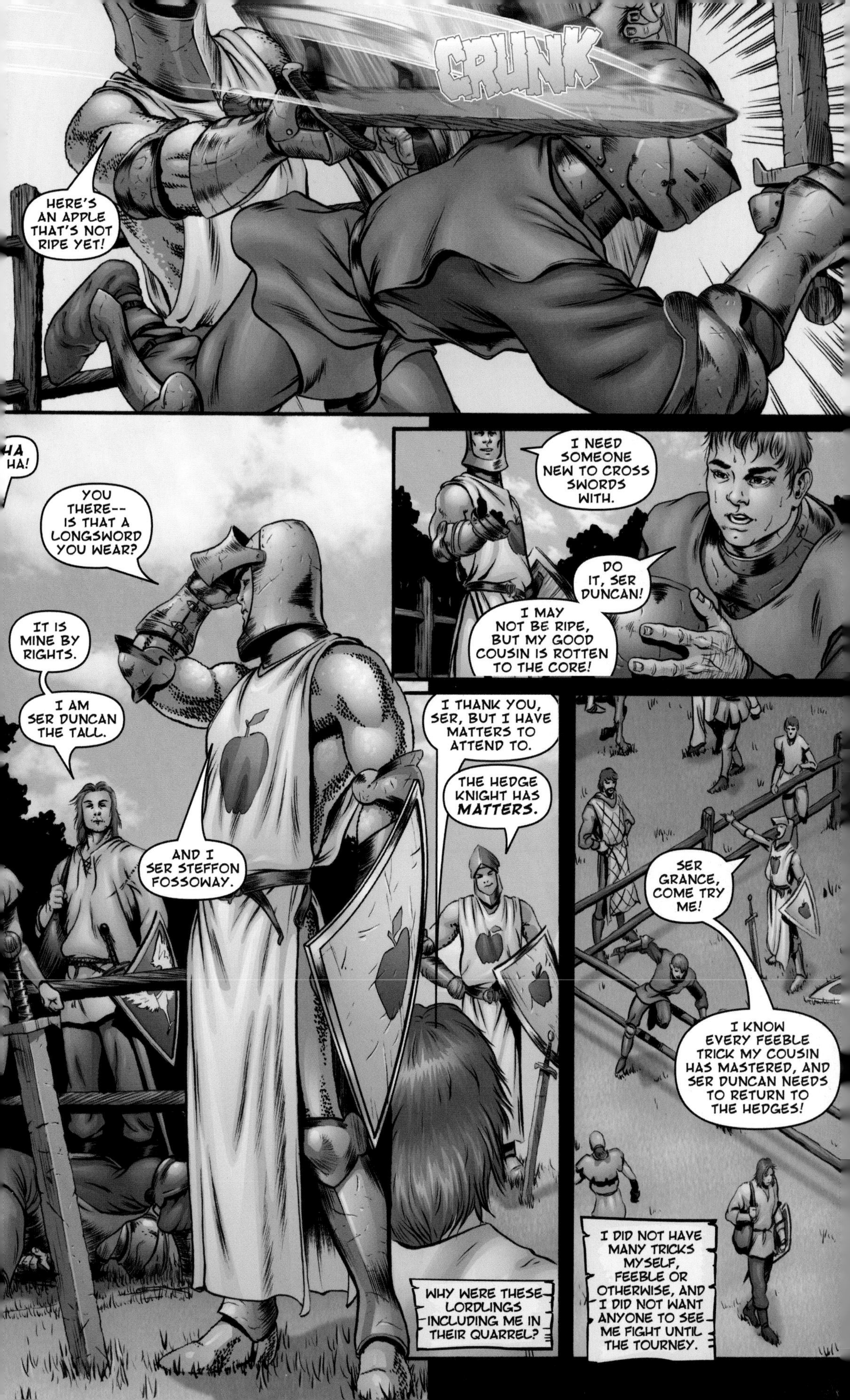
CRUNK
HERE'S AN APPLE THAT'S NOT RIPE YET!
HA HA!
YOU THERE-- IS THAT A LONGSWORD YOU WEAR?
IT IS MINE BY RIGHTS.
I AM SER DUNCAN THE TALL.
AND I SER STEFFON FOSSOWAY.
I NEED SOMEONE NEW TO CROSS SWORDS WITH.
DO IT, SER DUNCAN!
I MAY NOT BE RIPE, BUT MY GOOD COUSIN IS ROTTEN TO THE CORE!
I THANK YOU, SER, BUT I HAVE MATTERS TO ATTEND TO.
THE HEDGE KNIGHT HAS MATTERS.
WHY WERE THESE LORDLINGS INCLUDING ME IN THEIR QUARREL?
SER GRANCE, COME TRY ME!
I KNOW EVERY FEEBLE TRICK MY COUSIN HAS MASTERED, AND SER DUNCAN NEEDS TO RETURN TO THE HEDGES!
I DID NOT HAVE MANY TRICKS MYSELF, FEEBLE OR OTHERWISE, AND I DID NOT WANT ANYONE TO SEE ME FIGHT UNTIL THE TOURNEY.

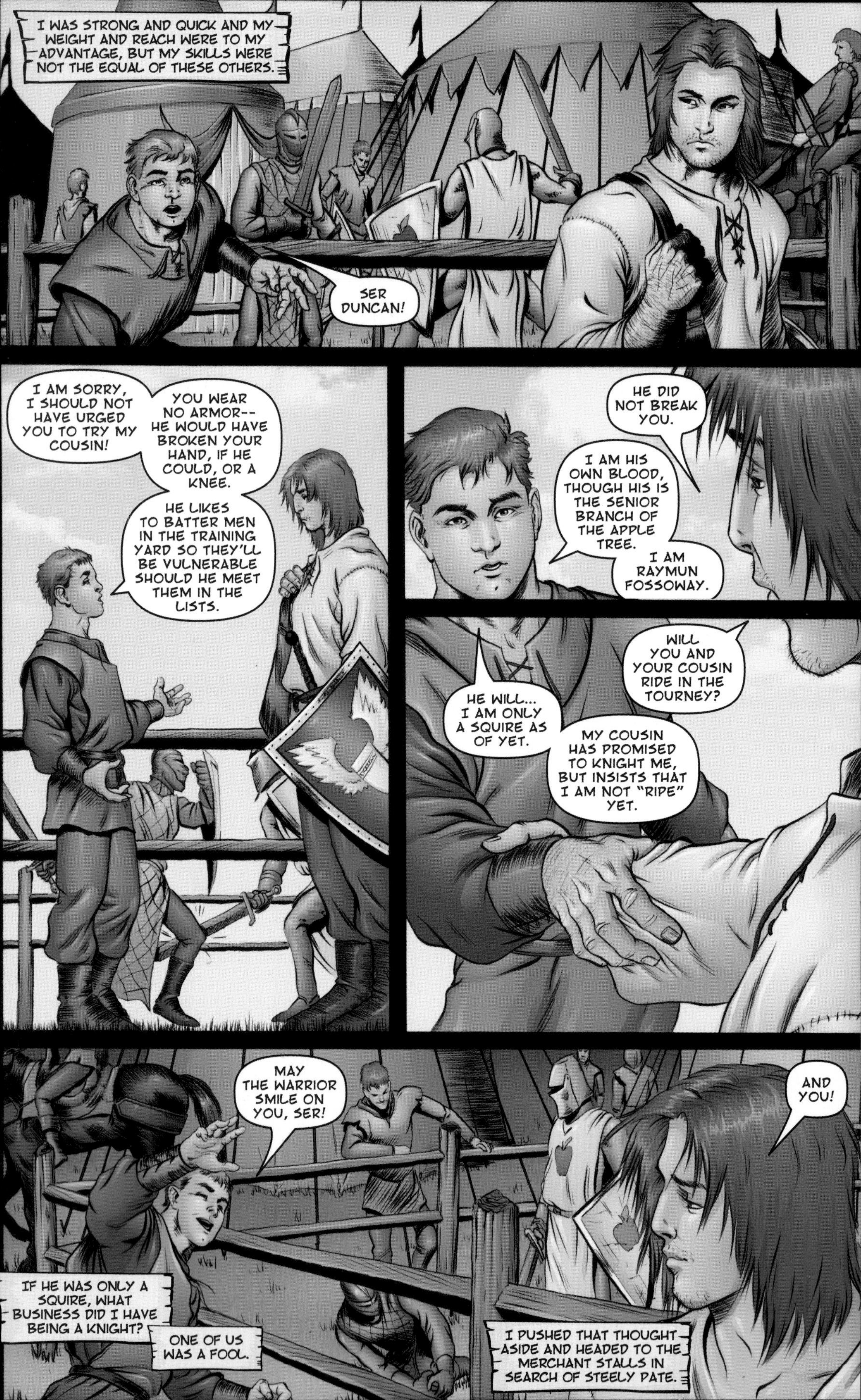
I WAS STRONG AND QUICK AND MY WEIGHT AND REACH WERE TO MY ADVANTAGE, BUT MY SKILLS WERE NOT THE EQUAL OF THESE OTHERS.
SER DUNCAN!
I AM SORRY, I SHOULD NOT HAVE URGED YOU TO TRY MY COUSIN!
YOU WEAR NO ARMOR-- HE WOULD HAVE BROKEN YOUR HAND, IF HE COULD, OR A KNEE.
HE LIKES TO BATTER MEN IN THE TRAINING YARD SO THEY'LL BE VULNERABLE SHOULD HE MEET THEM IN THE LISTS.
HE DID NOT BREAK YOU.
I AM HIS OWN BLOOD, THOUGH HIS IS THE SENIOR BRANCH OF THE APPLE TREE.
I AM RAYMUN FOSSOWAY.
WILL YOU AND YOUR COUSIN RIDE IN THE TOURNEY?
HE WILL... I AM ONLY A SQUIRE AS OF YET.
MY COUSIN HAS PROMISED TO KNIGHT ME, BUT INSISTS THAT I AM NOT "RIPE" YET.
MAY THE WARRIOR SMILE ON YOU, SER!
AND YOU!
IF HE WAS ONLY A SQUIRE, WHAT BUSINESS DID I HAVE BEING A KNIGHT?
ONE OF US WAS A FOOL.
I PUSHED THAT THOUGHT ASIDE AND HEADED TO THE MERCHANT STALLS IN SEARCH OF STEELY PATE.

ISSUE THREE
COVER A

MIKE S. MILLER

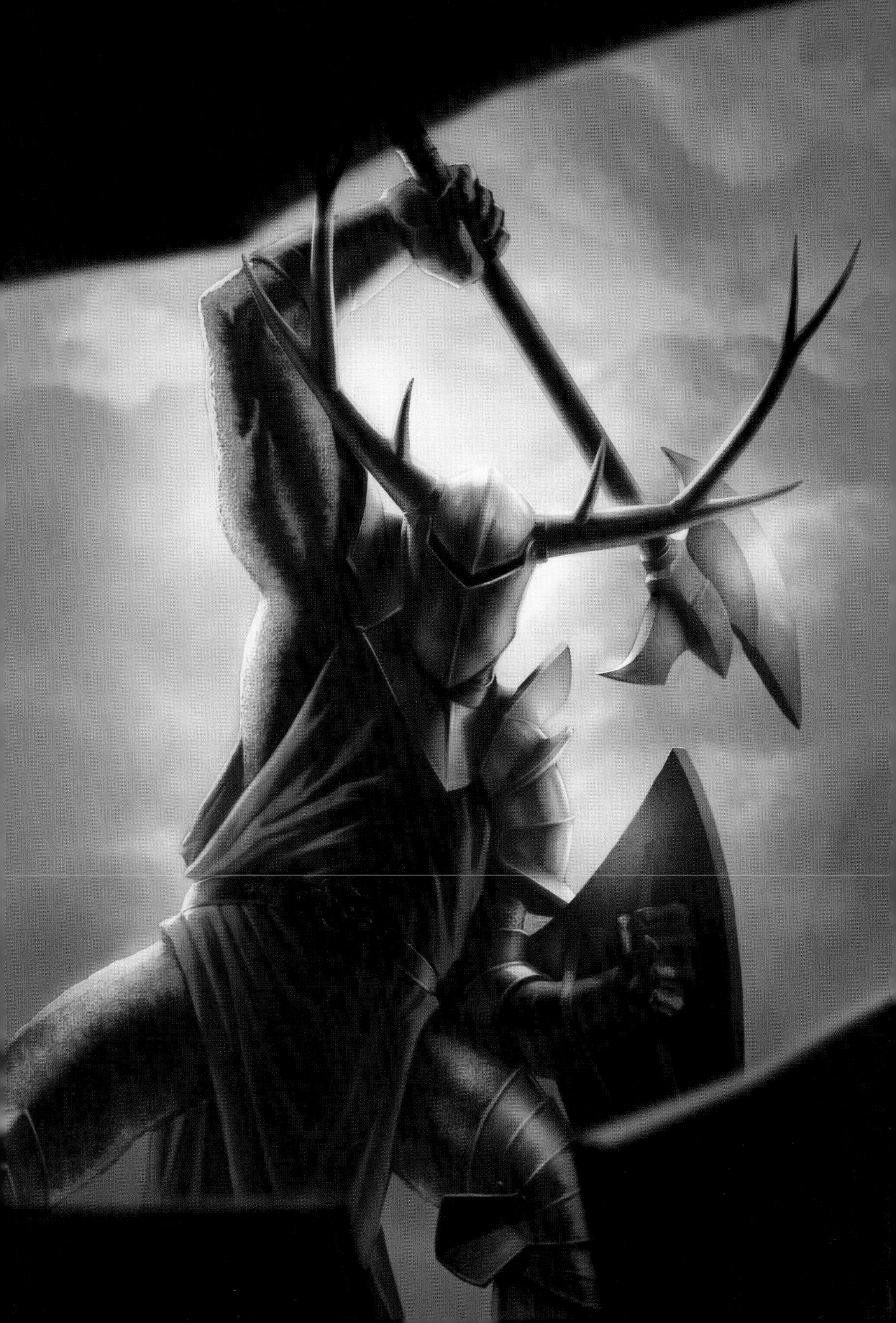

ISSUE THREE
COVER B
Tom Mandrake

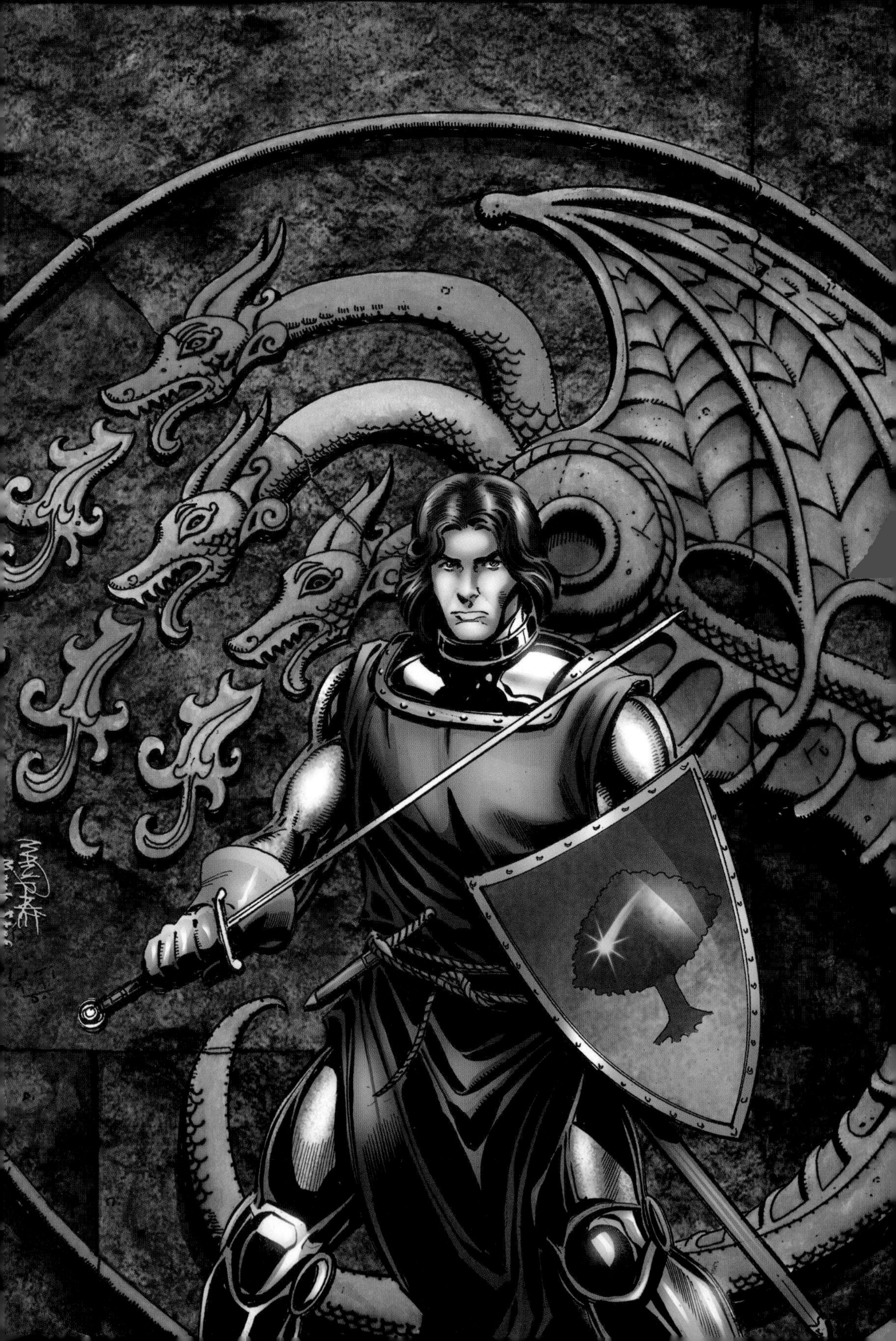

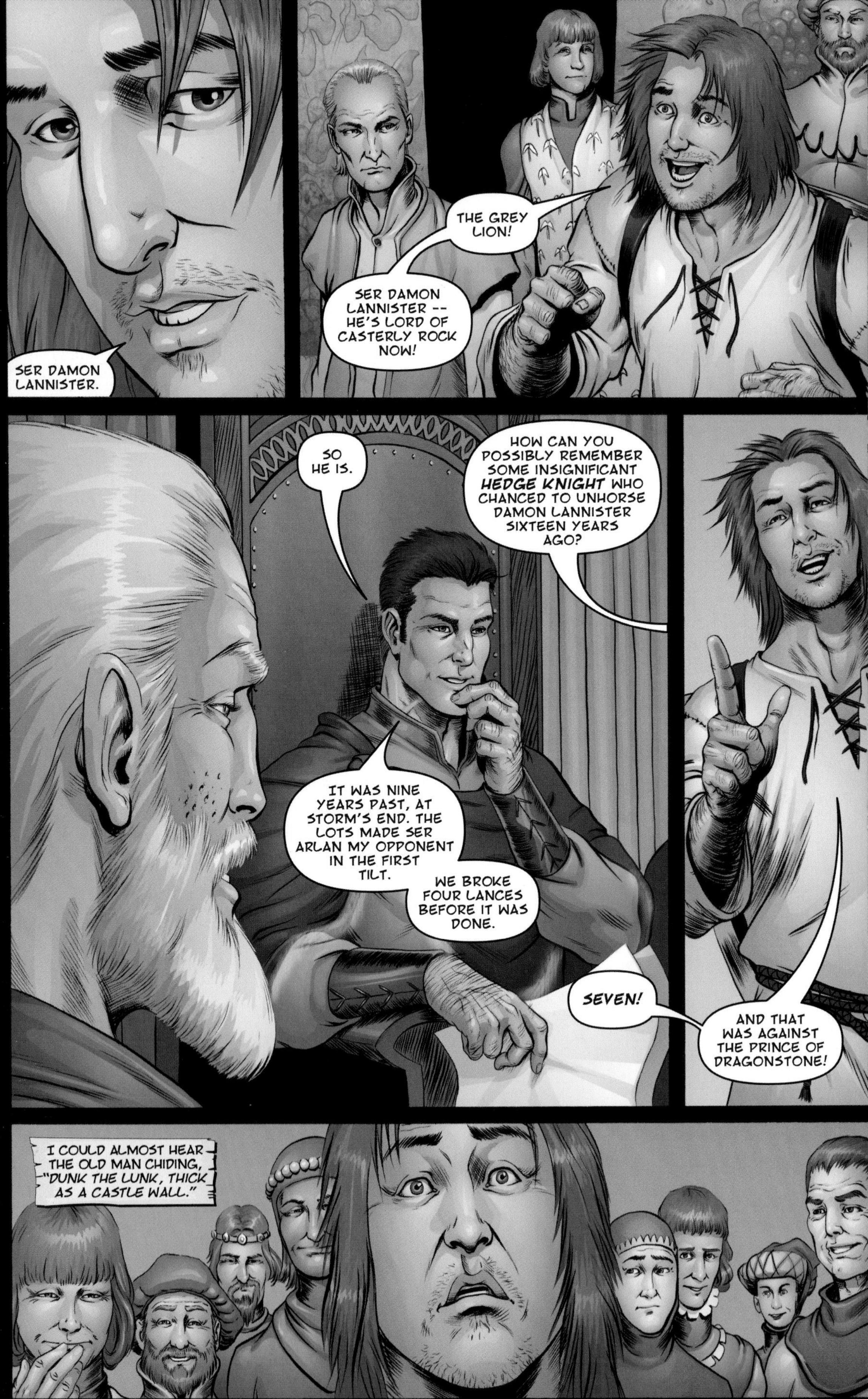
SER DAMON LANNISTER.
THE GREY LION!
SER DAMON LANNISTER -- HE'S LORD OF CASTERLY ROCK NOW!
SO HE IS.
HOW CAN YOU POSSIBLY REMEMBER SOME INSIGNIFICANT **HEDGE KNIGHT** WHO CHANCED TO UNHORSE DAMON LANNISTER SIXTEEN YEARS AGO?
IT WAS NINE YEARS PAST, AT STORM'S END. THE LOTS MADE SER ARLAN MY OPPONENT IN THE FIRST TILT.
WE BROKE FOUR LANCES BEFORE IT WAS DONE.
SEVEN!
AND THAT WAS AGAINST THE PRINCE OF DRAGONSTONE!
I COULD ALMOST HEAR THE OLD MAN CHIDING, "DUNK THE LUNK, THICK AS A CASTLE WALL."

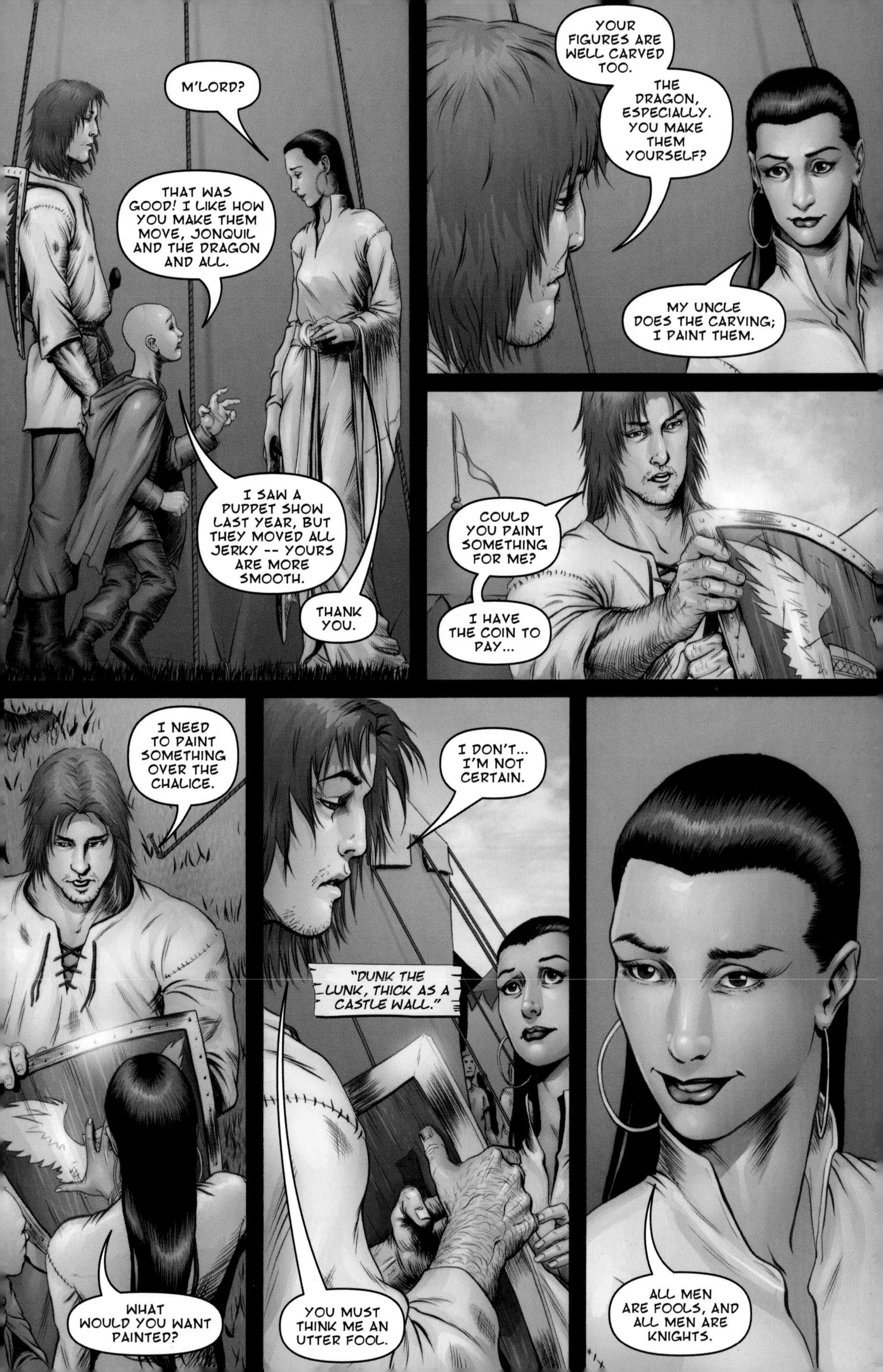
M'LORD?
THAT WAS GOOD! I LIKE HOW YOU MAKE THEM MOVE, JONQUIL AND THE DRAGON AND ALL.
I SAW A PUPPET SHOW LAST YEAR, BUT THEY MOVED ALL JERKY -- YOURS ARE MORE SMOOTH.
THANK YOU.
YOUR FIGURES ARE WELL CARVED TOO.
THE DRAGON, ESPECIALLY. YOU MAKE THEM YOURSELF?
MY UNCLE DOES THE CARVING; I PAINT THEM.
COULD YOU PAINT SOMETHING FOR ME?
I HAVE THE COIN TO PAY...
I NEED TO PAINT SOMETHING OVER THE CHALICE.
WHAT WOULD YOU WANT PAINTED?
I DON'T... I'M NOT CERTAIN.
"DUNK THE LUNK, THICK AS A CASTLE WALL."
YOU MUST THINK ME AN UTTER FOOL.
ALL MEN ARE FOOLS, AND ALL MEN ARE KNIGHTS.

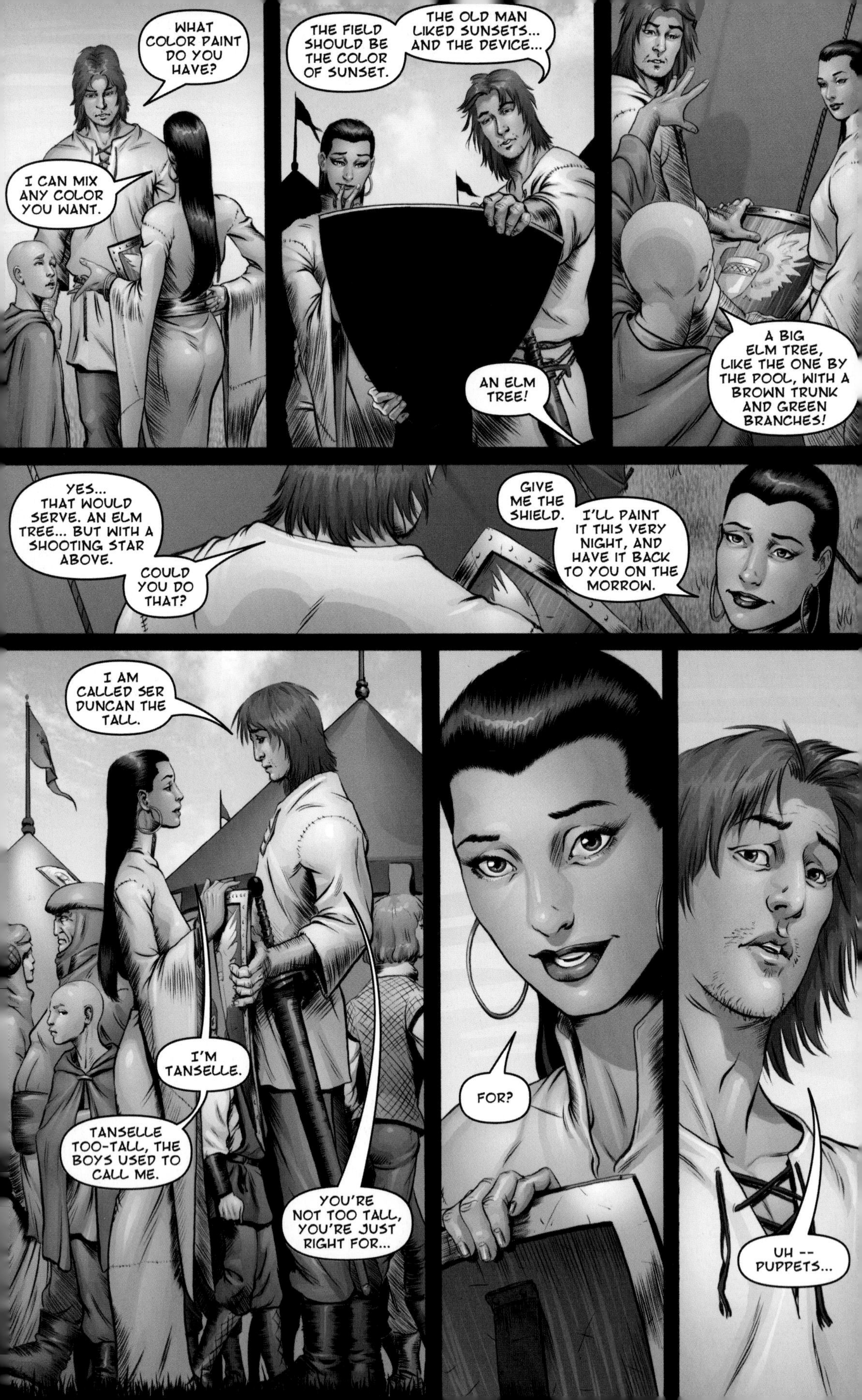
WHAT COLOR PAINT DO YOU HAVE?
I CAN MIX ANY COLOR YOU WANT.
THE FIELD SHOULD BE THE COLOR OF SUNSET.
THE OLD MAN LIKED SUNSETS... AND THE DEVICE...
AN ELM TREE!
A BIG ELM TREE, LIKE THE ONE BY THE POOL, WITH A BROWN TRUNK AND GREEN BRANCHES!
YES... THAT WOULD SERVE. AN ELM TREE... BUT WITH A SHOOTING STAR ABOVE.
COULD YOU DO THAT?
GIVE ME THE SHIELD.
I'LL PAINT IT THIS VERY NIGHT, AND HAVE IT BACK TO YOU ON THE MORROW.
I AM CALLED SER DUNCAN THE TALL.
I'M TANSELLE.
TANSELLE TOO-TALL, THE BOYS USED TO CALL ME.
YOU'RE NOT TOO TALL, YOU'RE JUST RIGHT FOR...
FOR?
UH -- PUPPETS...

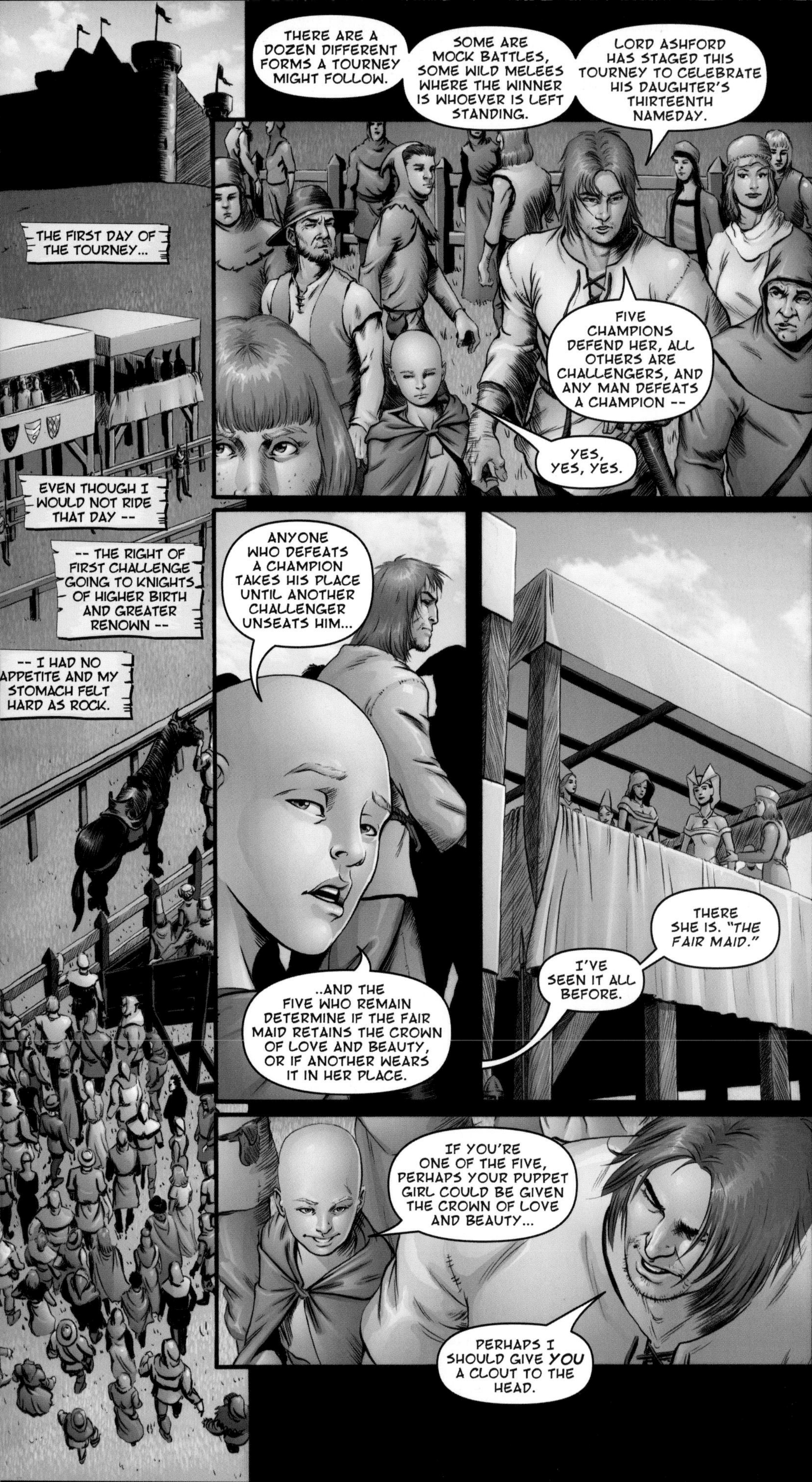
THE FIRST DAY OF THE TOURNEY...
THERE ARE A DOZEN DIFFERENT FORMS A TOURNEY MIGHT FOLLOW.
SOME ARE MOCK BATTLES, SOME WILD MELEES WHERE THE WINNER IS WHOEVER IS LEFT STANDING.
LORD ASHFORD HAS STAGED THIS TOURNEY TO CELEBRATE HIS DAUGHTER'S THIRTEENTH NAMEDAY.
FIVE CHAMPIONS DEFEND HER, ALL OTHERS ARE CHALLENGERS, AND ANY MAN DEFEATS A CHAMPION --
YES, YES, YES.
EVEN THOUGH I WOULD NOT RIDE THAT DAY --
-- THE RIGHT OF FIRST CHALLENGE GOING TO KNIGHTS OF HIGHER BIRTH AND GREATER RENOWN --
-- I HAD NO APPETITE AND MY STOMACH FELT HARD AS ROCK.
ANYONE WHO DEFEATS A CHAMPION TAKES HIS PLACE UNTIL ANOTHER CHALLENGER UNSEATS HIM...
..AND THE FIVE WHO REMAIN DETERMINE IF THE FAIR MAID RETAINS THE CROWN OF LOVE AND BEAUTY, OR IF ANOTHER WEARS IT IN HER PLACE.
THERE SHE IS. "THE FAIR MAID."
I'VE SEEN IT ALL BEFORE.
IF YOU'RE ONE OF THE FIVE, PERHAPS YOUR PUPPET GIRL COULD BE GIVEN THE CROWN OF LOVE AND BEAUTY...
PERHAPS I SHOULD GIVE YOU A CLOUT TO THE HEAD.

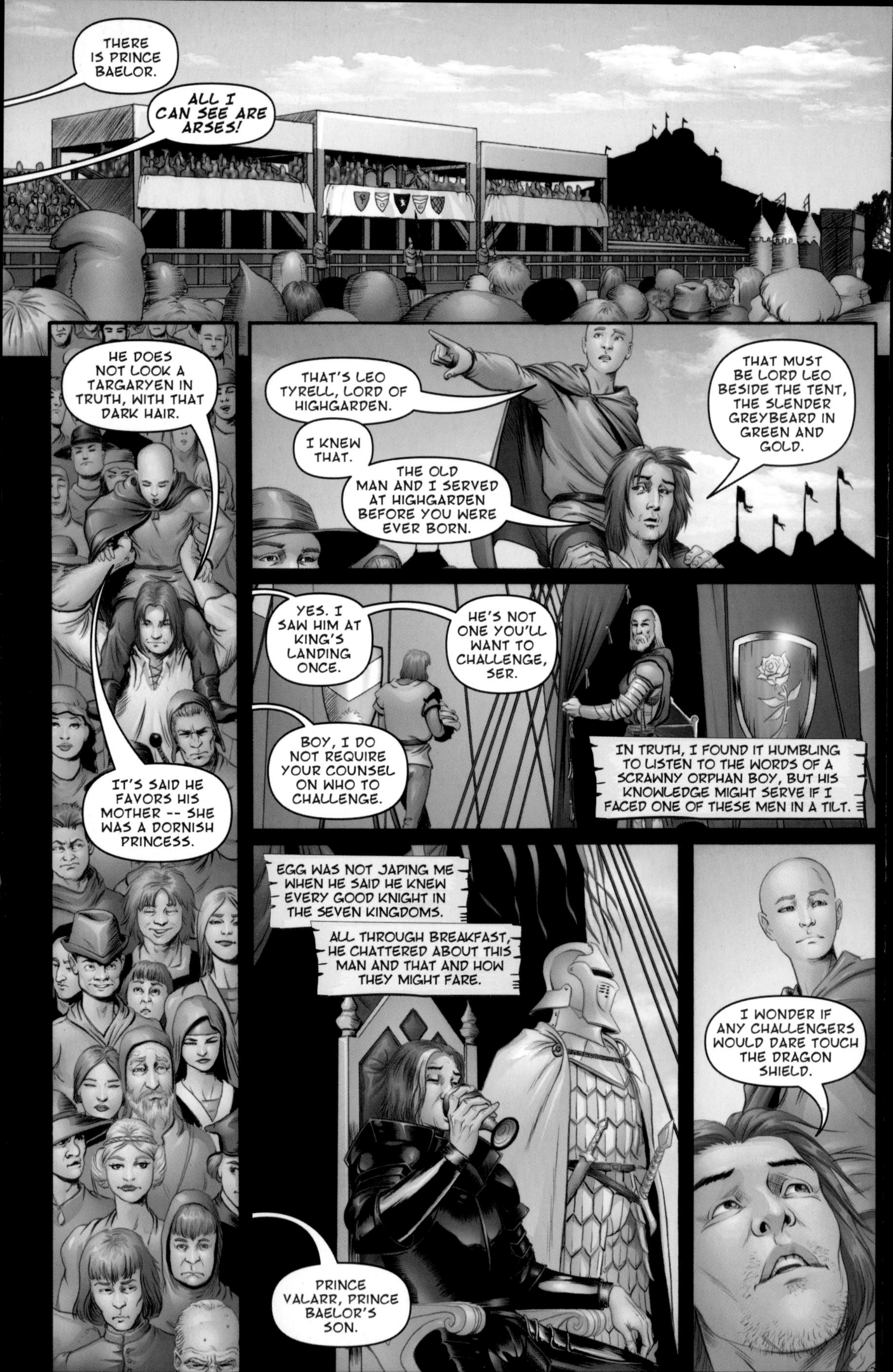
THERE IS PRINCE BAELOR.
ALL I CAN SEE ARE ARSES!
HE DOES NOT LOOK A TARGARYEN IN TRUTH, WITH THAT DARK HAIR.
IT'S SAID HE FAVORS HIS MOTHER -- SHE WAS A DORNISH PRINCESS.
THAT'S LEO TYRELL, LORD OF HIGHGARDEN.
I KNEW THAT.
THE OLD MAN AND I SERVED AT HIGHGARDEN BEFORE YOU WERE EVER BORN.
THAT MUST BE LORD LEO BESIDE THE TENT, THE SLENDER GREYBEARD IN GREEN AND GOLD.
YES. I SAW HIM AT KING'S LANDING ONCE.
HE'S NOT ONE YOU'LL WANT TO CHALLENGE, SER.
BOY, I DO NOT REQUIRE YOUR COUNSEL ON WHO TO CHALLENGE.
IN TRUTH, I FOUND IT HUMBLING TO LISTEN TO THE WORDS OF A SCRAWNY ORPHAN BOY, BUT HIS KNOWLEDGE MIGHT SERVE IF I FACED ONE OF THESE MEN IN A TILT.
EGG WAS NOT JAPING ME WHEN HE SAID HE KNEW EVERY GOOD KNIGHT IN THE SEVEN KINGDOMS.
ALL THROUGH BREAKFAST, HE CHATTERED ABOUT THIS MAN AND THAT AND HOW THEY MIGHT FARE.
PRINCE VALARR, PRINCE BAELOR'S SON.
I WONDER IF ANY CHALLENGERS WOULD DARE TOUCH THE DRAGON SHIELD.

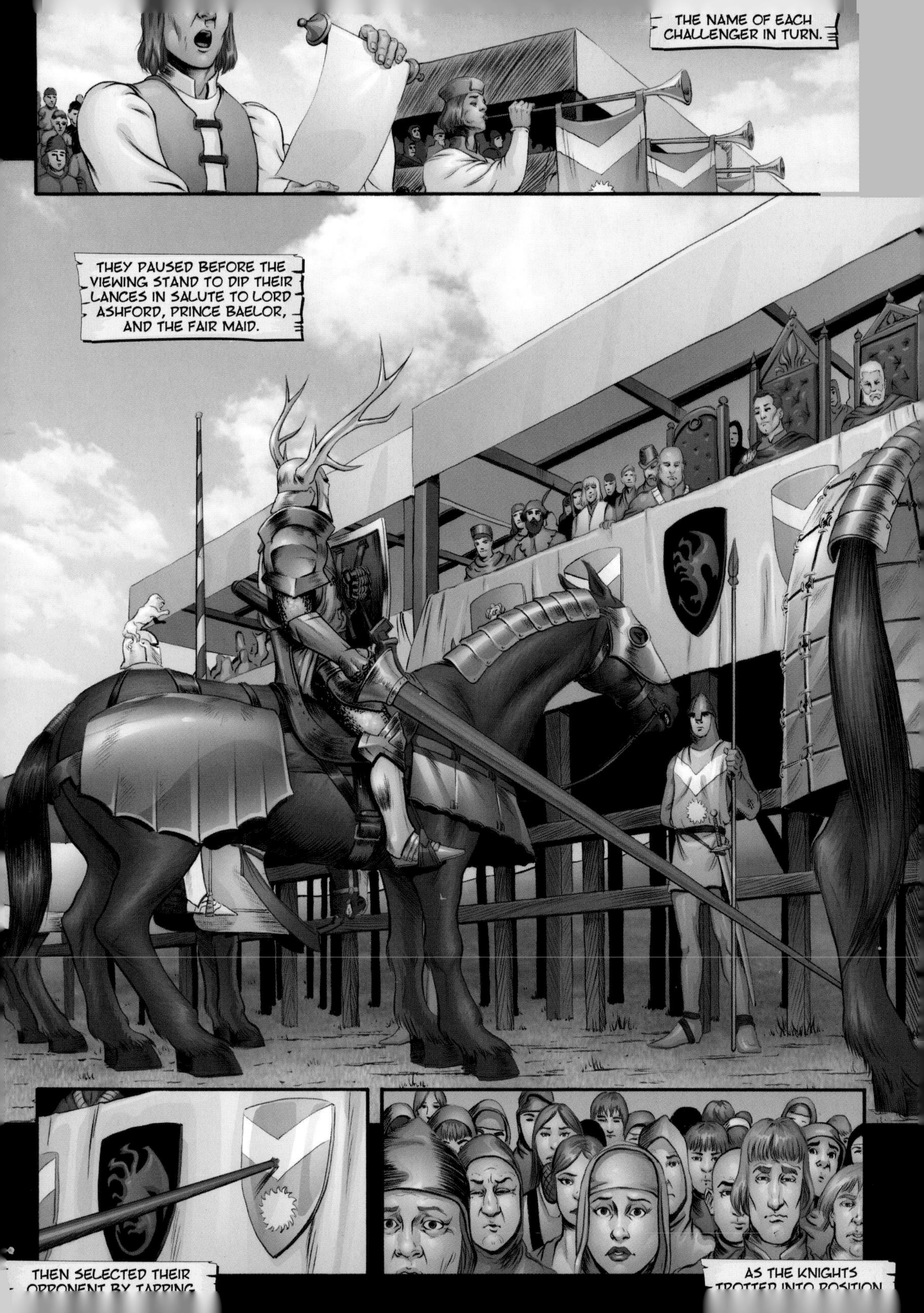
THE NAME OF EACH CHALLENGER IN TURN.
THEY PAUSED BEFORE THE VIEWING STAND TO DIP THEIR LANCES IN SALUTE TO LORD ASHFORD, PRINCE BAELOR, AND THE FAIR MAID.
THEN SELECTED THEIR
AS THE KNIGHTS

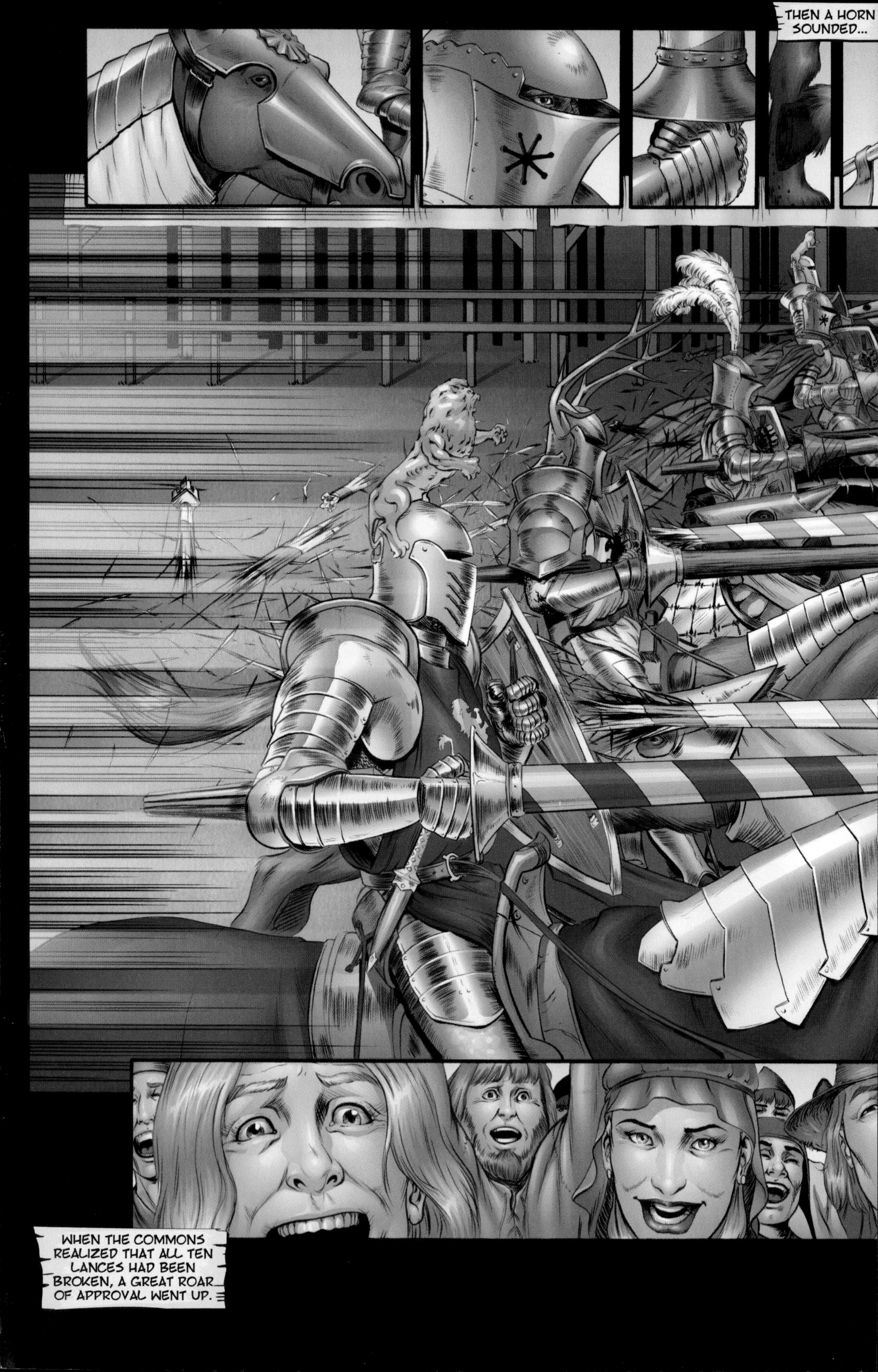
THEN A HORN SOUNDED...
WHEN THE COMMONS REALIZED THAT ALL TEN LANCES HAD BEEN BROKEN, A GREAT ROAR OF APPROVAL WENT UP.

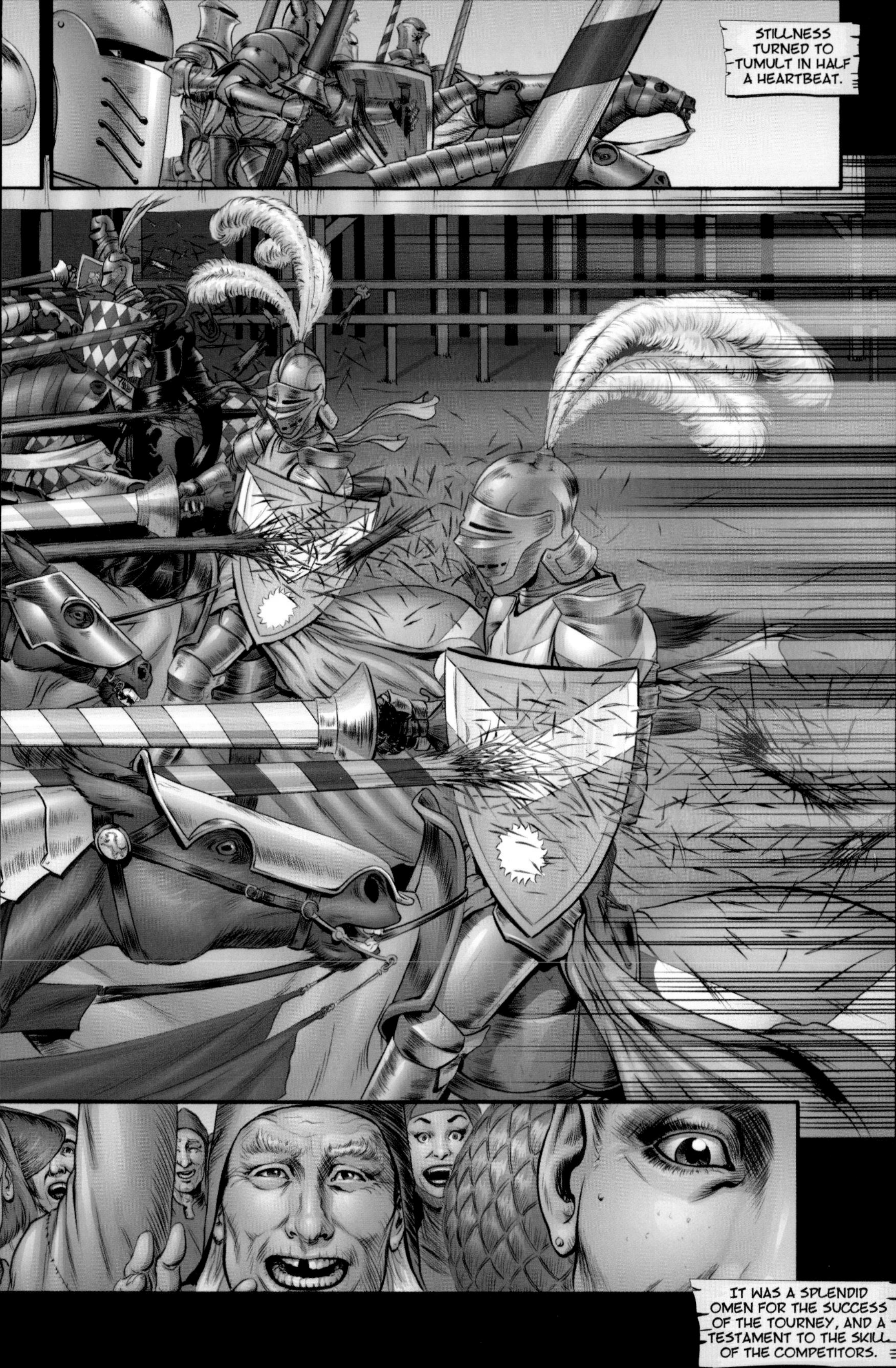
STILLNESS TURNED TO TUMULT IN HALF A HEARTBEAT.
IT WAS A SPLENDID OMEN FOR THE SUCCESS OF THE TOURNEY, AND A TESTAMENT TO THE SKILL OF THE COMPETITORS.

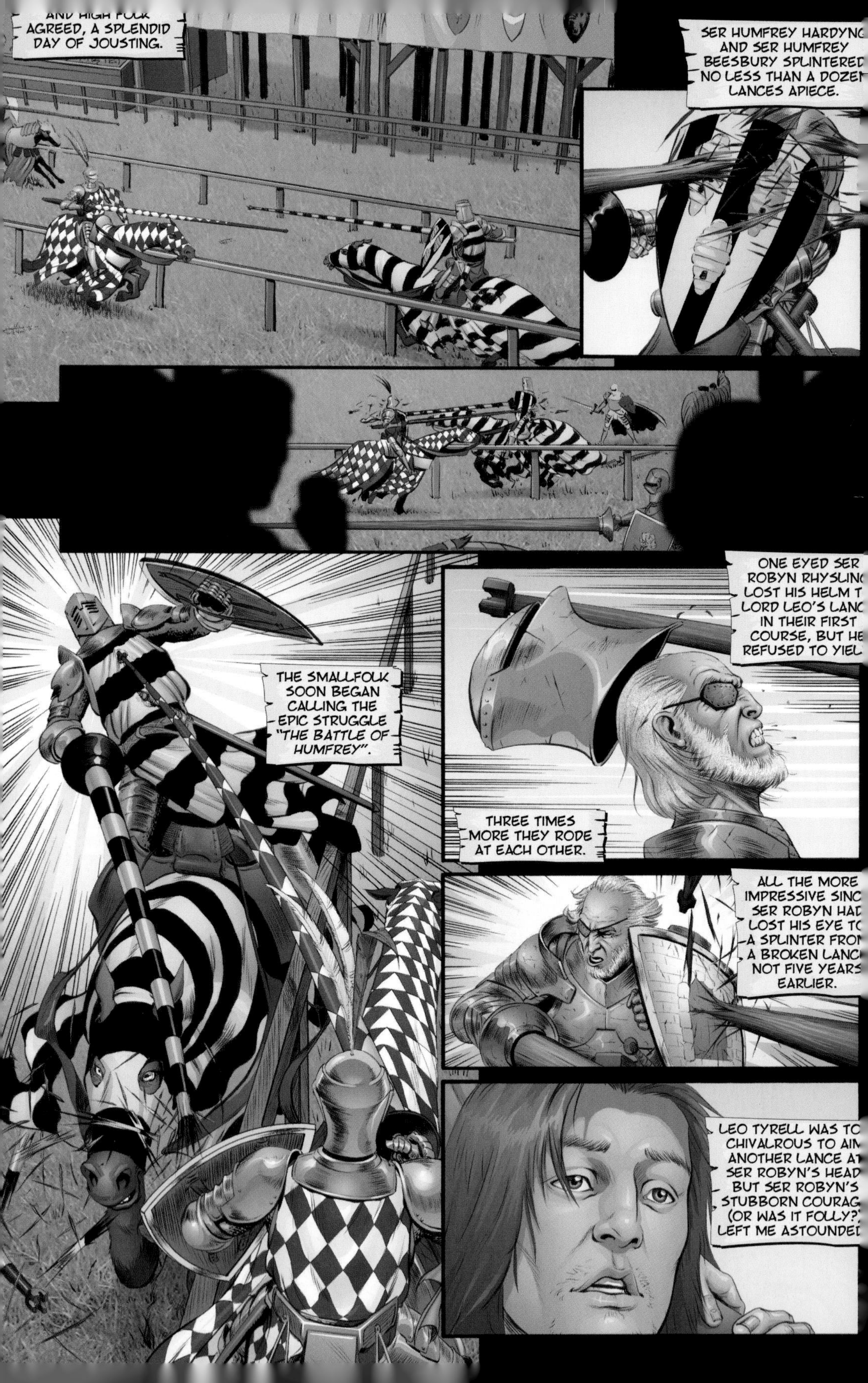
AND HIGH FOLK AGREED, A SPLENDID DAY OF JOUSTING.
SER HUMFREY HARDYNG AND SER HUMFREY BEESBURY SPLINTERED NO LESS THAN A DOZEN LANCES APIECE.
THE SMALLFOLK SOON BEGAN CALLING THE EPIC STRUGGLE "THE BATTLE OF HUMFREY".
ONE EYED SER ROBYN RHYSLING LOST HIS HELM TO LORD LEO'S LANCE IN THEIR FIRST COURSE, BUT HE REFUSED TO YIELD.
THREE TIMES MORE THEY RODE AT EACH OTHER.
ALL THE MORE IMPRESSIVE SINCE SER ROBYN HAD LOST HIS EYE TO A SPLINTER FROM A BROKEN LANCE NOT FIVE YEARS EARLIER.
LEO TYRELL WAS TOO CHIVALROUS TO AIM ANOTHER LANCE AT SER ROBYN'S HEAD, BUT SER ROBYN'S STUBBORN COURAGE (OR WAS IT FOLLY?) LEFT ME ASTOUNDED.

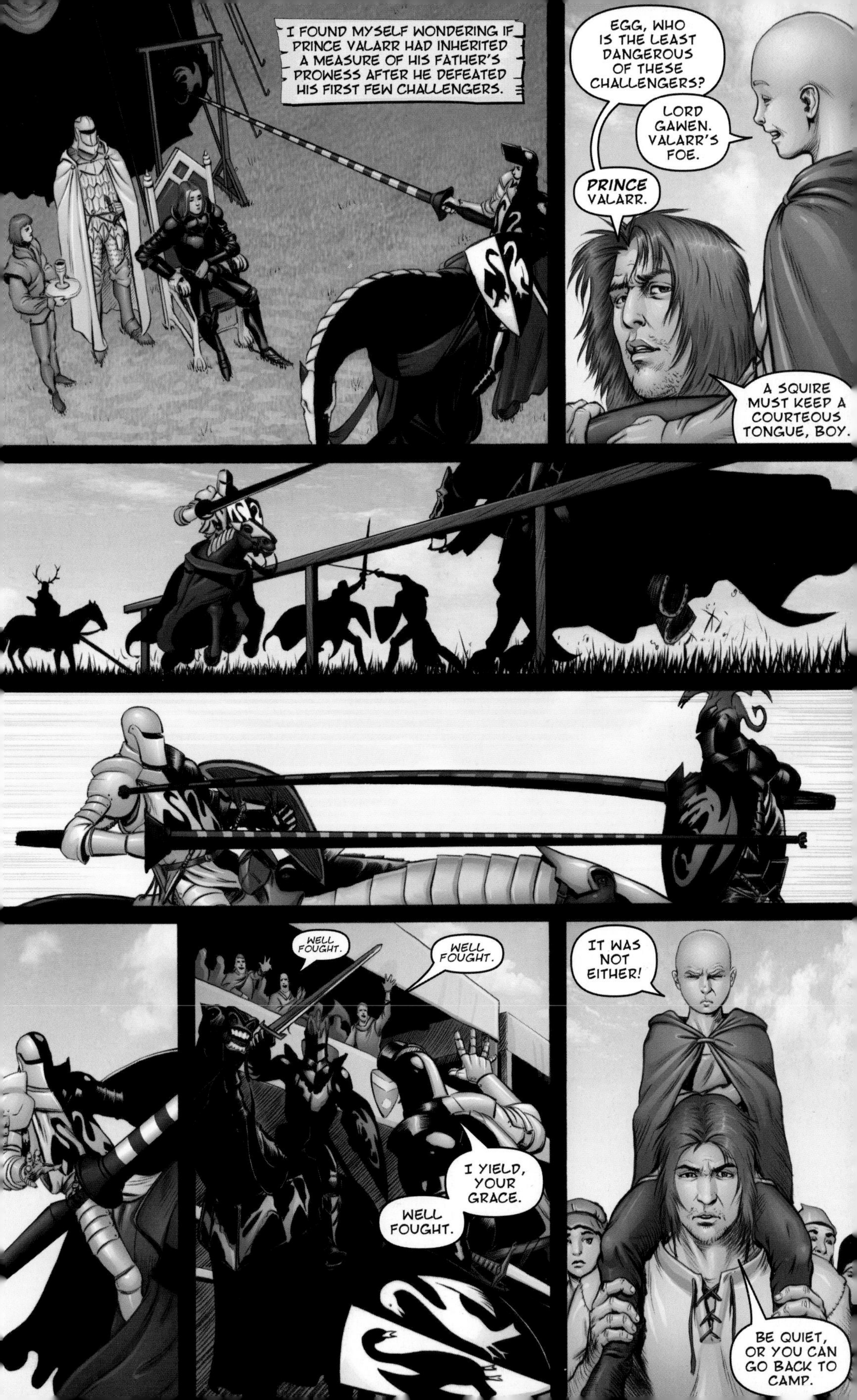
I FOUND MYSELF WONDERING IF PRINCE VALARR HAD INHERITED A MEASURE OF HIS FATHER'S PROWESS AFTER HE DEFEATED HIS FIRST FEW CHALLENGERS.
EGG, WHO IS THE LEAST DANGEROUS OF THESE CHALLENGERS?
LORD GAWEN. VALARR'S FOE.
PRINCE VALARR.
A SQUIRE MUST KEEP A COURTEOUS TONGUE, BOY.
WELL FOUGHT.
WELL FOUGHT.
I YIELD, YOUR GRACE.
WELL FOUGHT.
IT WAS NOT EITHER!
BE QUIET, OR YOU CAN GO BACK TO CAMP.

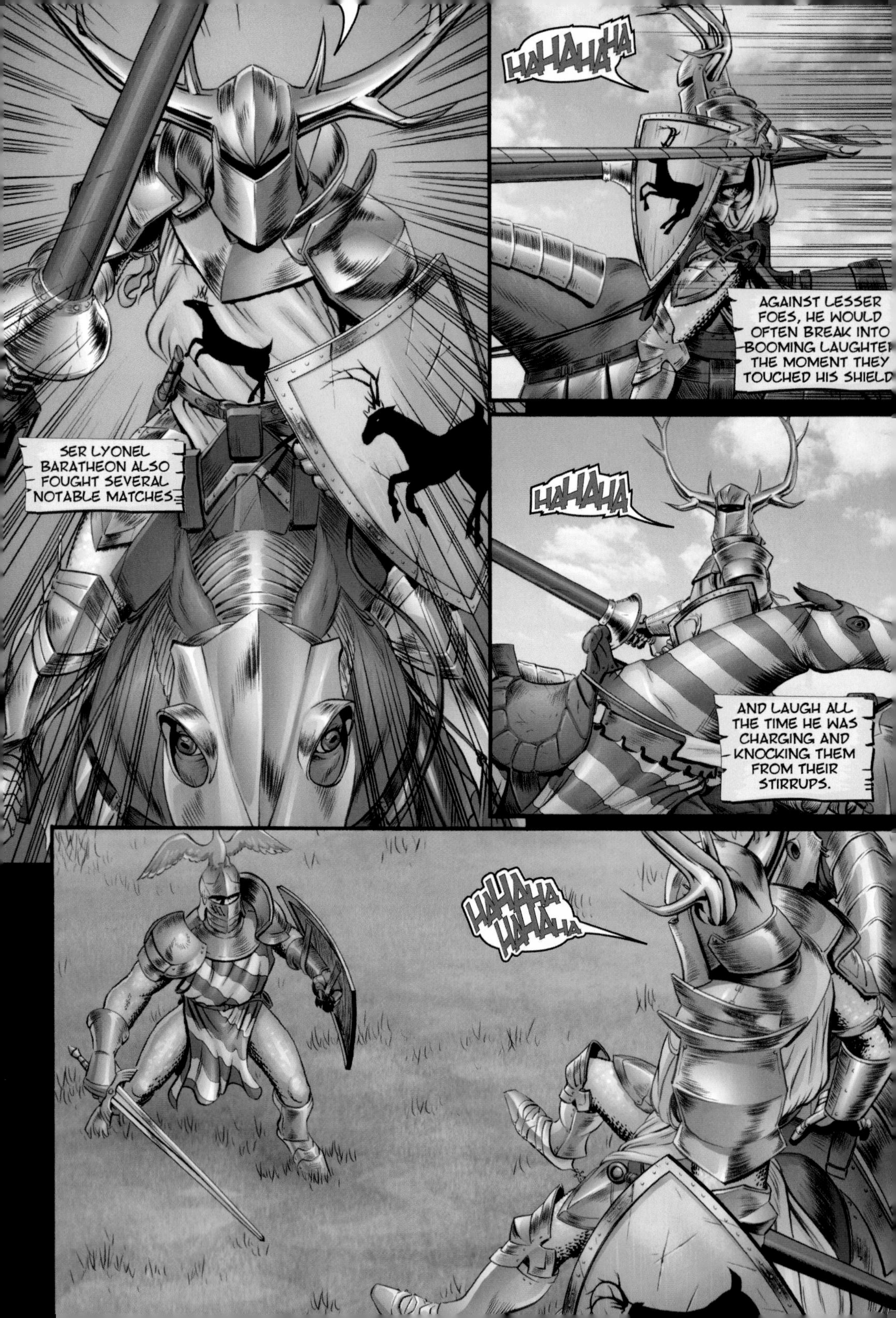
SER LYONEL BARATHEON ALSO FOUGHT SEVERAL NOTABLE MATCHES.
HAHAHAHA
AGAINST LESSER FOES, HE WOULD OFTEN BREAK INTO BOOMING LAUGHTER THE MOMENT THEY TOUCHED HIS SHIELD
HAHAHA
AND LAUGH ALL THE TIME HE WAS CHARGING AND KNOCKING THEM FROM THEIR STIRRUPS.
HAHAHA HAHAHAHA

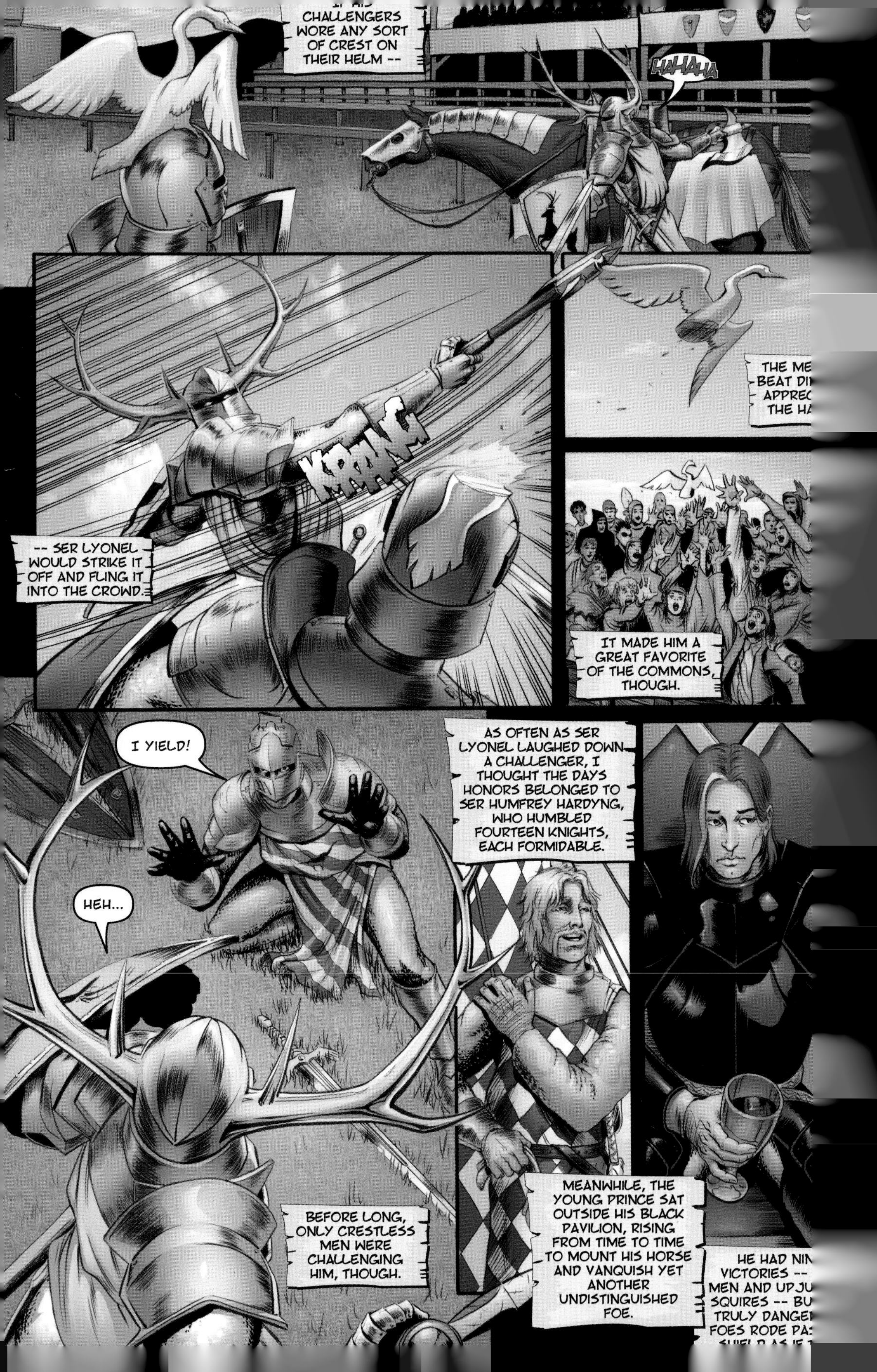
CHALLENGERS WORE ANY SORT OF CREST ON THEIR HELM --
HAHAHA
KRAANG
-- SER LYONEL WOULD STRIKE IT OFF AND FLING IT INTO THE CROWD.
THE ME
BEAT DI
APPREC
THE HA
IT MADE HIM A GREAT FAVORITE OF THE COMMONS, THOUGH.
I YIELD!
HEH...
BEFORE LONG, ONLY CRESTLESS MEN WERE CHALLENGING HIM, THOUGH.
AS OFTEN AS SER LYONEL LAUGHED DOWN A CHALLENGER, I THOUGHT THE DAYS HONORS BELONGED TO SER HUMFREY HARDYNG, WHO HUMBLED FOURTEEN KNIGHTS, EACH FORMIDABLE.
MEANWHILE, THE YOUNG PRINCE SAT OUTSIDE HIS BLACK PAVILION, RISING FROM TIME TO TIME TO MOUNT HIS HORSE AND VANQUISH YET ANOTHER UNDISTINGUISHED FOE.
HE HAD NIN
VICTORIES --
MEN AND UPJU
SQUIRES -- BU
TRULY DANGE
FOES RODE PA

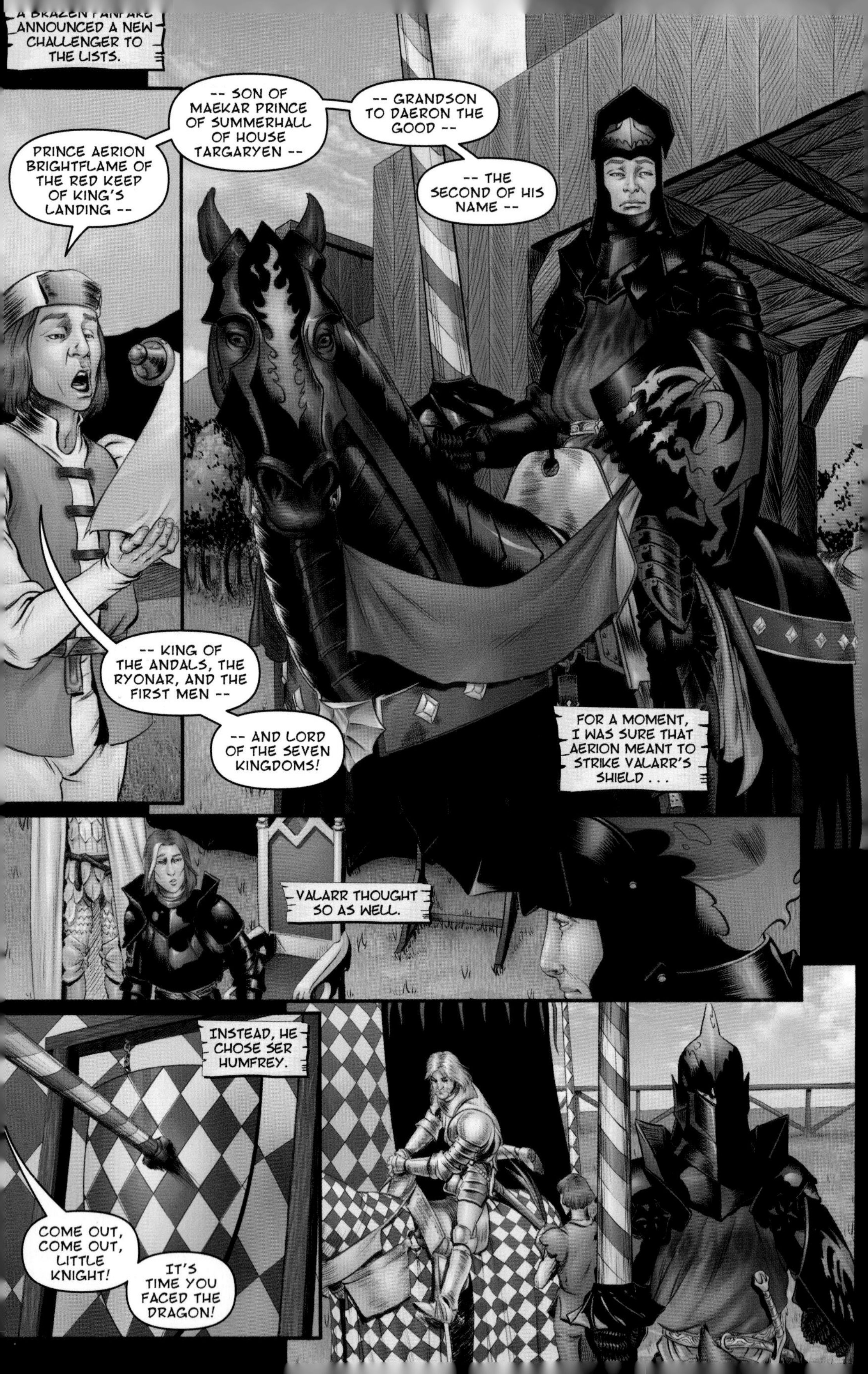
A BRAZEN FANFARE ANNOUNCED A NEW CHALLENGER TO THE LISTS.
PRINCE AERION BRIGHTFLAME OF THE RED KEEP OF KING'S LANDING --
-- SON OF MAEKAR PRINCE OF SUMMERHALL OF HOUSE TARGARYEN --
-- GRANDSON TO DAERON THE GOOD --
-- THE SECOND OF HIS NAME --
-- KING OF THE ANDALS, THE RYONAR, AND THE FIRST MEN --
-- AND LORD OF THE SEVEN KINGDOMS!
FOR A MOMENT, I WAS SURE THAT AERION MEANT TO STRIKE VALARR'S SHIELD . . .
VALARR THOUGHT SO AS WELL.
INSTEAD, HE CHOSE SER HUMFREY.
COME OUT, COME OUT, LITTLE KNIGHT!
IT'S TIME YOU FACED THE DRAGON!

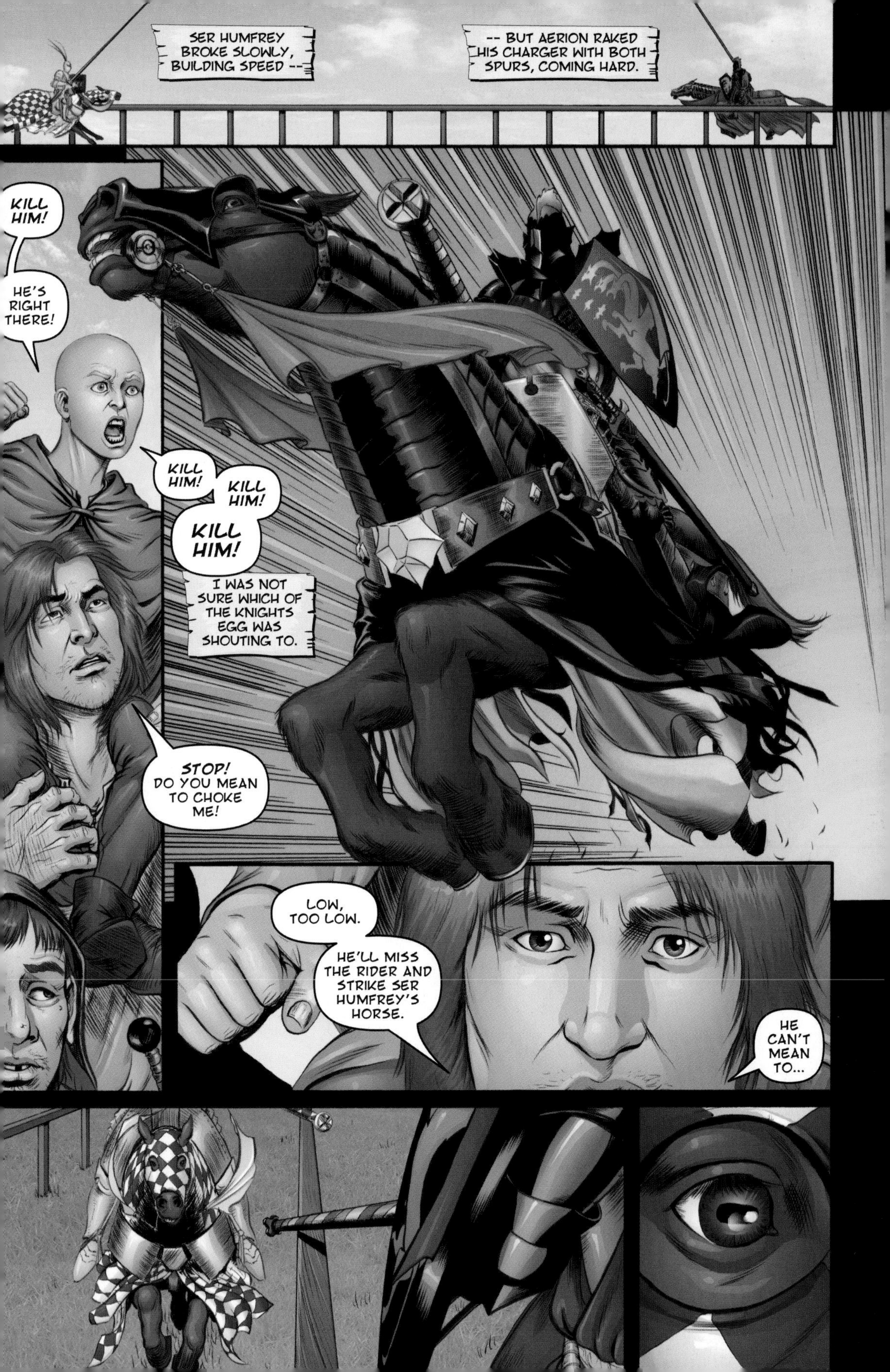
SER HUMFREY BROKE SLOWLY, BUILDING SPEED --
-- BUT AERION RAKED HIS CHARGER WITH BOTH SPURS, COMING HARD.
KILL HIM!
HE'S RIGHT THERE!
KILL HIM!
KILL HIM!
KILL HIM!
I WAS NOT SURE WHICH OF THE KNIGHTS EGG WAS SHOUTING TO.
STOP! DO YOU MEAN TO CHOKE ME!
LOW, TOO LOW.
HE'LL MISS THE RIDER AND STRIKE SER HUMFREY'S HORSE.
HE CAN'T MEAN TO...

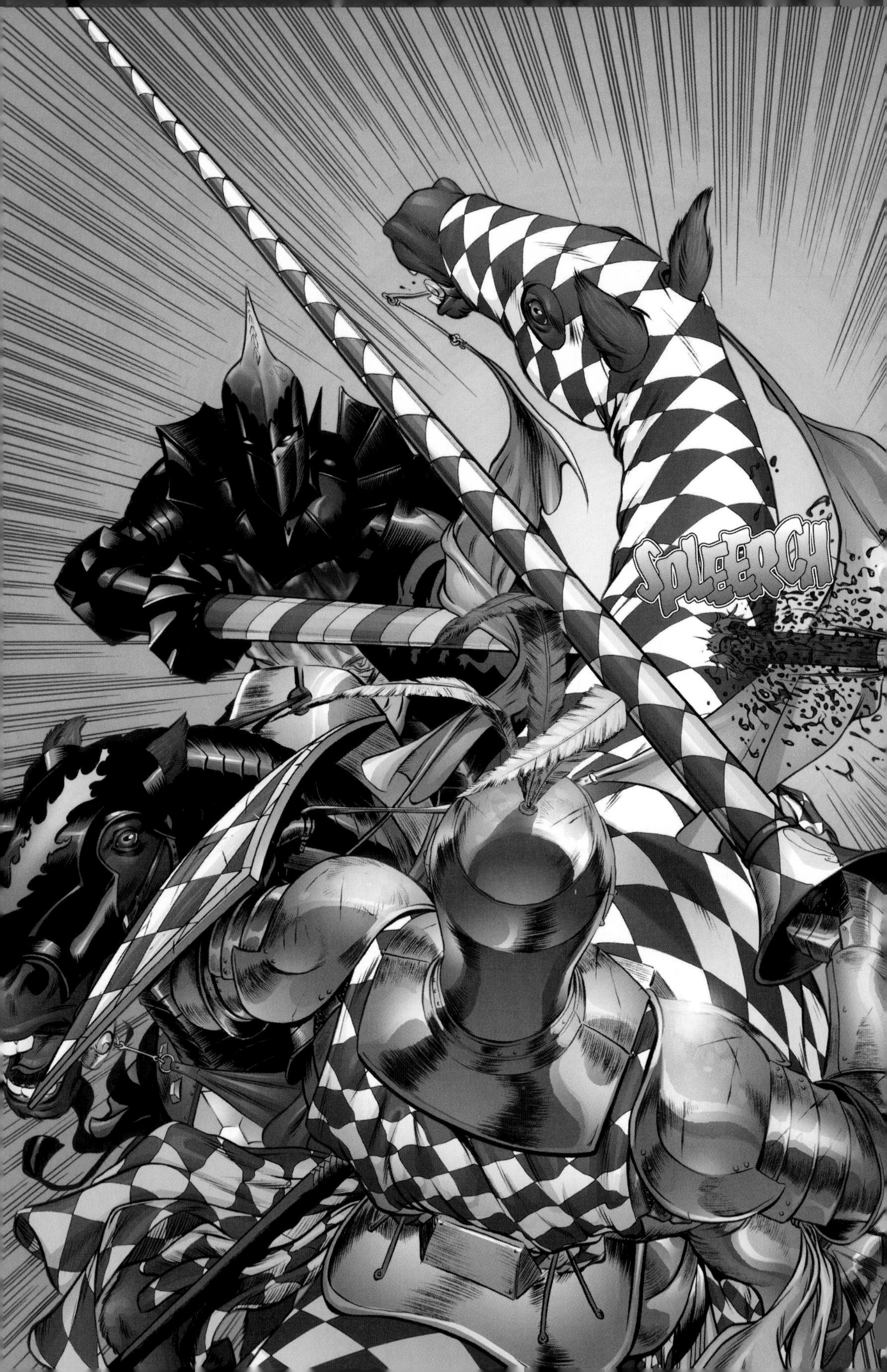
SPLEERCH

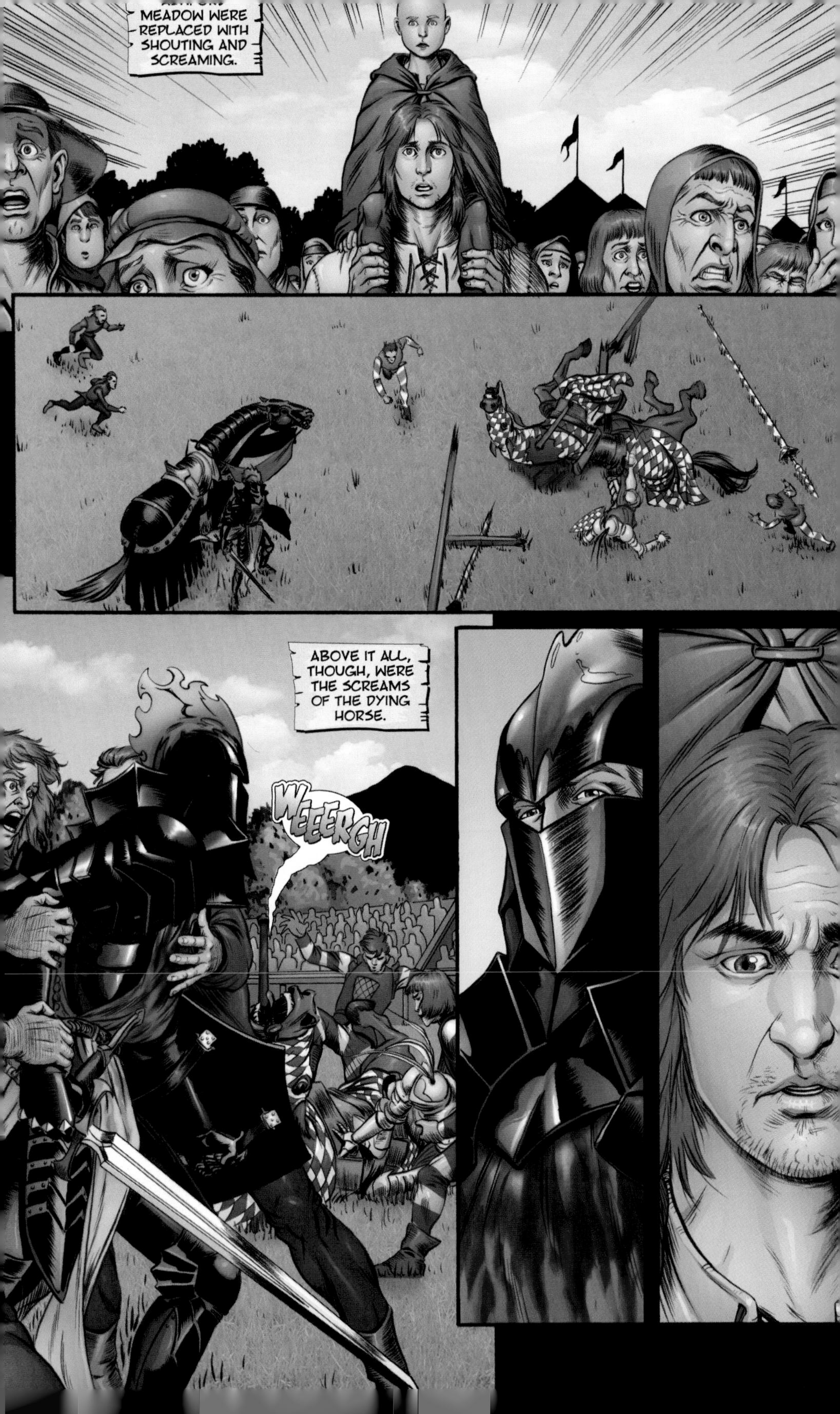
MEADOW WERE REPLACED WITH SHOUTING AND SCREAMING.
ABOVE IT ALL, THOUGH, WERE THE SCREAMS OF THE DYING HORSE.
WEEERGH

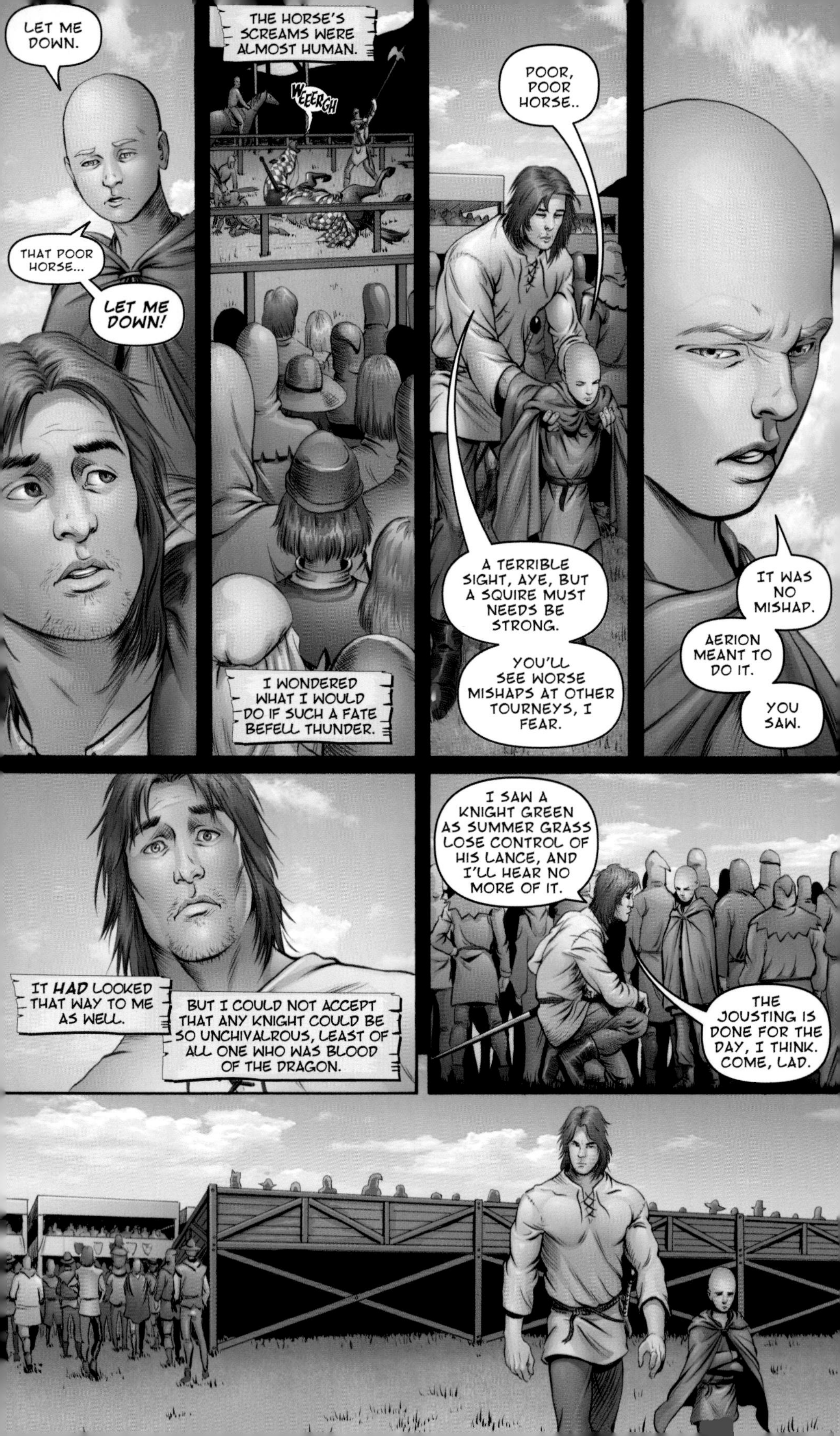
LET ME DOWN.
THAT POOR HORSE...
LET ME DOWN!
THE HORSE'S SCREAMS WERE ALMOST HUMAN.
WEEERGH
I WONDERED WHAT I WOULD DO IF SUCH A FATE BEFELL THUNDER.
POOR, POOR HORSE..
A TERRIBLE SIGHT, AYE, BUT A SQUIRE MUST NEEDS BE STRONG.
YOU'LL SEE WORSE MISHAPS AT OTHER TOURNEYS, I FEAR.
IT WAS NO MISHAP.
AERION MEANT TO DO IT.
YOU SAW.
IT HAD LOOKED THAT WAY TO ME AS WELL.
BUT I COULD NOT ACCEPT THAT ANY KNIGHT COULD BE SO UNCHIVALROUS, LEAST OF ALL ONE WHO WAS BLOOD OF THE DRAGON.
I SAW A KNIGHT GREEN AS SUMMER GRASS LOSE CONTROL OF HIS LANCE, AND I'LL HEAR NO MORE OF IT.
THE JOUSTING IS DONE FOR THE DAY, I THINK. COME, LAD.

ISSUE FOUR
COVER A

MIKE S. MILLER

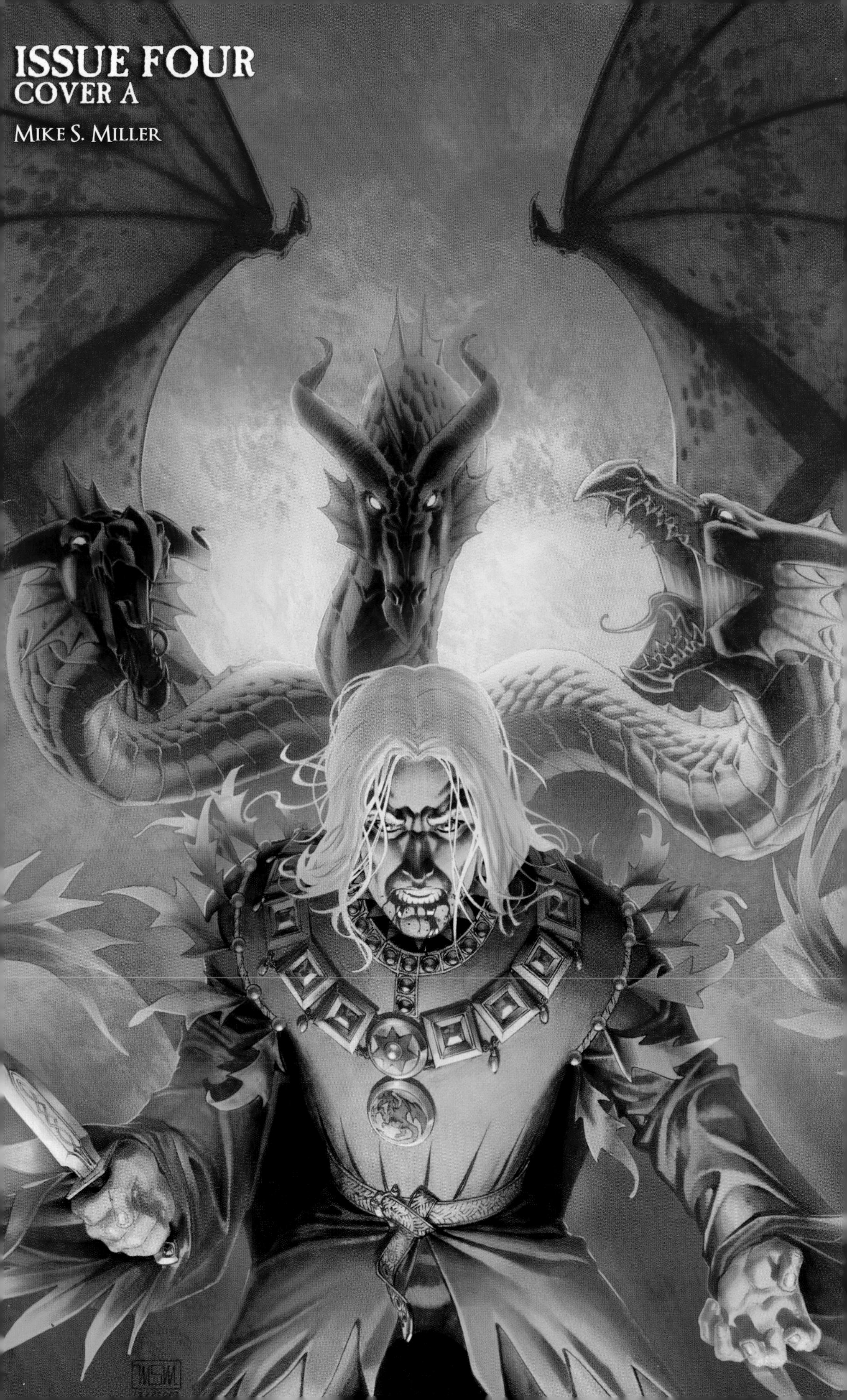

ISSUE FOUR
COVER B

Tom Yeates

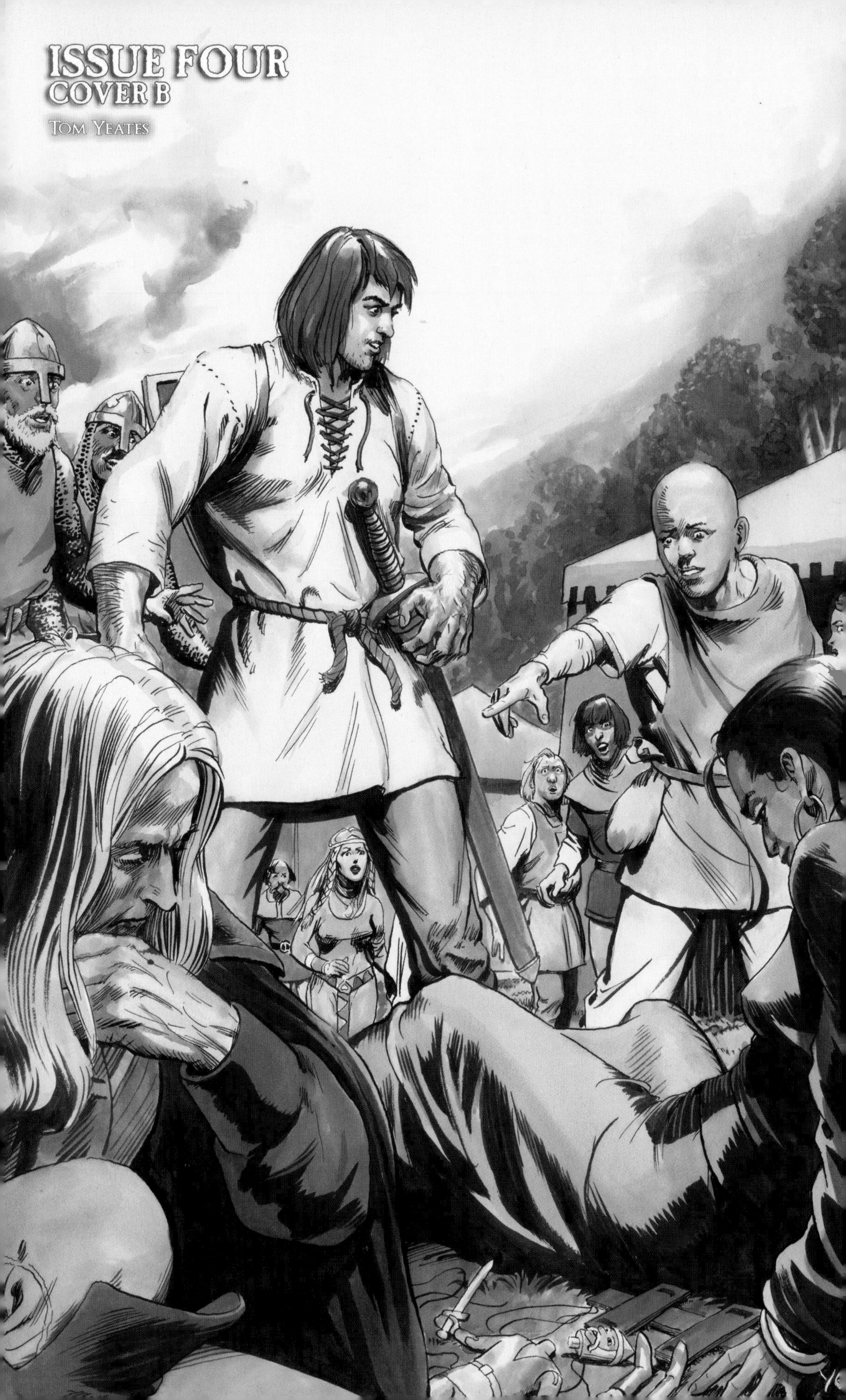

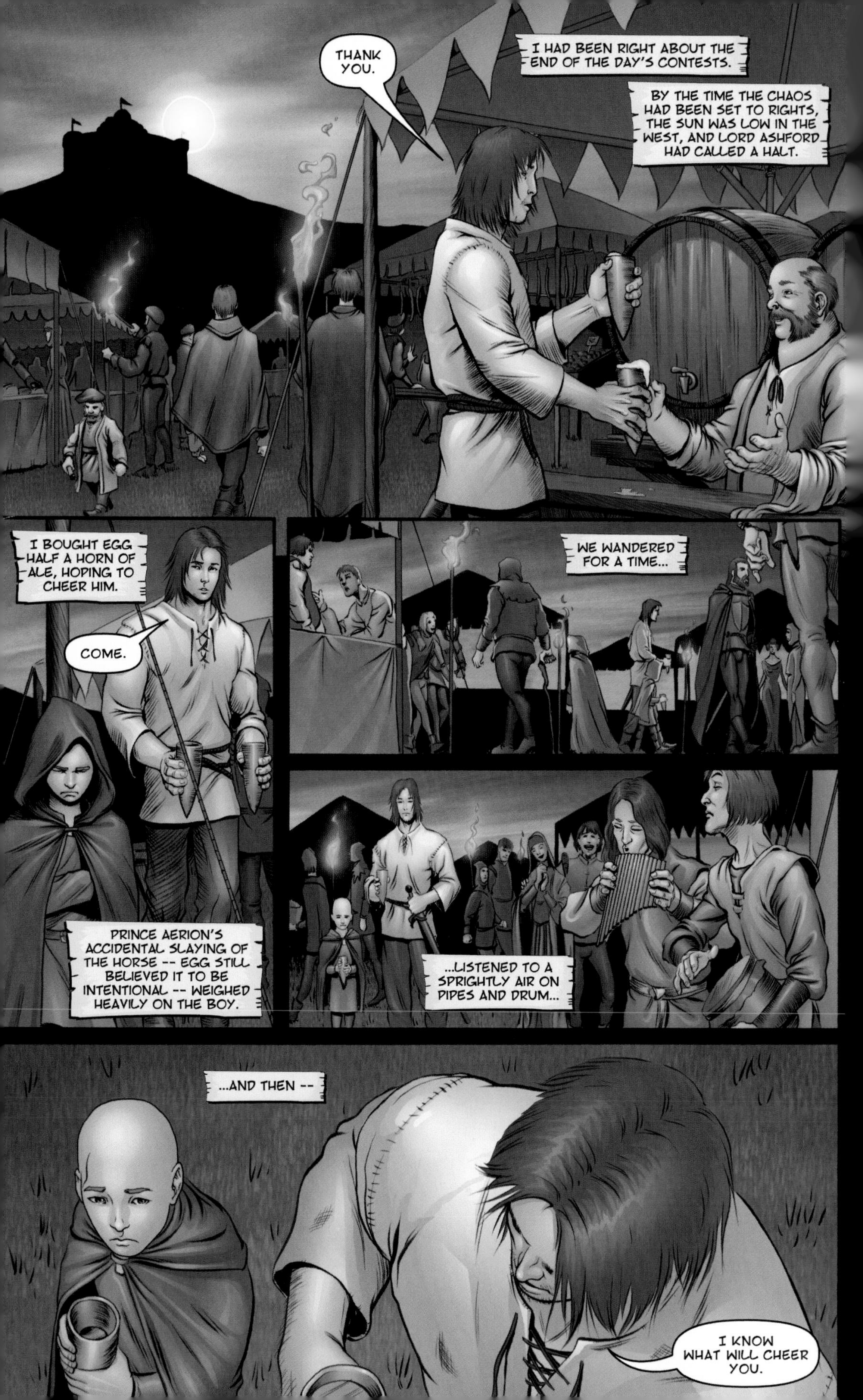

THANK YOU.
I HAD BEEN RIGHT ABOUT THE END OF THE DAY'S CONTESTS.
BY THE TIME THE CHAOS HAD BEEN SET TO RIGHTS, THE SUN WAS LOW IN THE WEST, AND LORD ASHFORD HAD CALLED A HALT.
I BOUGHT EGG HALF A HORN OF ALE, HOPING TO CHEER HIM.
COME.
PRINCE AERION'S ACCIDENTAL SLAYING OF THE HORSE -- EGG STILL BELIEVED IT TO BE INTENTIONAL -- WEIGHED HEAVILY ON THE BOY.
WE WANDERED FOR A TIME...
...LISTENED TO A SPRIGHTLY AIR ON PIPES AND DRUM...
...AND THEN --
I KNOW WHAT WILL CHEER YOU.

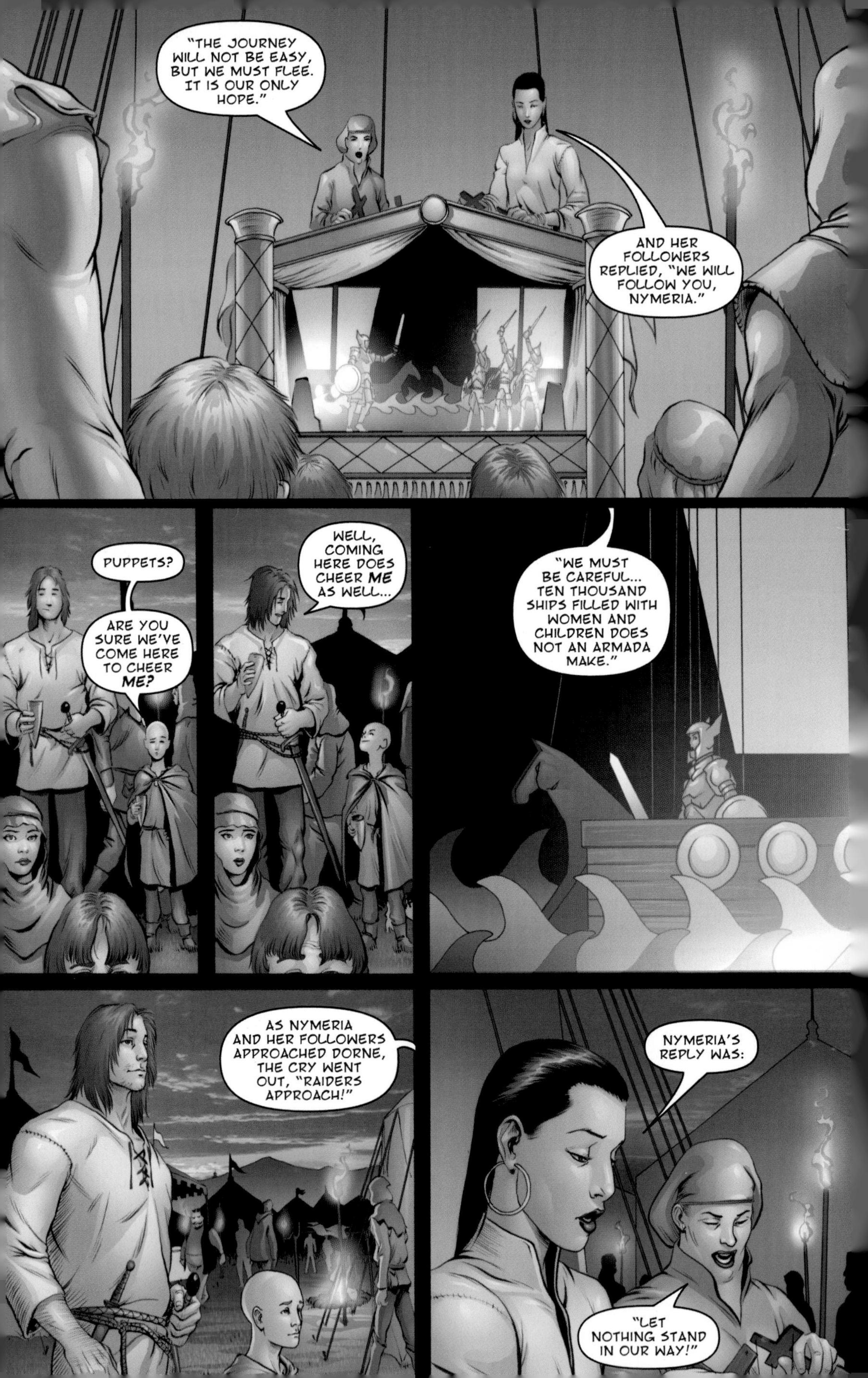
"THE JOURNEY WILL NOT BE EASY, BUT WE MUST FLEE. IT IS OUR ONLY HOPE."
AND HER FOLLOWERS REPLIED, "WE WILL FOLLOW YOU, NYMERIA."
PUPPETS?
ARE YOU SURE WE'VE COME HERE TO CHEER **ME?**
WELL, COMING HERE DOES CHEER **ME** AS WELL...
"WE MUST BE CAREFUL... TEN THOUSAND SHIPS FILLED WITH WOMEN AND CHILDREN DOES NOT AN ARMADA MAKE."
AS NYMERIA AND HER FOLLOWERS APPROACHED DORNE, THE CRY WENT OUT, "RAIDERS APPROACH!"
NYMERIA'S REPLY WAS:
"LET NOTHING STAND IN OUR WAY!"

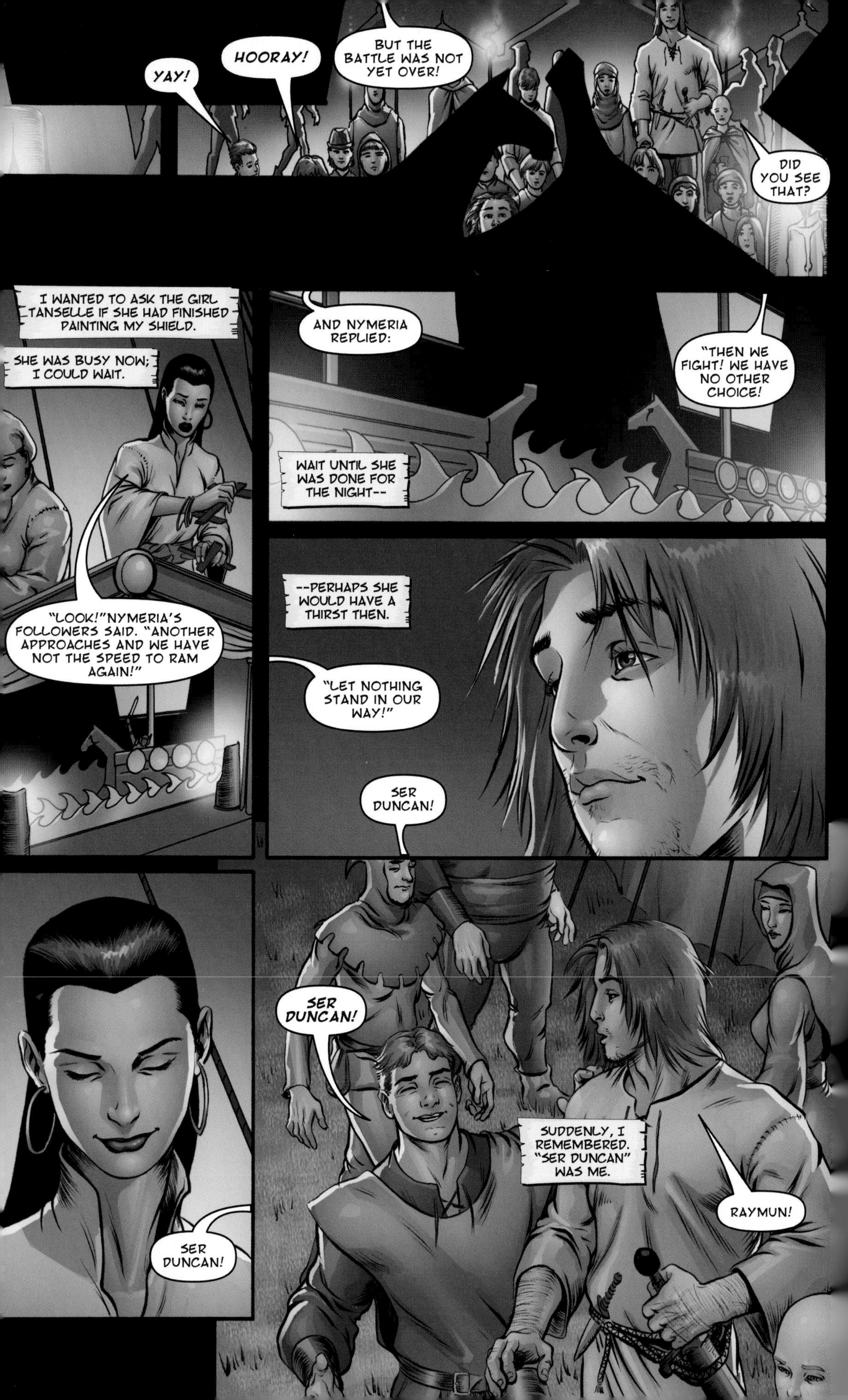

YAY!
HOORAY!
BUT THE BATTLE WAS NOT YET OVER!
DID YOU SEE THAT?
I WANTED TO ASK THE GIRL TANSELLE IF SHE HAD FINISHED PAINTING MY SHIELD.
SHE WAS BUSY NOW; I COULD WAIT.
"LOOK!" NYMERIA'S FOLLOWERS SAID. "ANOTHER APPROACHES AND WE HAVE NOT THE SPEED TO RAM AGAIN!"
AND NYMERIA REPLIED:
"THEN WE FIGHT! WE HAVE NO OTHER CHOICE!
WAIT UNTIL SHE WAS DONE FOR THE NIGHT--
--PERHAPS SHE WOULD HAVE A THIRST THEN.
"LET NOTHING STAND IN OUR WAY!"
SER DUNCAN!
SER DUNCAN!
SER DUNCAN!
SUDDENLY, I REMEMBERED. "SER DUNCAN" WAS ME.
RAYMUN!

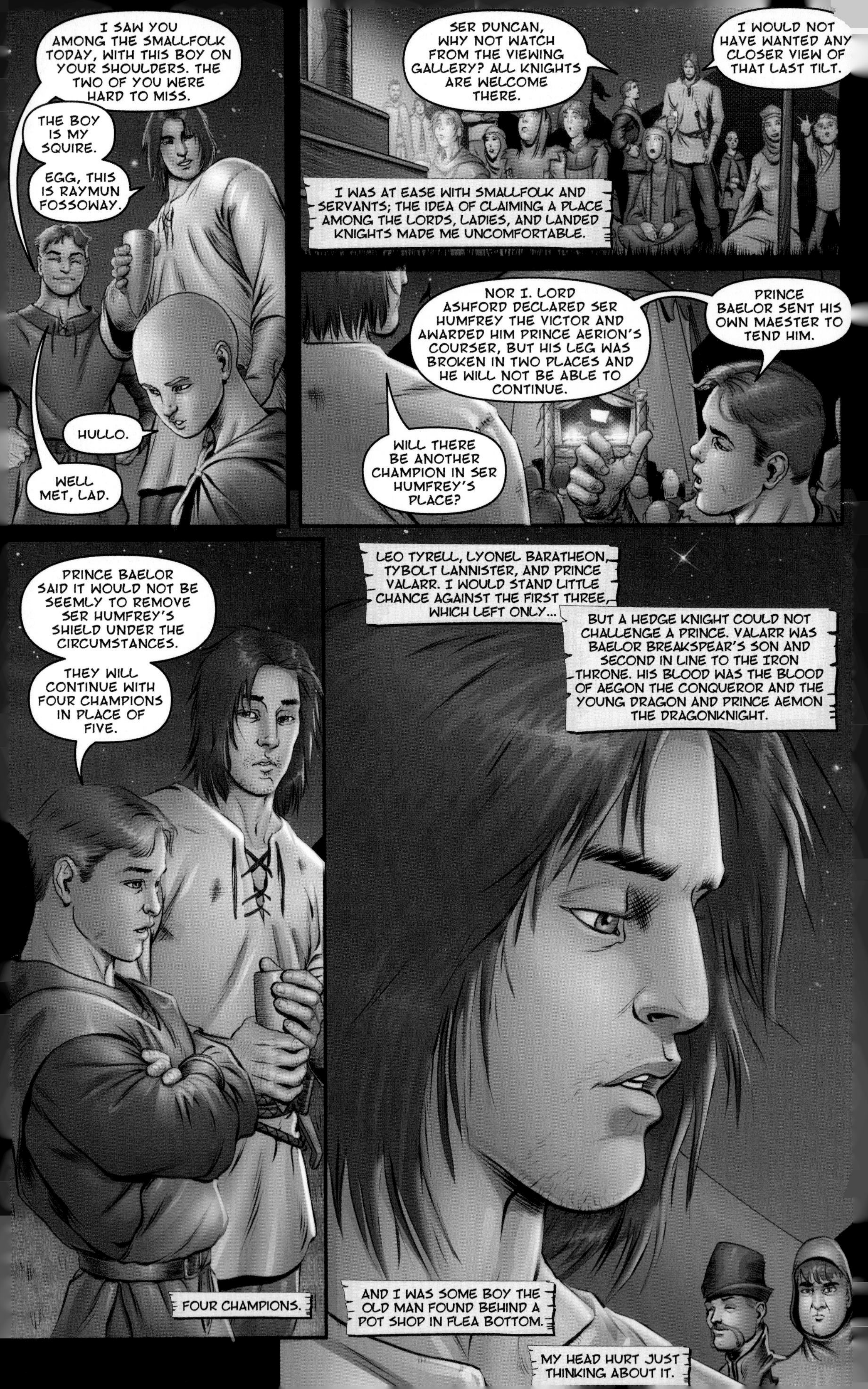
I SAW YOU AMONG THE SMALLFOLK TODAY, WITH THIS BOY ON YOUR SHOULDERS. THE TWO OF YOU WERE HARD TO MISS.
THE BOY IS MY SQUIRE.
EGG, THIS IS RAYMUN FOSSOWAY.
HULLO.
WELL MET, LAD.
SER DUNCAN, WHY NOT WATCH FROM THE VIEWING GALLERY? ALL KNIGHTS ARE WELCOME THERE.
I WOULD NOT HAVE WANTED ANY CLOSER VIEW OF THAT LAST TILT.
I WAS AT EASE WITH SMALLFOLK AND SERVANTS; THE IDEA OF CLAIMING A PLACE AMONG THE LORDS, LADIES, AND LANDED KNIGHTS MADE ME UNCOMFORTABLE.
NOR I. LORD ASHFORD DECLARED SER HUMFREY THE VICTOR AND AWARDED HIM PRINCE AERION'S COURSER, BUT HIS LEG WAS BROKEN IN TWO PLACES AND HE WILL NOT BE ABLE TO CONTINUE.
PRINCE BAELOR SENT HIS OWN MAESTER TO TEND HIM.
WILL THERE BE ANOTHER CHAMPION IN SER HUMFREY'S PLACE?
PRINCE BAELOR SAID IT WOULD NOT BE SEEMLY TO REMOVE SER HUMFREY'S SHIELD UNDER THE CIRCUMSTANCES.
THEY WILL CONTINUE WITH FOUR CHAMPIONS IN PLACE OF FIVE.
FOUR CHAMPIONS.
LEO TYRELL, LYONEL BARATHEON, TYBOLT LANNISTER, AND PRINCE VALARR. I WOULD STAND LITTLE CHANCE AGAINST THE FIRST THREE, WHICH LEFT ONLY...
BUT A HEDGE KNIGHT COULD NOT CHALLENGE A PRINCE. VALARR WAS BAELOR BREAKSPEAR'S SON AND SECOND IN LINE TO THE IRON THRONE. HIS BLOOD WAS THE BLOOD OF AEGON THE CONQUEROR AND THE YOUNG DRAGON AND PRINCE AEMON THE DRAGONKNIGHT.
AND I WAS SOME BOY THE OLD MAN FOUND BEHIND A POT SHOP IN FLEA BOTTOM.
MY HEAD HURT JUST THINKING ABOUT IT.

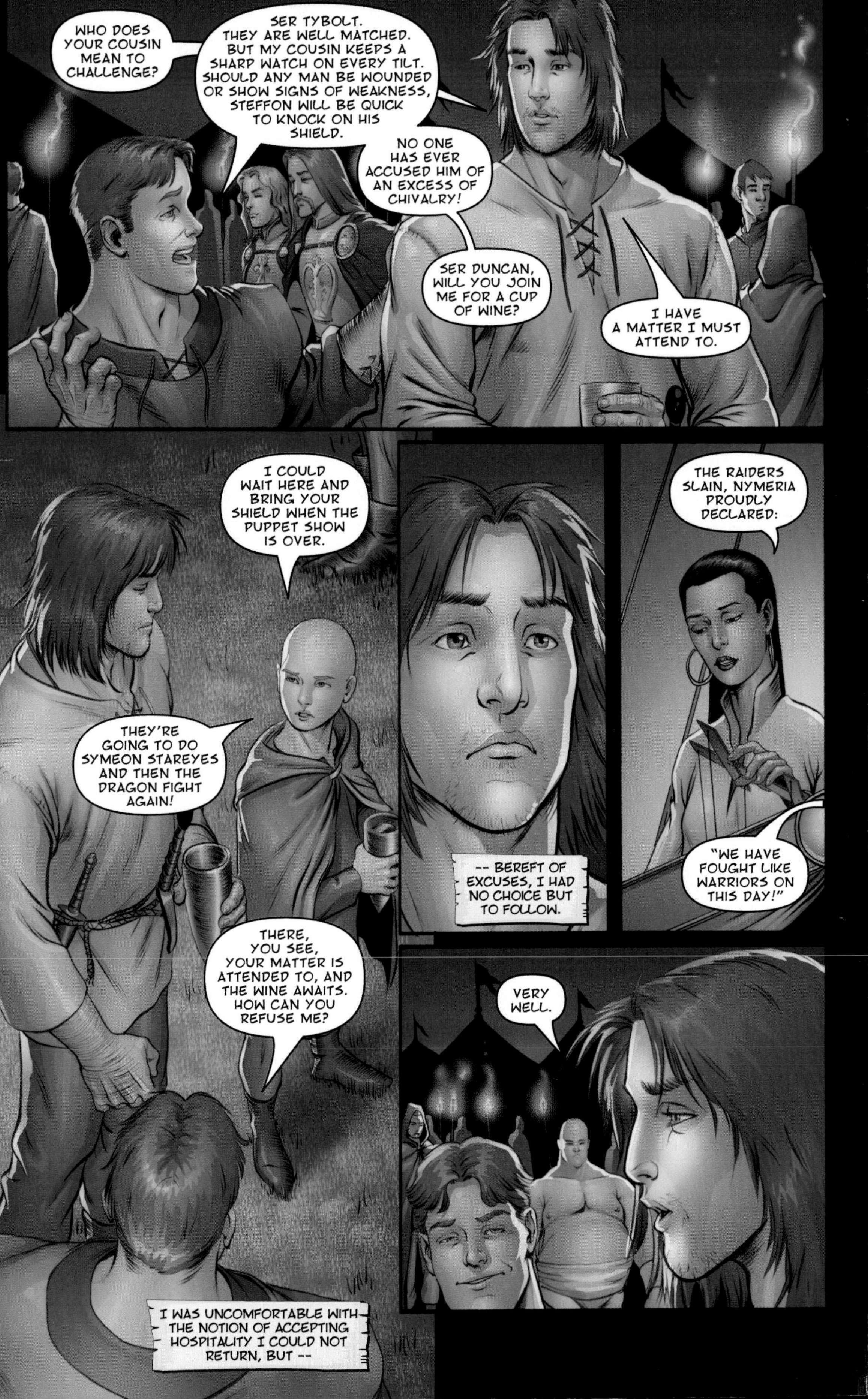
WHO DOES YOUR COUSIN MEAN TO CHALLENGE?
SER TYBOLT. THEY ARE WELL MATCHED. BUT MY COUSIN KEEPS A SHARP WATCH ON EVERY TILT. SHOULD ANY MAN BE WOUNDED OR SHOW SIGNS OF WEAKNESS, STEFFON WILL BE QUICK TO KNOCK ON HIS SHIELD.
NO ONE HAS EVER ACCUSED HIM OF AN EXCESS OF CHIVALRY!
SER DUNCAN, WILL YOU JOIN ME FOR A CUP OF WINE?
I HAVE A MATTER I MUST ATTEND TO.
I COULD WAIT HERE AND BRING YOUR SHIELD WHEN THE PUPPET SHOW IS OVER.
THEY'RE GOING TO DO SYMEON STAREYES AND THEN THE DRAGON FIGHT AGAIN!
THERE, YOU SEE, YOUR MATTER IS ATTENDED TO, AND THE WINE AWAITS. HOW CAN YOU REFUSE ME?
I WAS UNCOMFORTABLE WITH THE NOTION OF ACCEPTING HOSPITALITY I COULD NOT RETURN, BUT --
-- BEREFT OF EXCUSES, I HAD NO CHOICE BUT TO FOLLOW.
THE RAIDERS SLAIN, NYMERIA PROUDLY DECLARED:
"WE HAVE FOUGHT LIKE WARRIORS ON THIS DAY!"
VERY WELL.

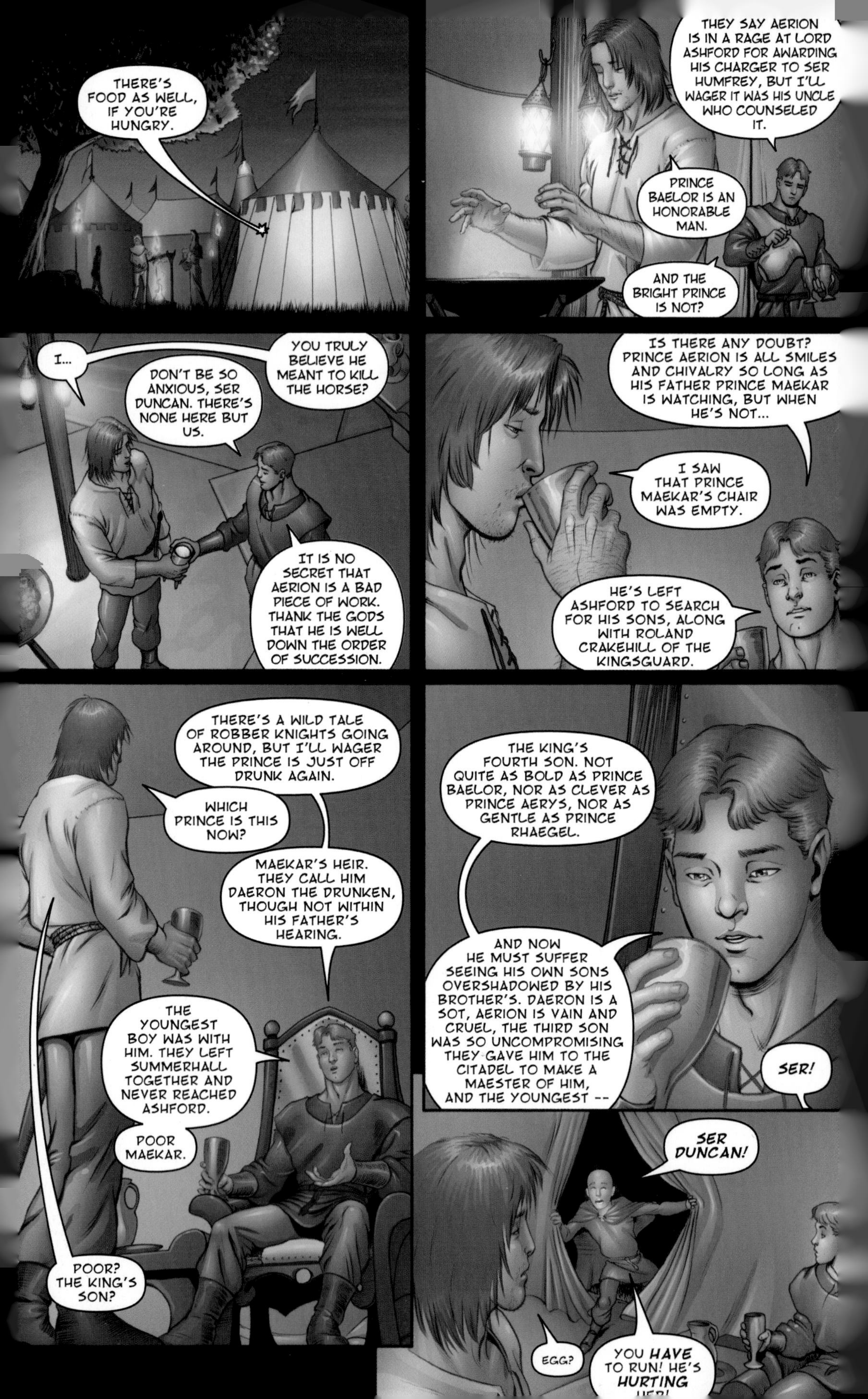
THERE'S FOOD AS WELL, IF YOU'RE HUNGRY.
THEY SAY AERION IS IN A RAGE AT LORD ASHFORD FOR AWARDING HIS CHARGER TO SER HUMFREY, BUT I'LL WAGER IT WAS HIS UNCLE WHO COUNSELED IT.
PRINCE BAELOR IS AN HONORABLE MAN.
AND THE BRIGHT PRINCE IS NOT?
YOU TRULY BELIEVE HE MEANT TO KILL THE HORSE?
I...
DON'T BE SO ANXIOUS, SER DUNCAN. THERE'S NONE HERE BUT US.
IT IS NO SECRET THAT AERION IS A BAD PIECE OF WORK. THANK THE GODS THAT HE IS WELL DOWN THE ORDER OF SUCCESSION.
IS THERE ANY DOUBT? PRINCE AERION IS ALL SMILES AND CHIVALRY SO LONG AS HIS FATHER PRINCE MAEKAR IS WATCHING, BUT WHEN HE'S NOT...
I SAW THAT PRINCE MAEKAR'S CHAIR WAS EMPTY.
HE'S LEFT ASHFORD TO SEARCH FOR HIS SONS, ALONG WITH ROLAND CRAKEHILL OF THE KINGSGUARD.
THERE'S A WILD TALE OF ROBBER KNIGHTS GOING AROUND, BUT I'LL WAGER THE PRINCE IS JUST OFF DRUNK AGAIN.
WHICH PRINCE IS THIS NOW?
MAEKAR'S HEIR. THEY CALL HIM DAERON THE DRUNKEN, THOUGH NOT WITHIN HIS FATHER'S HEARING.
THE YOUNGEST BOY WAS WITH HIM. THEY LEFT SUMMERHALL TOGETHER AND NEVER REACHED ASHFORD.
POOR MAEKAR.
POOR? THE KING'S SON?
THE KING'S FOURTH SON. NOT QUITE AS BOLD AS PRINCE BAELOR, NOR AS CLEVER AS PRINCE AERYS, NOR AS GENTLE AS PRINCE RHAEGEL.
AND NOW HE MUST SUFFER SEEING HIS OWN SONS OVERSHADOWED BY HIS BROTHER'S. DAERON IS A SOT, AERION IS VAIN AND CRUEL, THE THIRD SON WAS SO UNCOMPROMISING THEY GAVE HIM TO THE CITADEL TO MAKE A MAESTER OF HIM, AND THE YOUNGEST --
SER!
SER DUNCAN!
EGG?
YOU HAVE TO RUN! HE'S HURTING

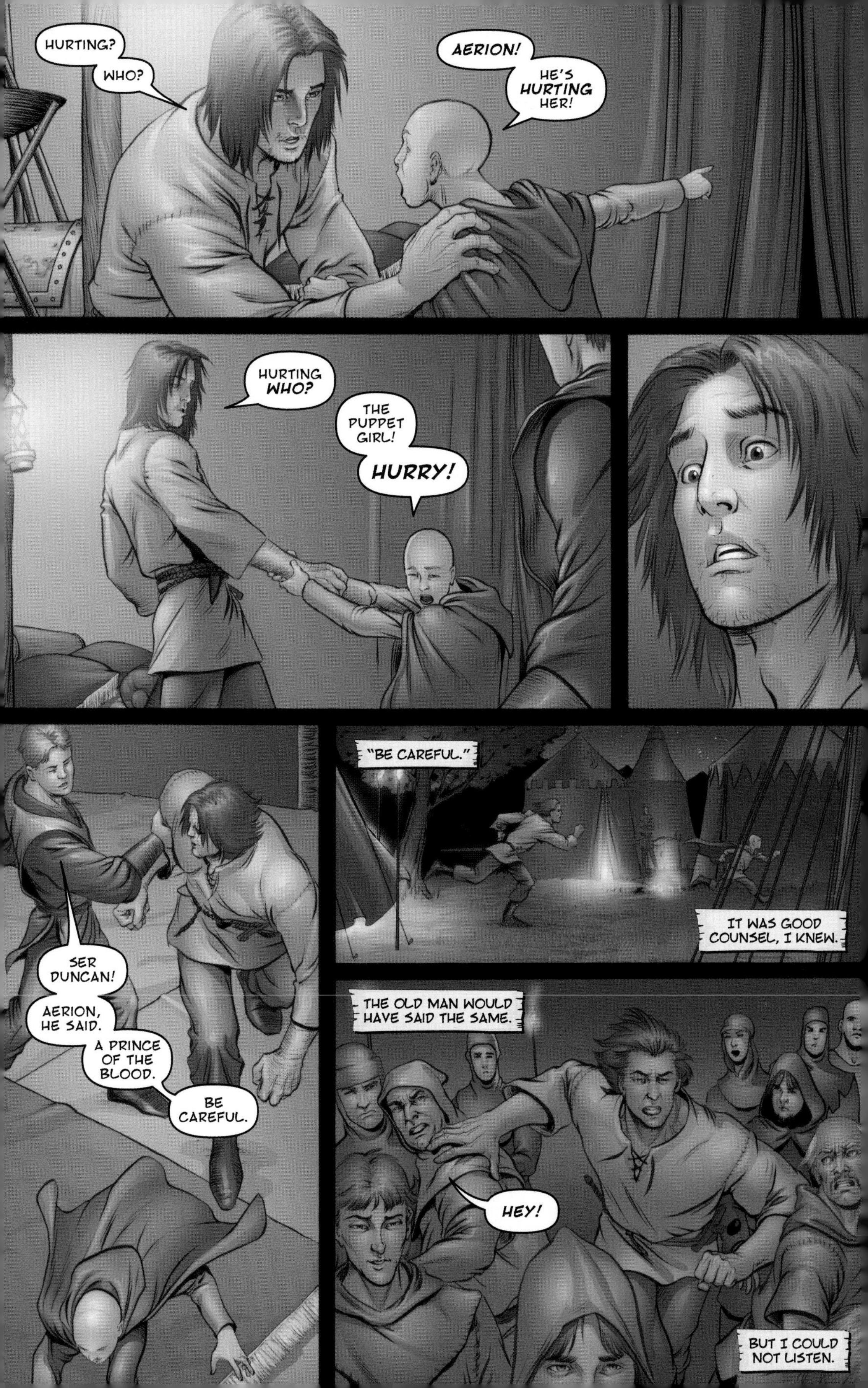
HURTING?
WHO?
AERION!
HE'S HURTING HER!
HURTING WHO?
THE PUPPET GIRL!
HURRY!
SER DUNCAN!
AERION, HE SAID.
A PRINCE OF THE BLOOD.
BE CAREFUL.
"BE CAREFUL."
IT WAS GOOD COUNSEL, I KNEW.
THE OLD MAN WOULD HAVE SAID THE SAME.
HEY!
BUT I COULD NOT LISTEN.

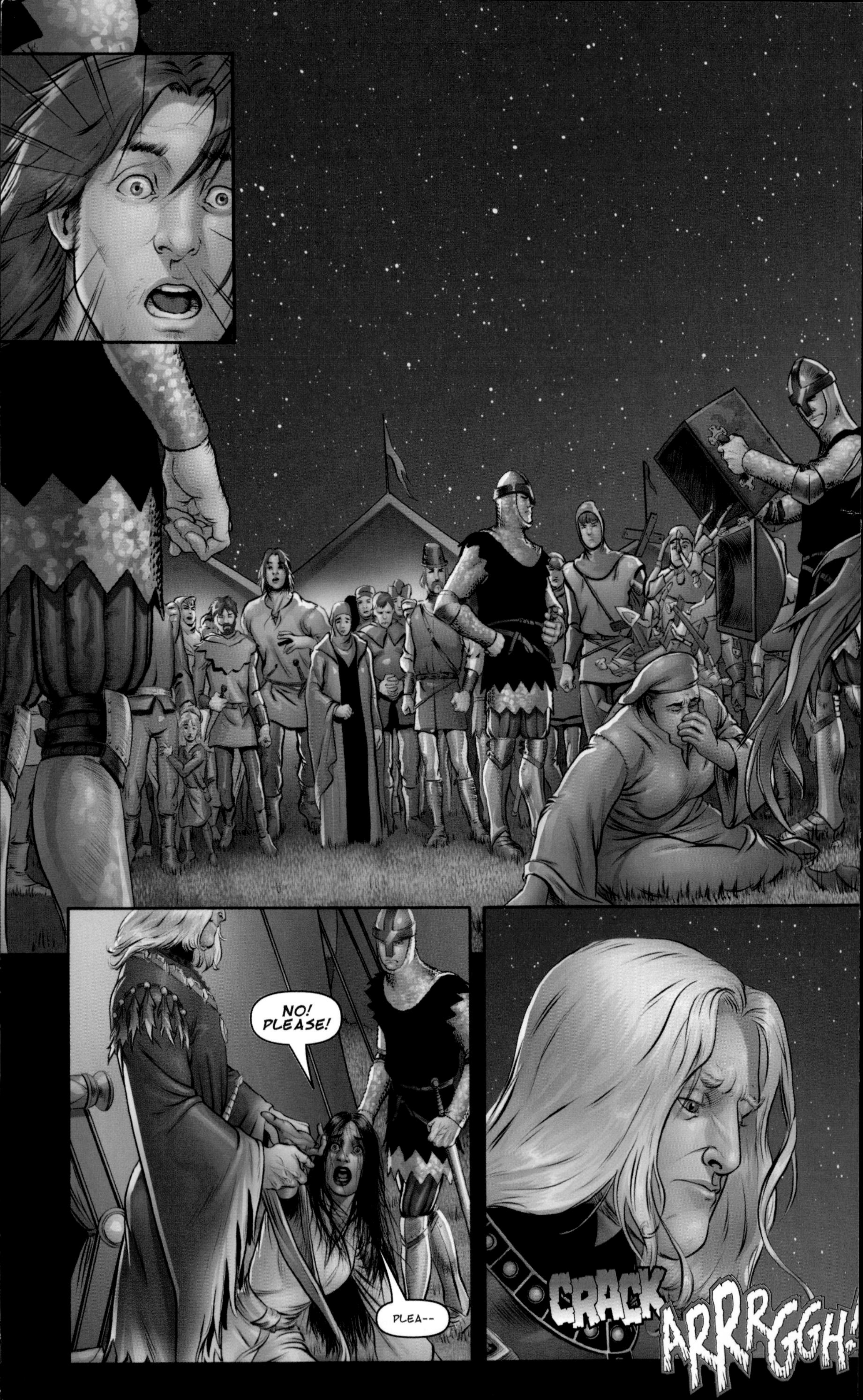
NO! PLEASE!
PLEA--
CRACK
ARRRGGH!

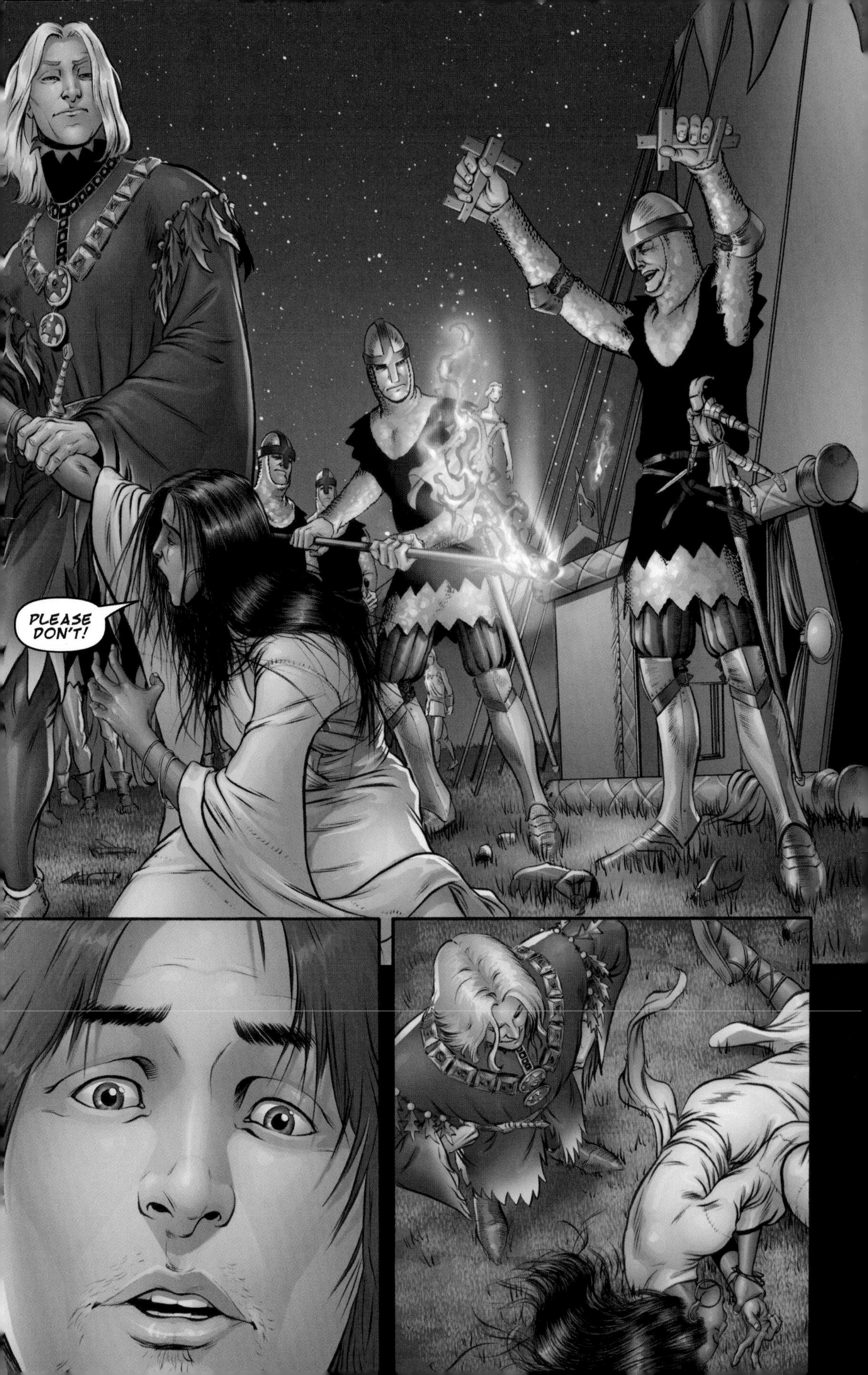
PLEASE DON'T!

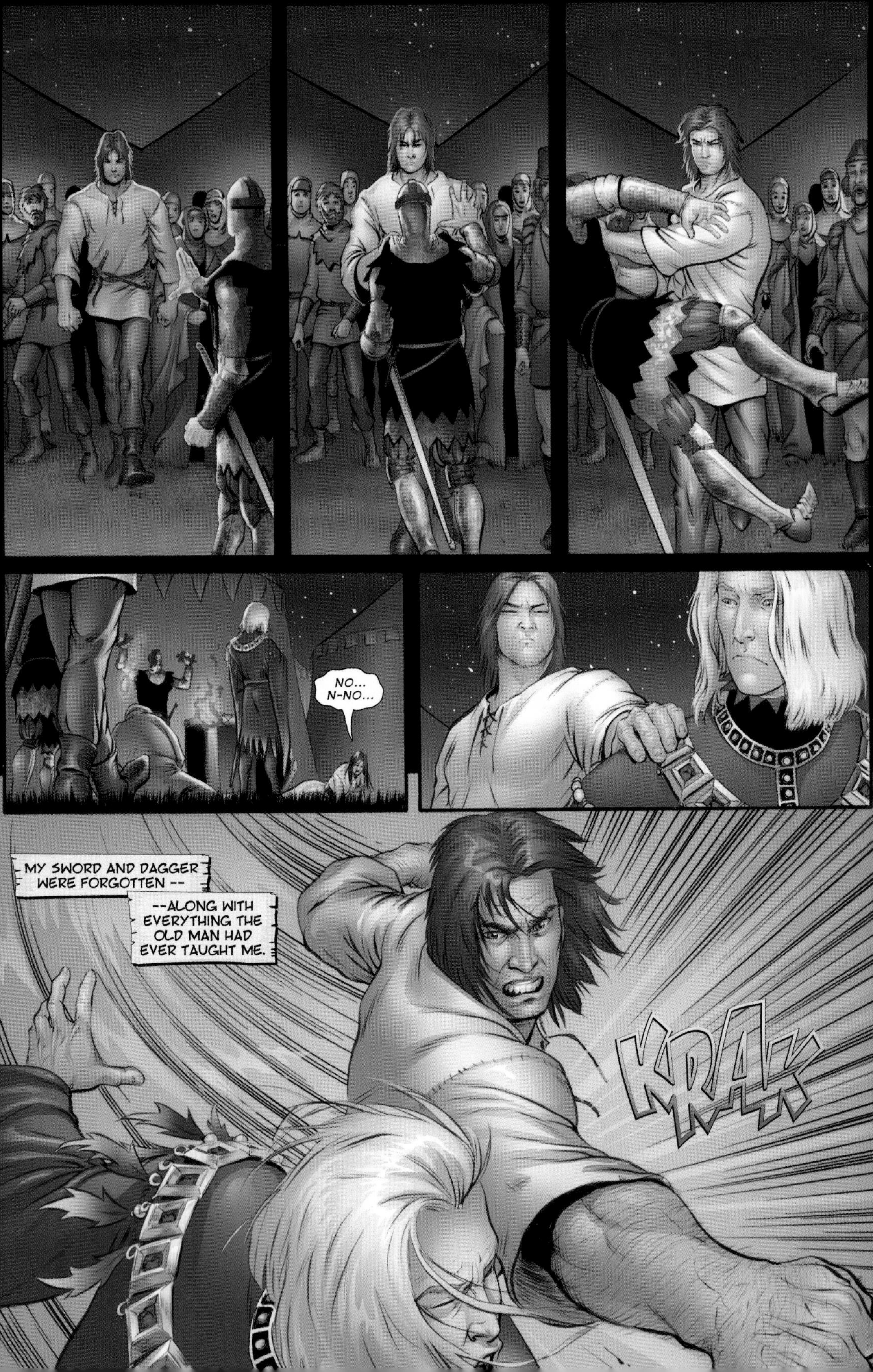
NO... N-NO...
MY SWORD AND DAGGER WERE FORGOTTEN --
--ALONG WITH EVERYTHING THE OLD MAN HAD EVER TAUGHT ME.
KRAK

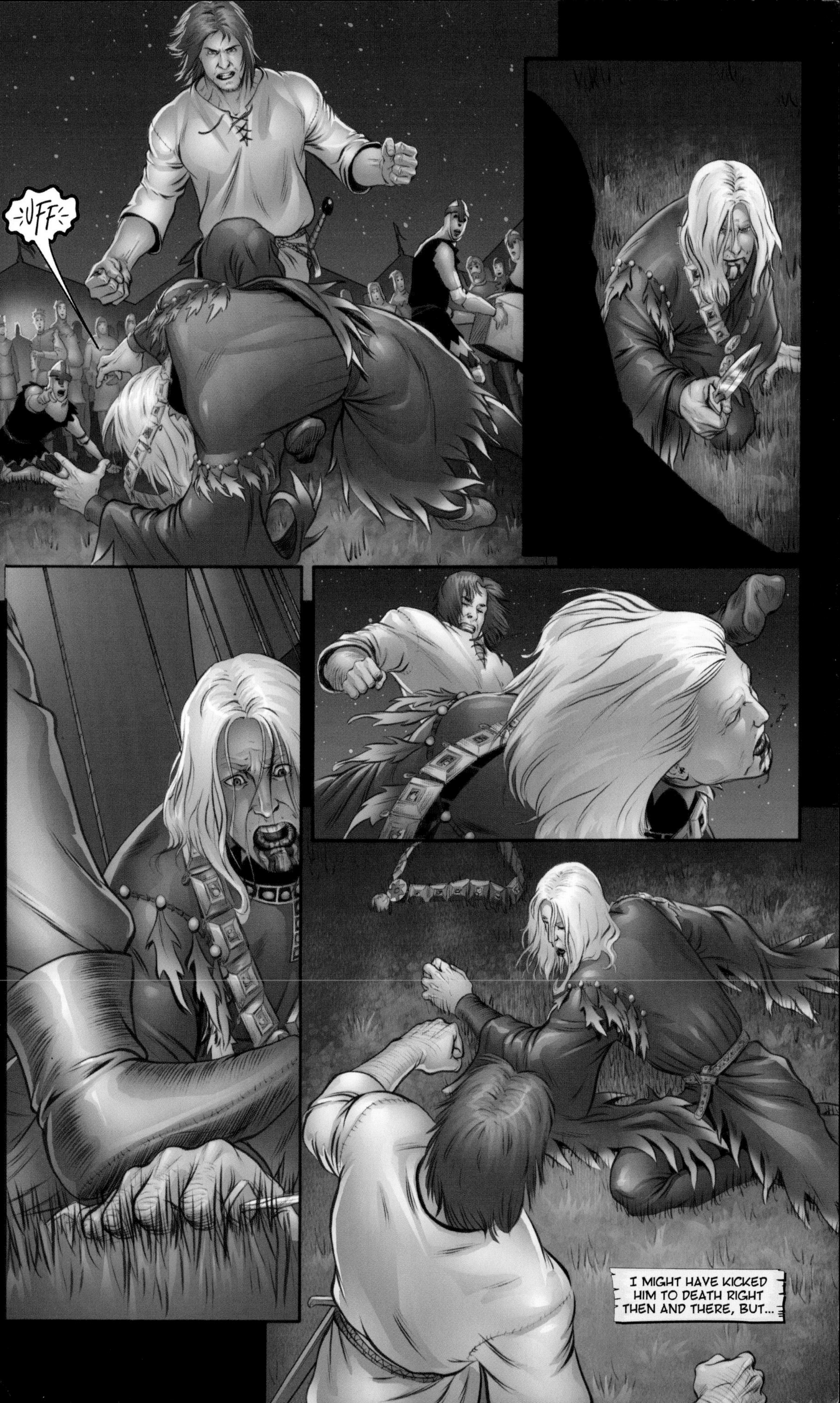
UFF
I MIGHT HAVE KICKED HIM TO DEATH RIGHT THEN AND THERE, BUT...

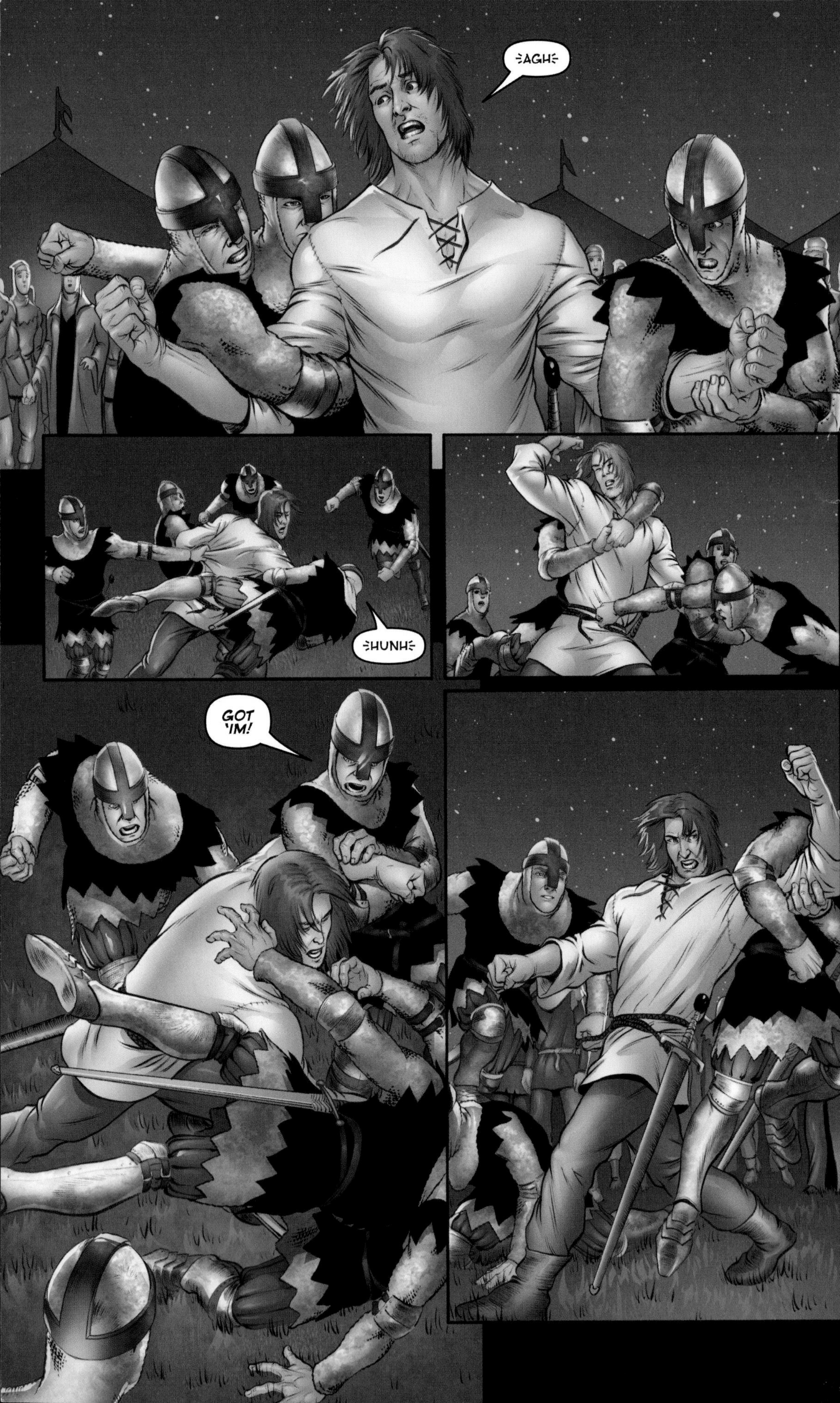

AGH
HUNH
GOT 'IM!

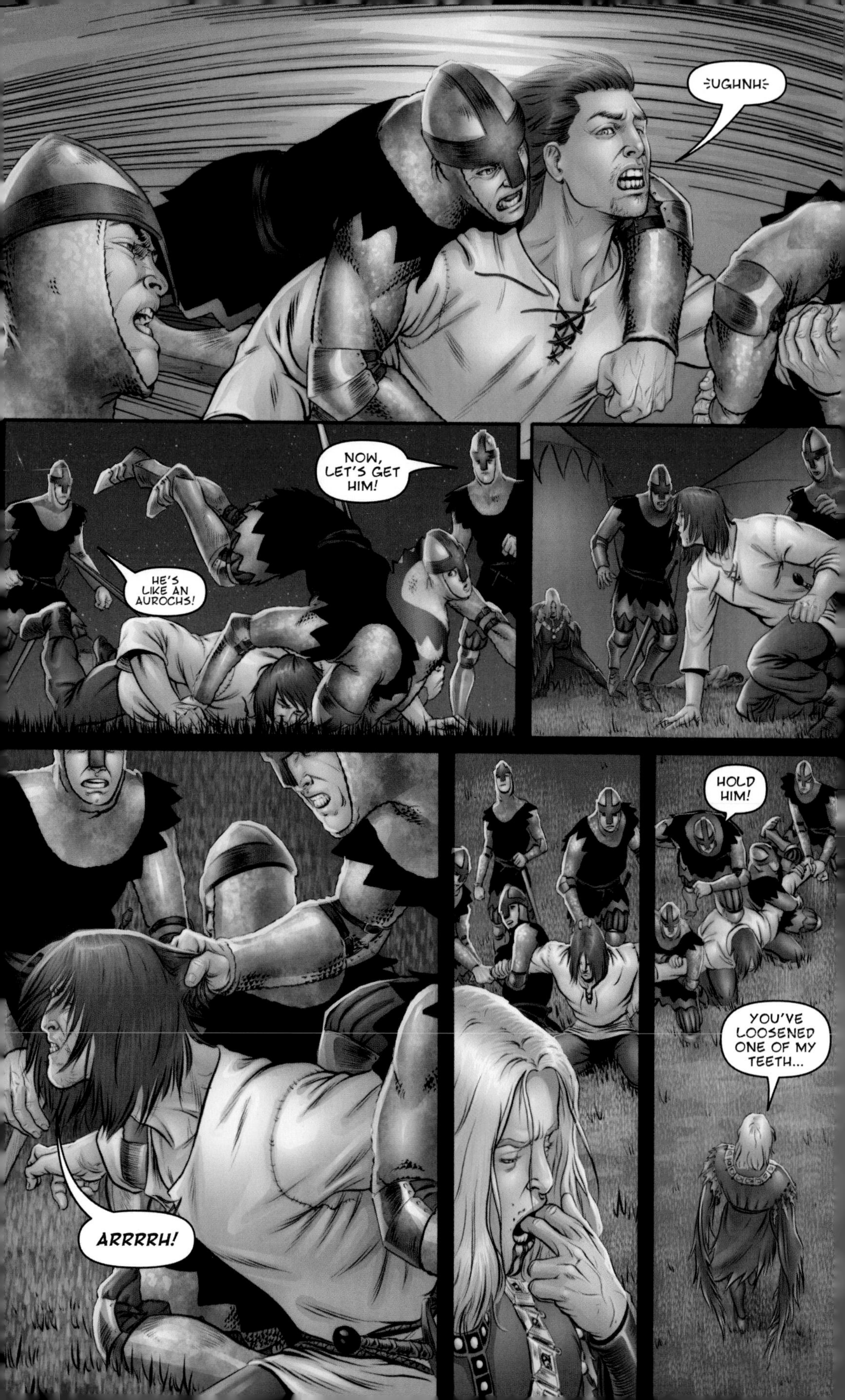
UGHNH
NOW, LET'S GET HIM!
HE'S LIKE AN AUROCHS!
ARRRRH!
HOLD HIM!
YOU'VE LOOSENED ONE OF MY TEETH...

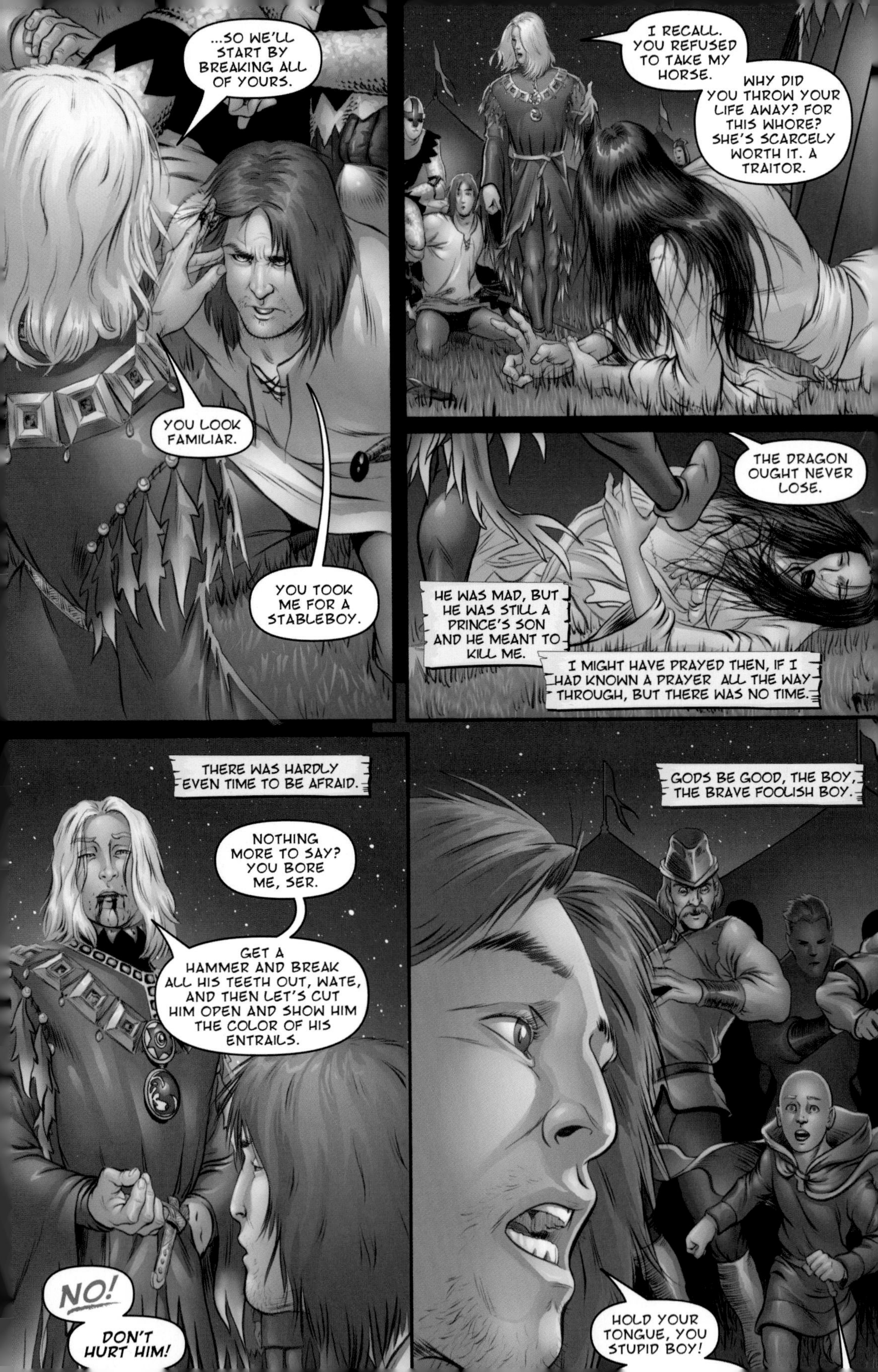
...SO WE'LL START BY BREAKING ALL OF YOURS.
YOU LOOK FAMILIAR.
YOU TOOK ME FOR A STABLEBOY.
I RECALL. YOU REFUSED TO TAKE MY HORSE.
WHY DID YOU THROW YOUR LIFE AWAY? FOR THIS WHORE? SHE'S SCARCELY WORTH IT. A TRAITOR.
THE DRAGON OUGHT NEVER LOSE.
HE WAS MAD, BUT HE WAS STILL A PRINCE'S SON AND HE MEANT TO KILL ME.
I MIGHT HAVE PRAYED THEN, IF I HAD KNOWN A PRAYER ALL THE WAY THROUGH, BUT THERE WAS NO TIME.
THERE WAS HARDLY EVEN TIME TO BE AFRAID.
NOTHING MORE TO SAY? YOU BORE ME, SER.
GET A HAMMER AND BREAK ALL HIS TEETH OUT, WATE, AND THEN LET'S CUT HIM OPEN AND SHOW HIM THE COLOR OF HIS ENTRAILS.
NO!
DON'T HURT HIM!
GODS BE GOOD, THE BOY, THE BRAVE FOOLISH BOY.
HOLD YOUR TONGUE, YOU STUPID BOY!

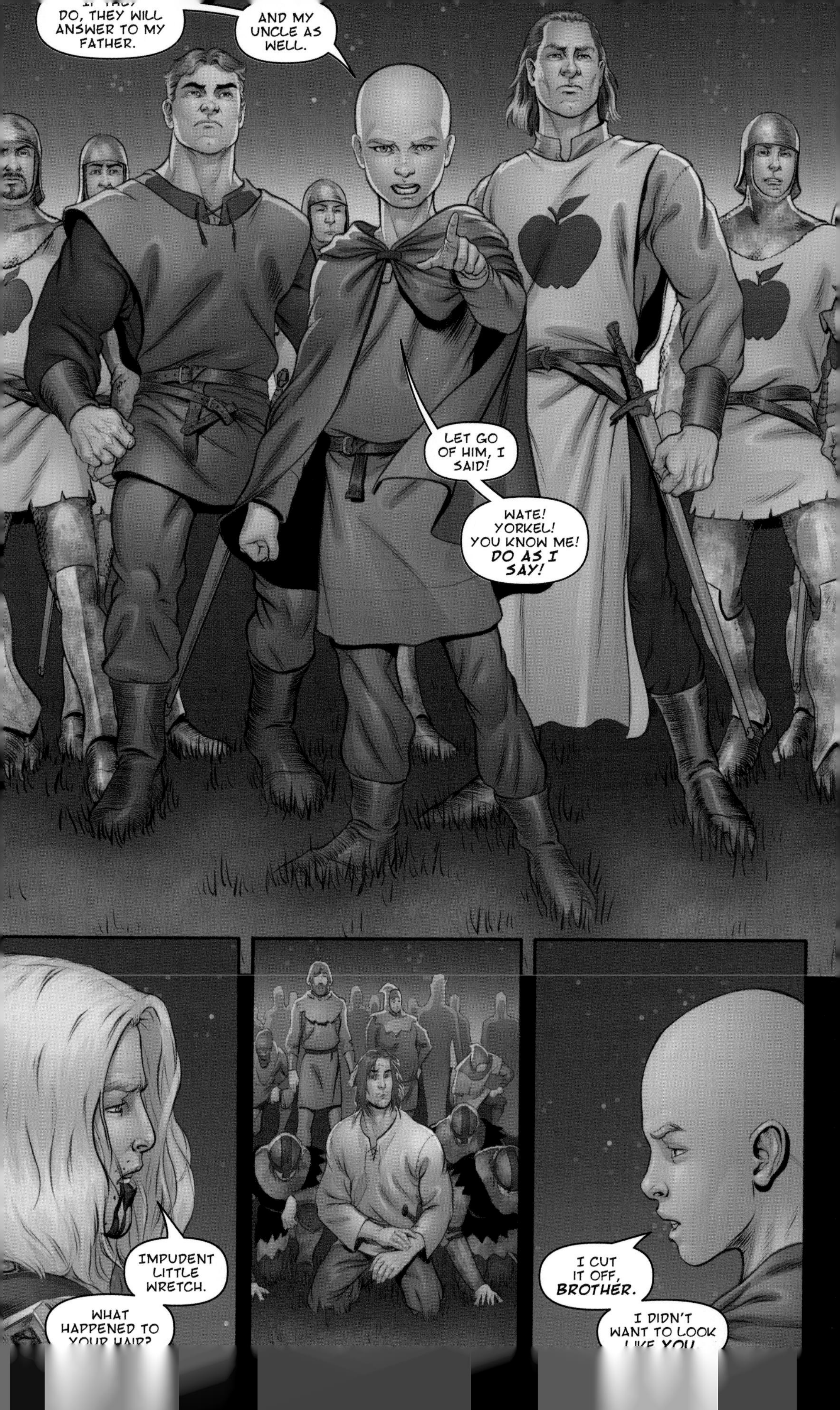
DO, THEY WILL ANSWER TO MY FATHER.
AND MY UNCLE AS WELL.
LET GO OF HIM, I SAID!
WATE! YORKEL! YOU KNOW ME! DO AS I SAY!
IMPUDENT LITTLE WRETCH.
WHAT HAPPENED TO
I CUT IT OFF, BROTHER.
I DIDN'T WANT TO LOOK

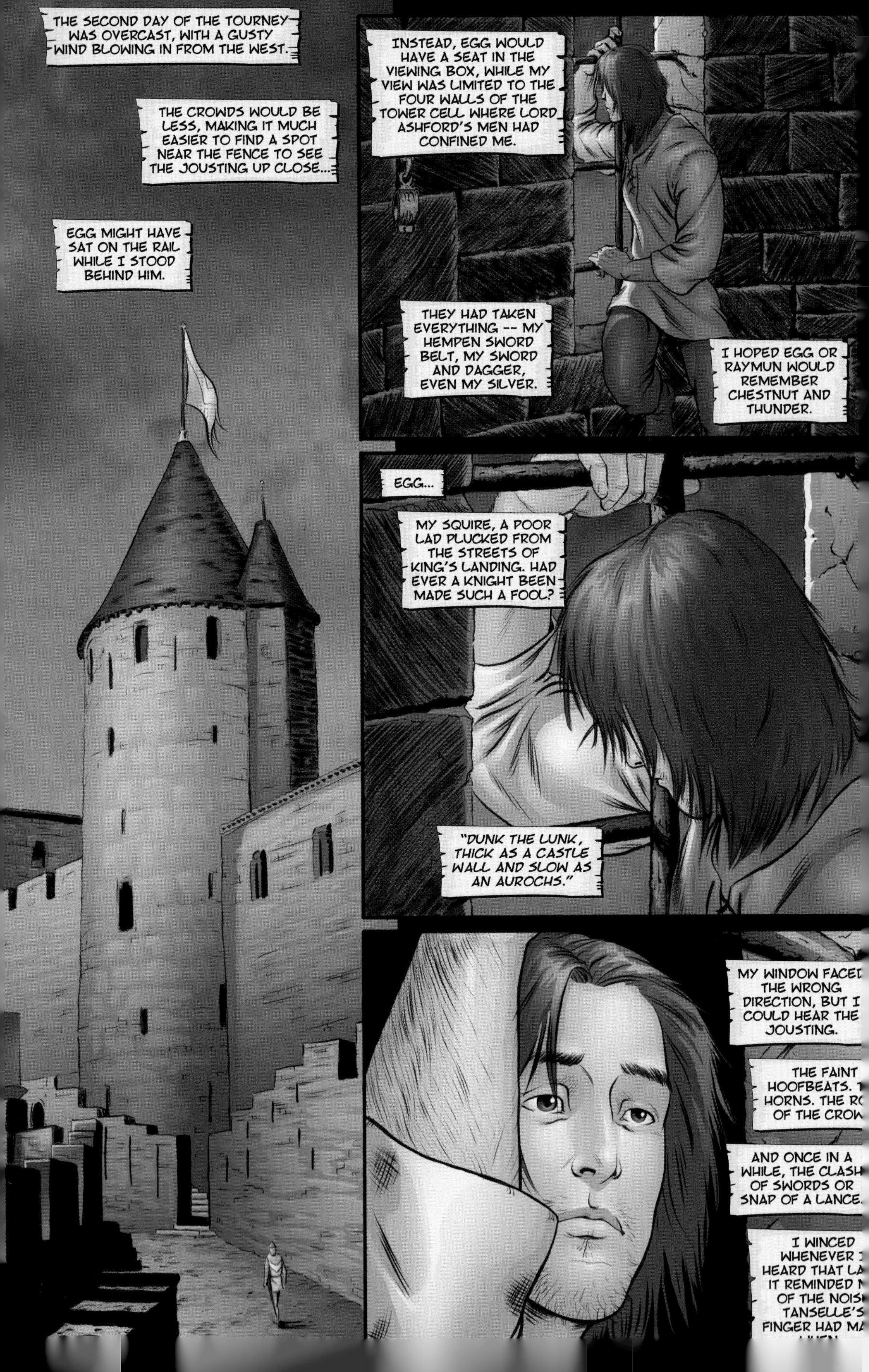
THE SECOND DAY OF THE TOURNEY WAS OVERCAST, WITH A GUSTY WIND BLOWING IN FROM THE WEST.
THE CROWDS WOULD BE LESS, MAKING IT MUCH EASIER TO FIND A SPOT NEAR THE FENCE TO SEE THE JOUSTING UP CLOSE...
EGG MIGHT HAVE SAT ON THE RAIL WHILE I STOOD BEHIND HIM.
INSTEAD, EGG WOULD HAVE A SEAT IN THE VIEWING BOX, WHILE MY VIEW WAS LIMITED TO THE FOUR WALLS OF THE TOWER CELL WHERE LORD ASHFORD'S MEN HAD CONFINED ME.
THEY HAD TAKEN EVERYTHING -- MY HEMPEN SWORD BELT, MY SWORD AND DAGGER, EVEN MY SILVER.
I HOPED EGG OR RAYMUN WOULD REMEMBER CHESTNUT AND THUNDER.
EGG...
MY SQUIRE, A POOR LAD PLUCKED FROM THE STREETS OF KING'S LANDING. HAD EVER A KNIGHT BEEN MADE SUCH A FOOL?
"DUNK THE LUNK, THICK AS A CASTLE WALL AND SLOW AS AN AUROCHS."
MY WINDOW FACED THE WRONG DIRECTION, BUT I COULD HEAR THE JOUSTING.
THE FAINT HOOFBEATS. HORNS. THE OF THE
AND ONCE IN A WHILE, THE OF SWORDS OR SNAP OF A LANCE.
I WINCED WHENEVER HEARD THAT IT REMINDED OF THE TANSELLE'S FINGER HAD

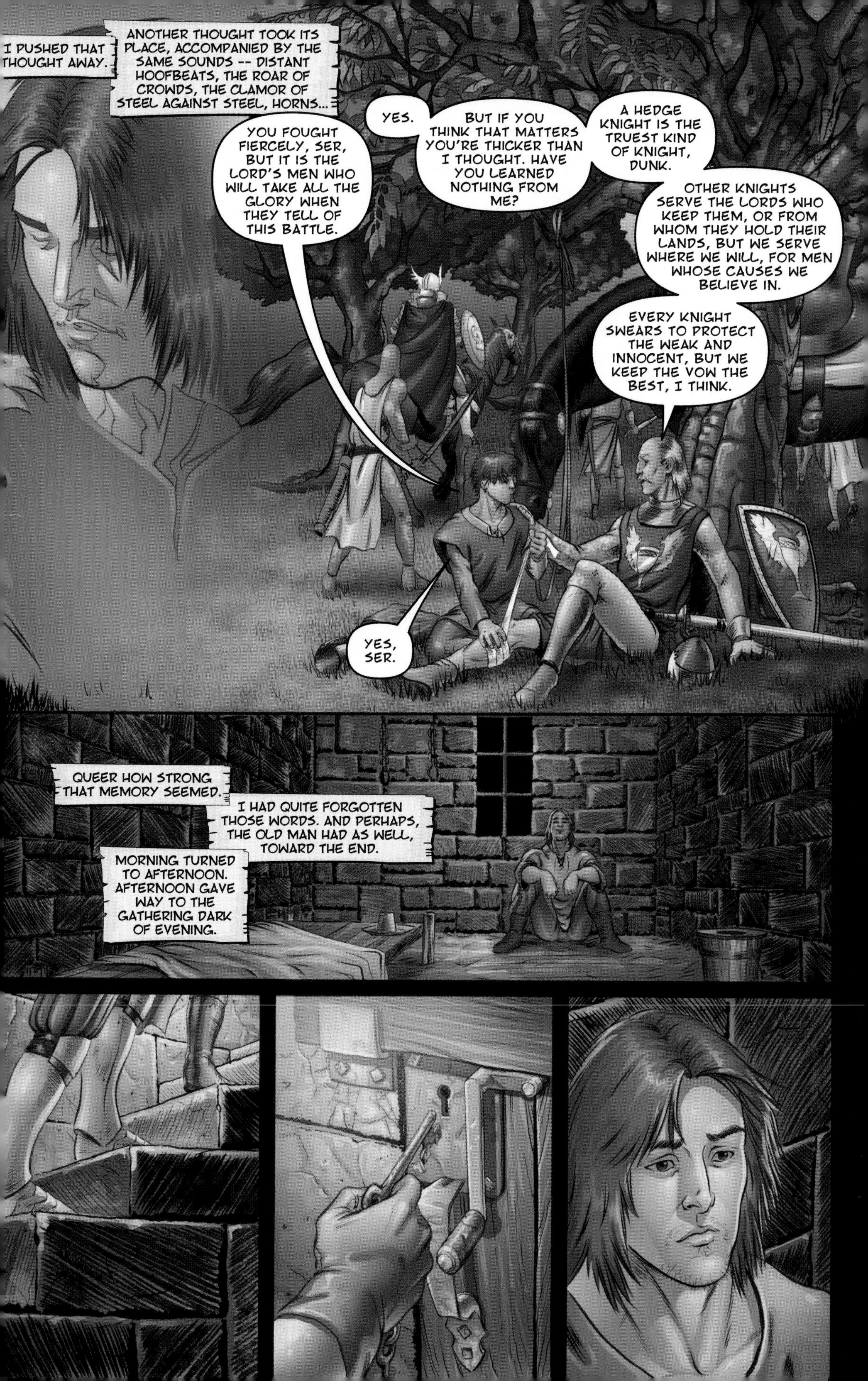
I PUSHED THAT THOUGHT AWAY.
ANOTHER THOUGHT TOOK ITS PLACE, ACCOMPANIED BY THE SAME SOUNDS -- DISTANT HOOFBEATS, THE ROAR OF CROWDS, THE CLAMOR OF STEEL AGAINST STEEL, HORNS...
YOU FOUGHT FIERCELY, SER, BUT IT IS THE LORD'S MEN WHO WILL TAKE ALL THE GLORY WHEN THEY TELL OF THIS BATTLE.
YES.
BUT IF YOU THINK THAT MATTERS YOU'RE THICKER THAN I THOUGHT. HAVE YOU LEARNED NOTHING FROM ME?
YES, SER.
A HEDGE KNIGHT IS THE TRUEST KIND OF KNIGHT, DUNK.
OTHER KNIGHTS SERVE THE LORDS WHO KEEP THEM, OR FROM WHOM THEY HOLD THEIR LANDS, BUT WE SERVE WHERE WE WILL, FOR MEN WHOSE CAUSES WE BELIEVE IN.
EVERY KNIGHT SWEARS TO PROTECT THE WEAK AND INNOCENT, BUT WE KEEP THE VOW THE BEST, I THINK.
QUEER HOW STRONG THAT MEMORY SEEMED.
I HAD QUITE FORGOTTEN THOSE WORDS. AND PERHAPS, THE OLD MAN HAD AS WELL, TOWARD THE END.
MORNING TURNED TO AFTERNOON. AFTERNOON GAVE WAY TO THE GATHERING DARK OF EVENING.

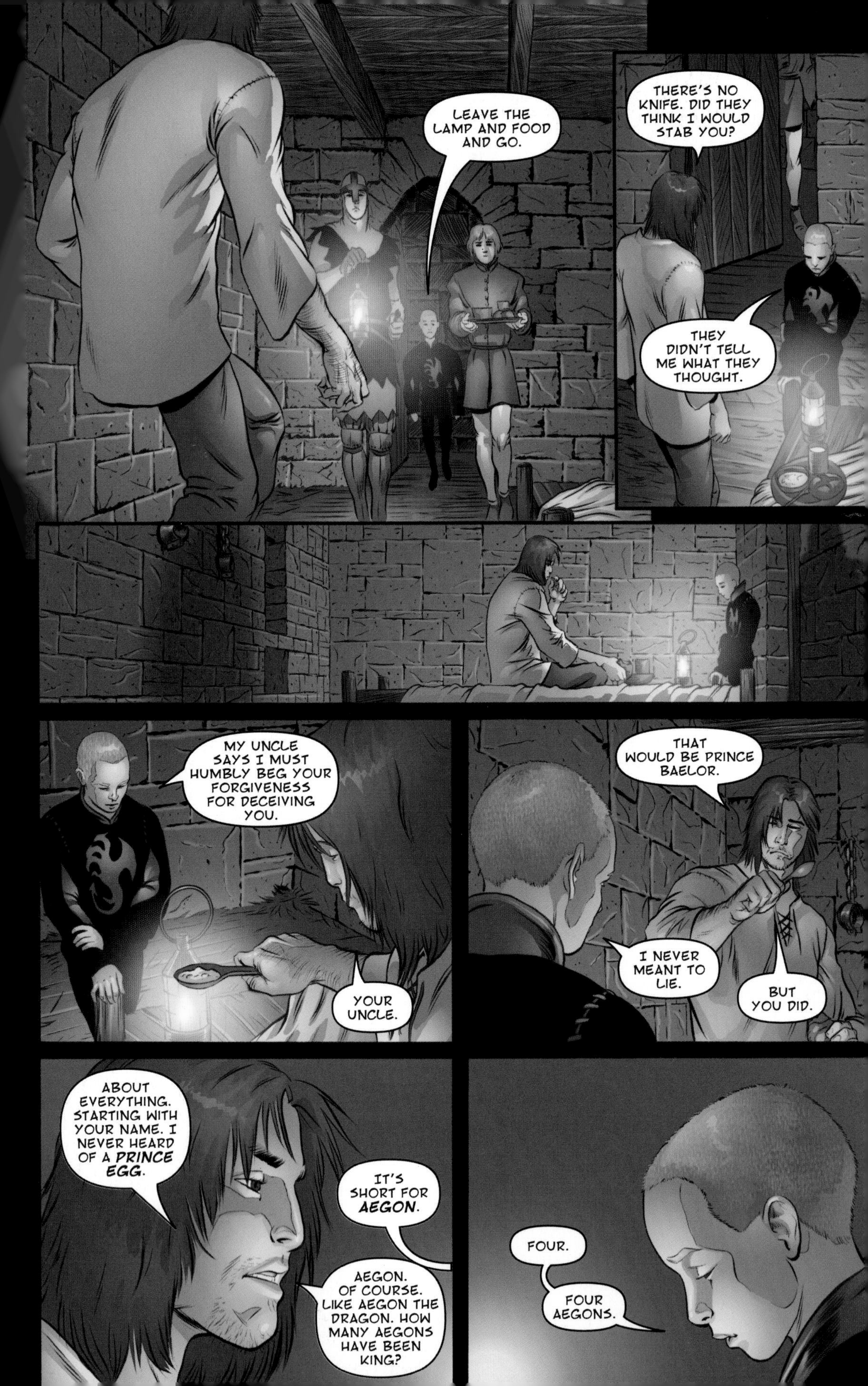
LEAVE THE LAMP AND FOOD AND GO.
THERE'S NO KNIFE. DID THEY THINK I WOULD STAB YOU?
THEY DIDN'T TELL ME WHAT THEY THOUGHT.
MY UNCLE SAYS I MUST HUMBLY BEG YOUR FORGIVENESS FOR DECEIVING YOU.
YOUR UNCLE.
THAT WOULD BE PRINCE BAELOR.
I NEVER MEANT TO LIE.
BUT YOU DID.
ABOUT EVERYTHING. STARTING WITH YOUR NAME. I NEVER HEARD OF A PRINCE EGG.
IT'S SHORT FOR AEGON.
AEGON. OF COURSE. LIKE AEGON THE DRAGON. HOW MANY AEGONS HAVE BEEN KING?
FOUR.
FOUR AEGONS.

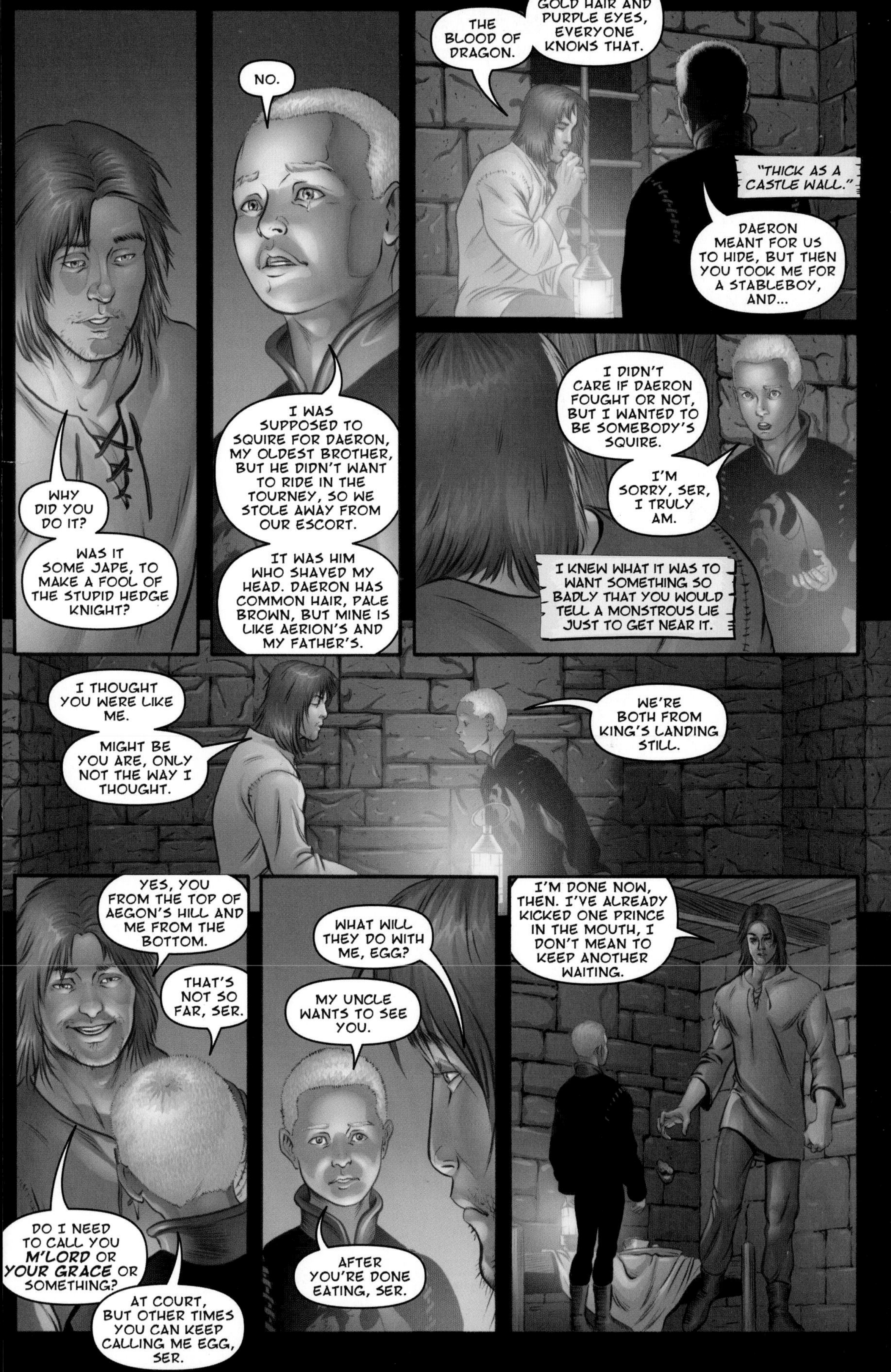
WHY DID YOU DO IT?
WAS IT SOME JAPE, TO MAKE A FOOL OF THE STUPID HEDGE KNIGHT?
NO.
I WAS SUPPOSED TO SQUIRE FOR DAERON, MY OLDEST BROTHER, BUT HE DIDN'T WANT TO RIDE IN THE TOURNEY, SO WE STOLE AWAY FROM OUR ESCORT.
IT WAS HIM WHO SHAVED MY HEAD. DAERON HAS COMMON HAIR, PALE BROWN, BUT MINE IS LIKE AERION'S AND MY FATHER'S.
THE BLOOD OF DRAGON.
SILVER-GOLD HAIR AND PURPLE EYES, EVERYONE KNOWS THAT.
"THICK AS A CASTLE WALL."
DAERON MEANT FOR US TO HIDE, BUT THEN YOU TOOK ME FOR A STABLEBOY, AND...
I DIDN'T CARE IF DAERON FOUGHT OR NOT, BUT I WANTED TO BE SOMEBODY'S SQUIRE.
I'M SORRY, SER, I TRULY AM.
I KNEW WHAT IT WAS TO WANT SOMETHING SO BADLY THAT YOU WOULD TELL A MONSTROUS LIE JUST TO GET NEAR IT.
I THOUGHT YOU WERE LIKE ME.
MIGHT BE YOU ARE, ONLY NOT THE WAY I THOUGHT.
WE'RE BOTH FROM KING'S LANDING STILL.
YES, YOU FROM THE TOP OF AEGON'S HILL AND ME FROM THE BOTTOM.
THAT'S NOT SO FAR, SER.
DO I NEED TO CALL YOU *M'LORD* OR *YOUR GRACE* OR SOMETHING?
AT COURT, BUT OTHER TIMES YOU CAN KEEP CALLING ME EGG, SER.
WHAT WILL THEY DO WITH ME, EGG?
MY UNCLE WANTS TO SEE YOU.
AFTER YOU'RE DONE EATING, SER.
I'M DONE NOW, THEN. I'VE ALREADY KICKED ONE PRINCE IN THE MOUTH, I DON'T MEAN TO KEEP ANOTHER WAITING.

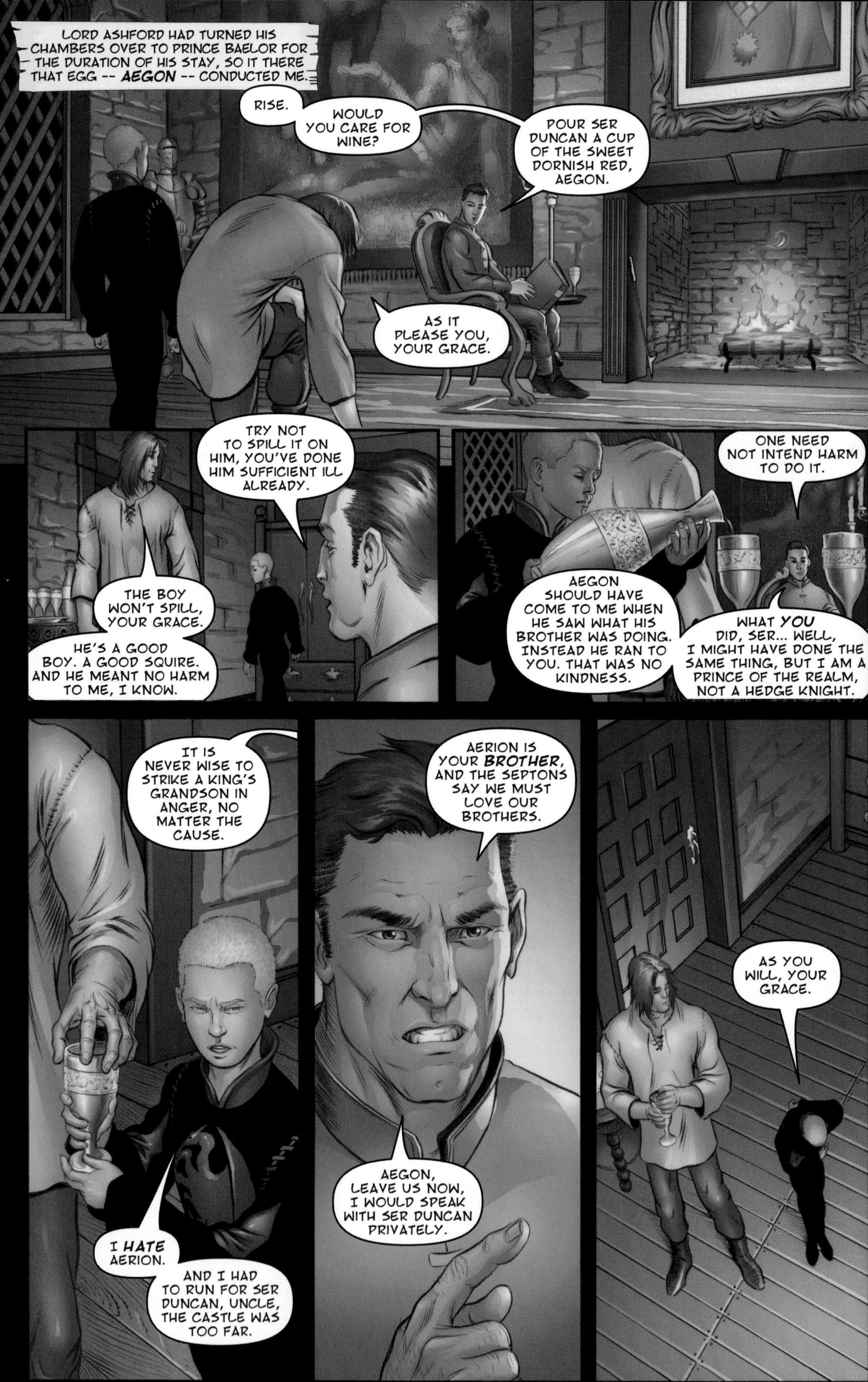
LORD ASHFORD HAD TURNED HIS CHAMBERS OVER TO PRINCE BAELOR FOR THE DURATION OF HIS STAY, SO IT THERE THAT EGG -- AEGON -- CONDUCTED ME.
RISE.
WOULD YOU CARE FOR WINE?
POUR SER DUNCAN A CUP OF THE SWEET DORNISH RED, AEGON.
AS IT PLEASE YOU, YOUR GRACE.
TRY NOT TO SPILL IT ON HIM, YOU'VE DONE HIM SUFFICIENT ILL ALREADY.
THE BOY WON'T SPILL, YOUR GRACE.
HE'S A GOOD BOY. A GOOD SQUIRE. AND HE MEANT NO HARM TO ME, I KNOW.
ONE NEED NOT INTEND HARM TO DO IT.
AEGON SHOULD HAVE COME TO ME WHEN HE SAW WHAT HIS BROTHER WAS DOING. INSTEAD HE RAN TO YOU. THAT WAS NO KINDNESS.
WHAT YOU DID, SER... WELL, I MIGHT HAVE DONE THE SAME THING, BUT I AM A PRINCE OF THE REALM, NOT A HEDGE KNIGHT.
IT IS NEVER WISE TO STRIKE A KING'S GRANDSON IN ANGER, NO MATTER THE CAUSE.
I HATE AERION.
AND I HAD TO RUN FOR SER DUNCAN, UNCLE, THE CASTLE WAS TOO FAR.
AERION IS YOUR BROTHER, AND THE SEPTONS SAY WE MUST LOVE OUR BROTHERS.
AEGON, LEAVE US NOW, I WOULD SPEAK WITH SER DUNCAN PRIVATELY.
AS YOU WILL, YOUR GRACE.

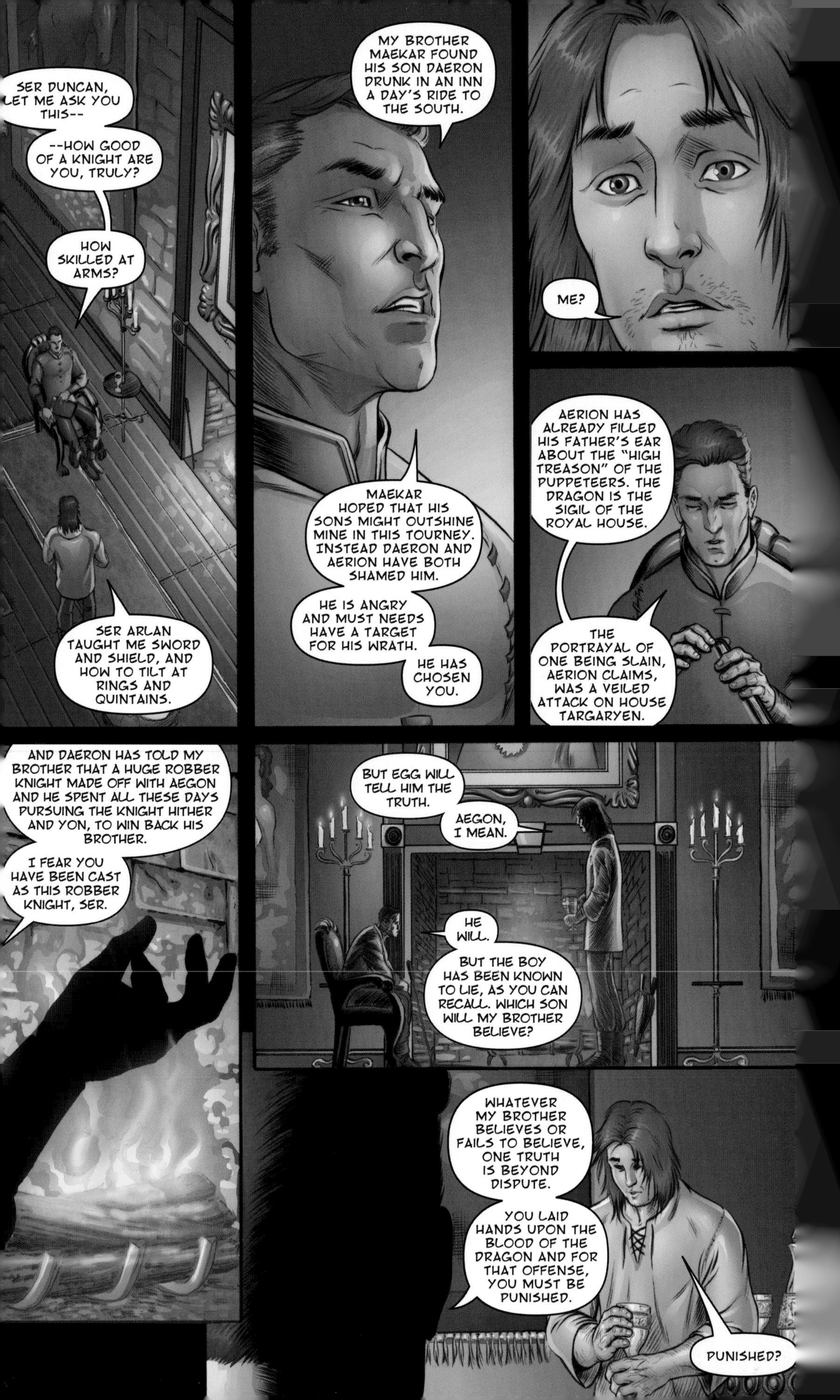

SER DUNCAN, LET ME ASK YOU THIS--
--HOW GOOD OF A KNIGHT ARE YOU, TRULY?
HOW SKILLED AT ARMS?
SER ARLAN TAUGHT ME SWORD AND SHIELD, AND HOW TO TILT AT RINGS AND QUINTAINS.
MY BROTHER MAEKAR FOUND HIS SON DAERON DRUNK IN AN INN A DAY'S RIDE TO THE SOUTH.
MAEKAR HOPED THAT HIS SONS MIGHT OUTSHINE MINE IN THIS TOURNEY. INSTEAD DAERON AND AERION HAVE BOTH SHAMED HIM.
HE IS ANGRY AND MUST NEEDS HAVE A TARGET FOR HIS WRATH.
HE HAS CHOSEN YOU.
ME?
AERION HAS ALREADY FILLED HIS FATHER'S EAR ABOUT THE "HIGH TREASON" OF THE PUPPETEERS. THE DRAGON IS THE SIGIL OF THE ROYAL HOUSE.
THE PORTRAYAL OF ONE BEING SLAIN, AERION CLAIMS, WAS A VEILED ATTACK ON HOUSE TARGARYEN.
AND DAERON HAS TOLD MY BROTHER THAT A HUGE ROBBER KNIGHT MADE OFF WITH AEGON AND HE SPENT ALL THESE DAYS PURSUING THE KNIGHT HITHER AND YON, TO WIN BACK HIS BROTHER.
I FEAR YOU HAVE BEEN CAST AS THIS ROBBER KNIGHT, SER.
BUT EGG WILL TELL HIM THE TRUTH.
AEGON, I MEAN.
HE WILL.
BUT THE BOY HAS BEEN KNOWN TO LIE, AS YOU CAN RECALL. WHICH SON WILL MY BROTHER BELIEVE?
WHATEVER MY BROTHER BELIEVES OR FAILS TO BELIEVE, ONE TRUTH IS BEYOND DISPUTE.
YOU LAID HANDS UPON THE BLOOD OF THE DRAGON AND FOR THAT OFFENSE, YOU MUST BE PUNISHED.
PUNISHED?

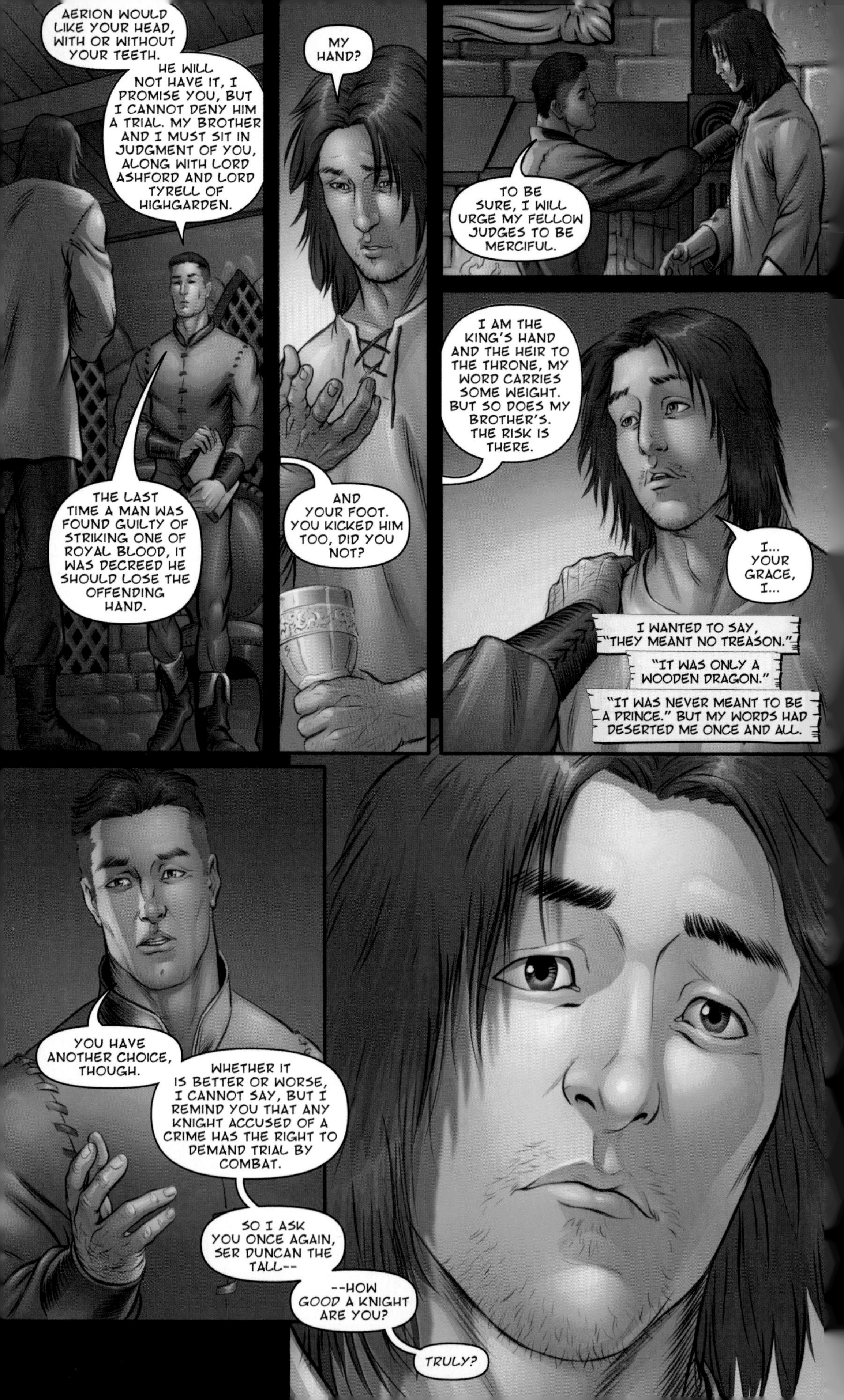

AERION WOULD LIKE YOUR HEAD, WITH OR WITHOUT YOUR TEETH.
HE WILL NOT HAVE IT, I PROMISE YOU, BUT I CANNOT DENY HIM A TRIAL. MY BROTHER AND I MUST SIT IN JUDGMENT OF YOU, ALONG WITH LORD ASHFORD AND LORD TYRELL OF HIGHGARDEN.
THE LAST TIME A MAN WAS FOUND GUILTY OF STRIKING ONE OF ROYAL BLOOD, IT WAS DECREED HE SHOULD LOSE THE OFFENDING HAND.
MY HAND?
AND YOUR FOOT. YOU KICKED HIM TOO, DID YOU NOT?
TO BE SURE, I WILL URGE MY FELLOW JUDGES TO BE MERCIFUL.
I AM THE KING'S HAND AND THE HEIR TO THE THRONE, MY WORD CARRIES SOME WEIGHT. BUT SO DOES MY BROTHER'S. THE RISK IS THERE.
I... YOUR GRACE, I...
I WANTED TO SAY, "THEY MEANT NO TREASON."
"IT WAS ONLY A WOODEN DRAGON."
"IT WAS NEVER MEANT TO BE A PRINCE." BUT MY WORDS HAD DESERTED ME ONCE AND ALL.
YOU HAVE ANOTHER CHOICE, THOUGH.
WHETHER IT IS BETTER OR WORSE, I CANNOT SAY, BUT I REMIND YOU THAT ANY KNIGHT ACCUSED OF A CRIME HAS THE RIGHT TO DEMAND TRIAL BY COMBAT.
SO I ASK YOU ONCE AGAIN, SER DUNCAN THE TALL--
--HOW GOOD A KNIGHT ARE YOU?
TRULY?

ISSUE FIVE
COVER A

MIKE S. MILLER

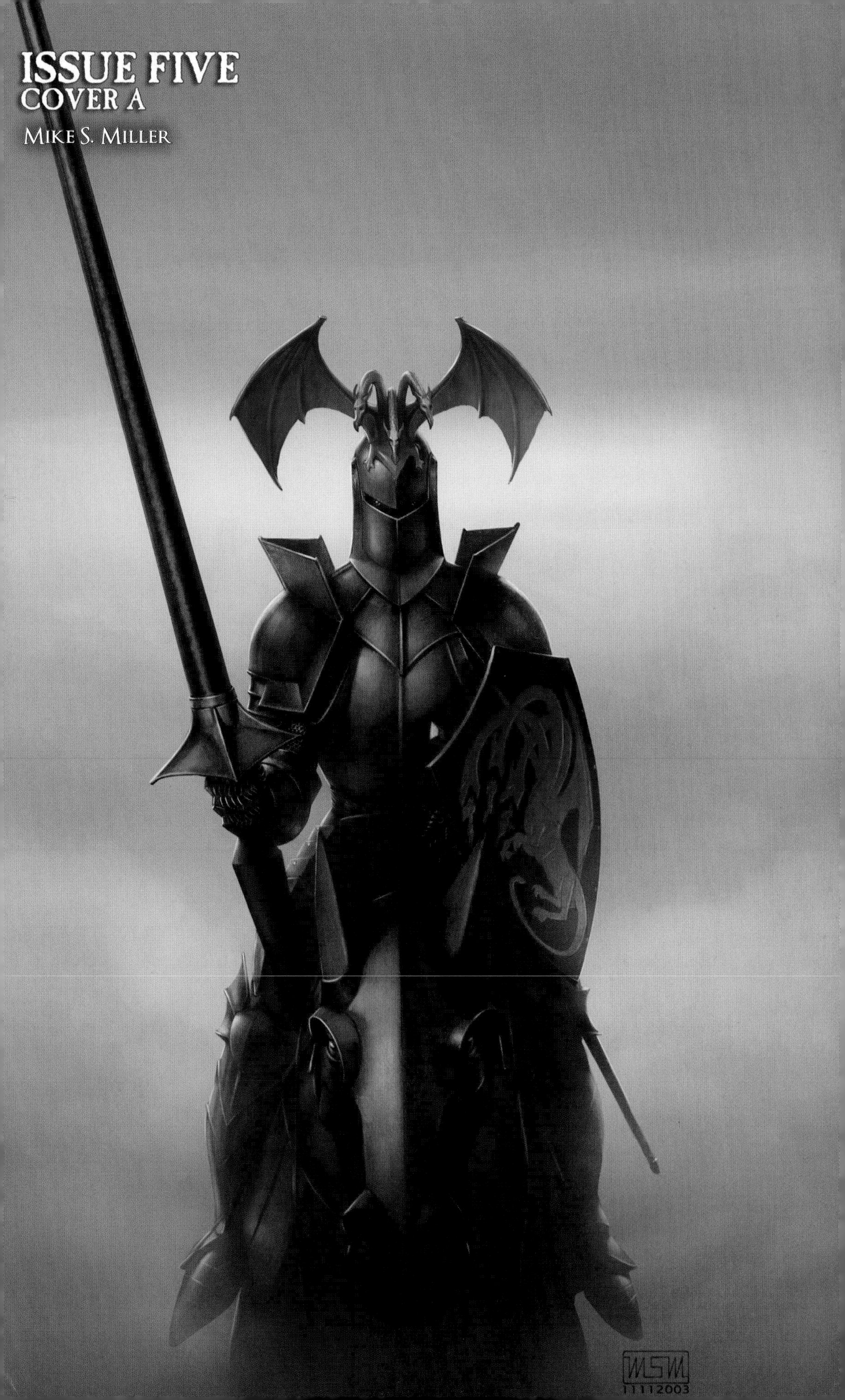
MSM
11112003

ISSUE FIVE
COVER B

TED NASMITH

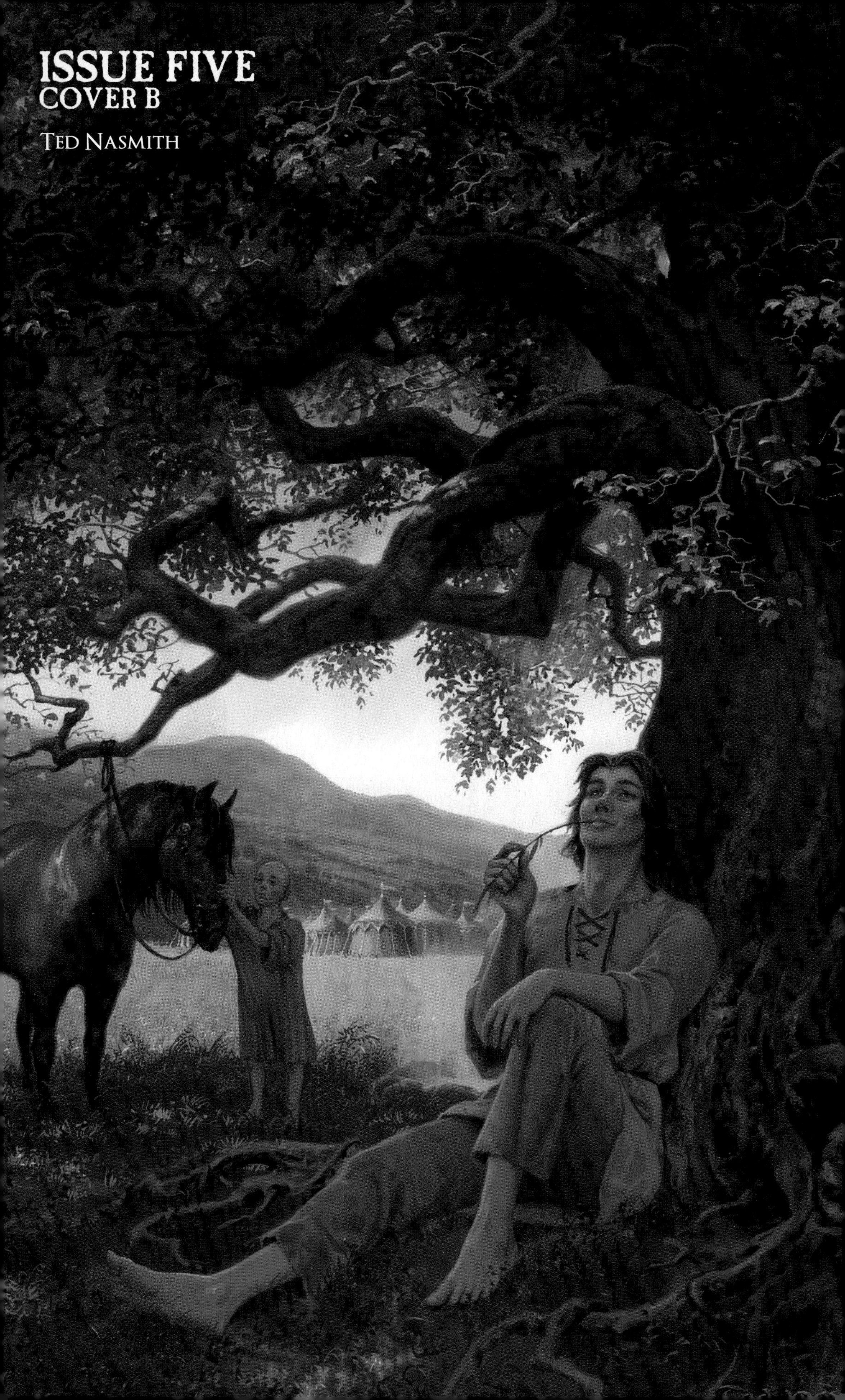

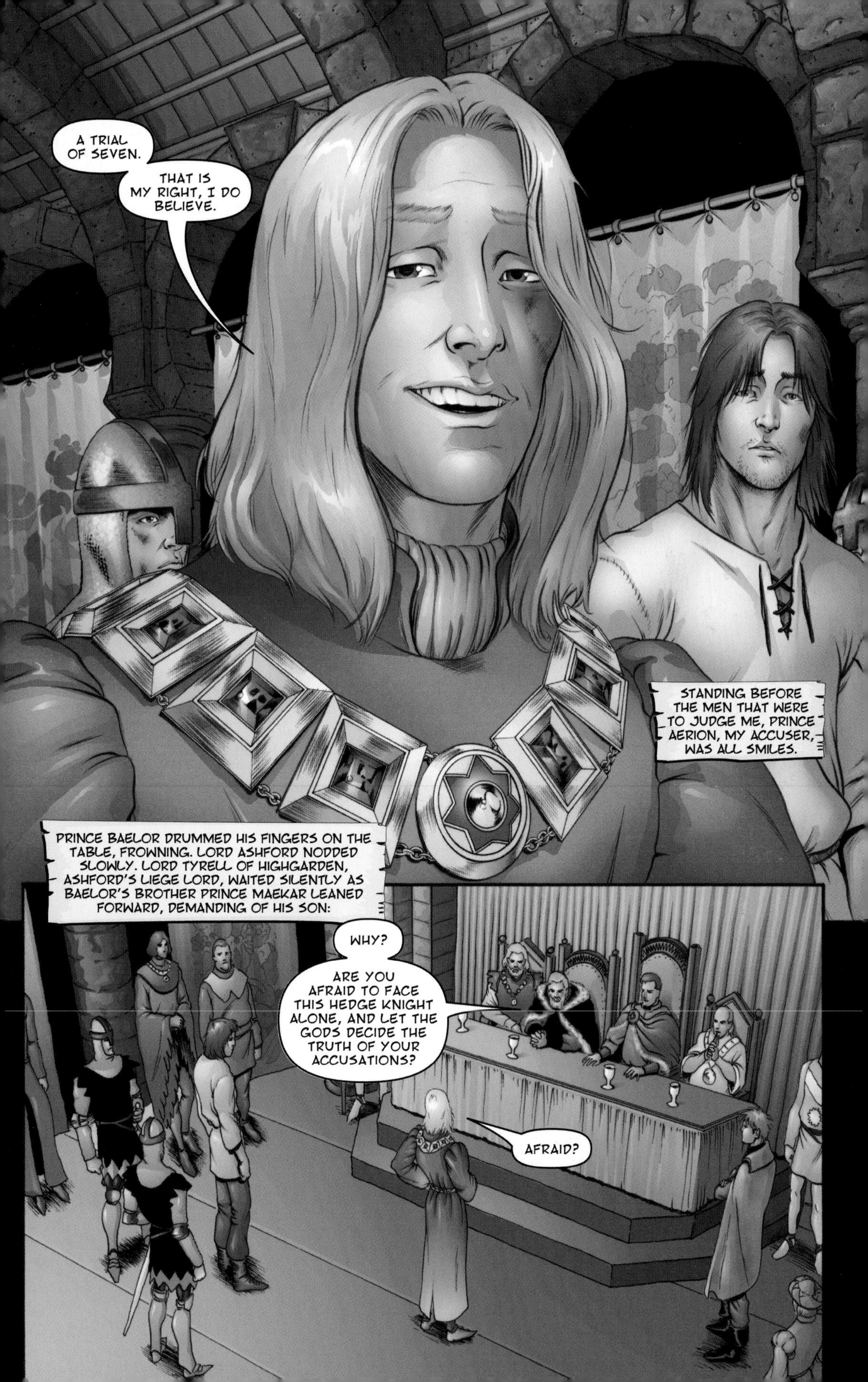
A TRIAL OF SEVEN.
THAT IS MY RIGHT, I DO BELIEVE.
STANDING BEFORE THE MEN THAT WERE TO JUDGE ME, PRINCE AERION, MY ACCUSER, WAS ALL SMILES.
PRINCE BAELOR DRUMMED HIS FINGERS ON THE TABLE, FROWNING. LORD ASHFORD NODDED SLOWLY. LORD TYRELL OF HIGHGARDEN, ASHFORD'S LIEGE LORD, WAITED SILENTLY AS BAELOR'S BROTHER PRINCE MAEKAR LEANED FORWARD, DEMANDING OF HIS SON:
WHY?
ARE YOU AFRAID TO FACE THIS HEDGE KNIGHT ALONE, AND LET THE GODS DECIDE THE TRUTH OF YOUR ACCUSATIONS?
AFRAID?

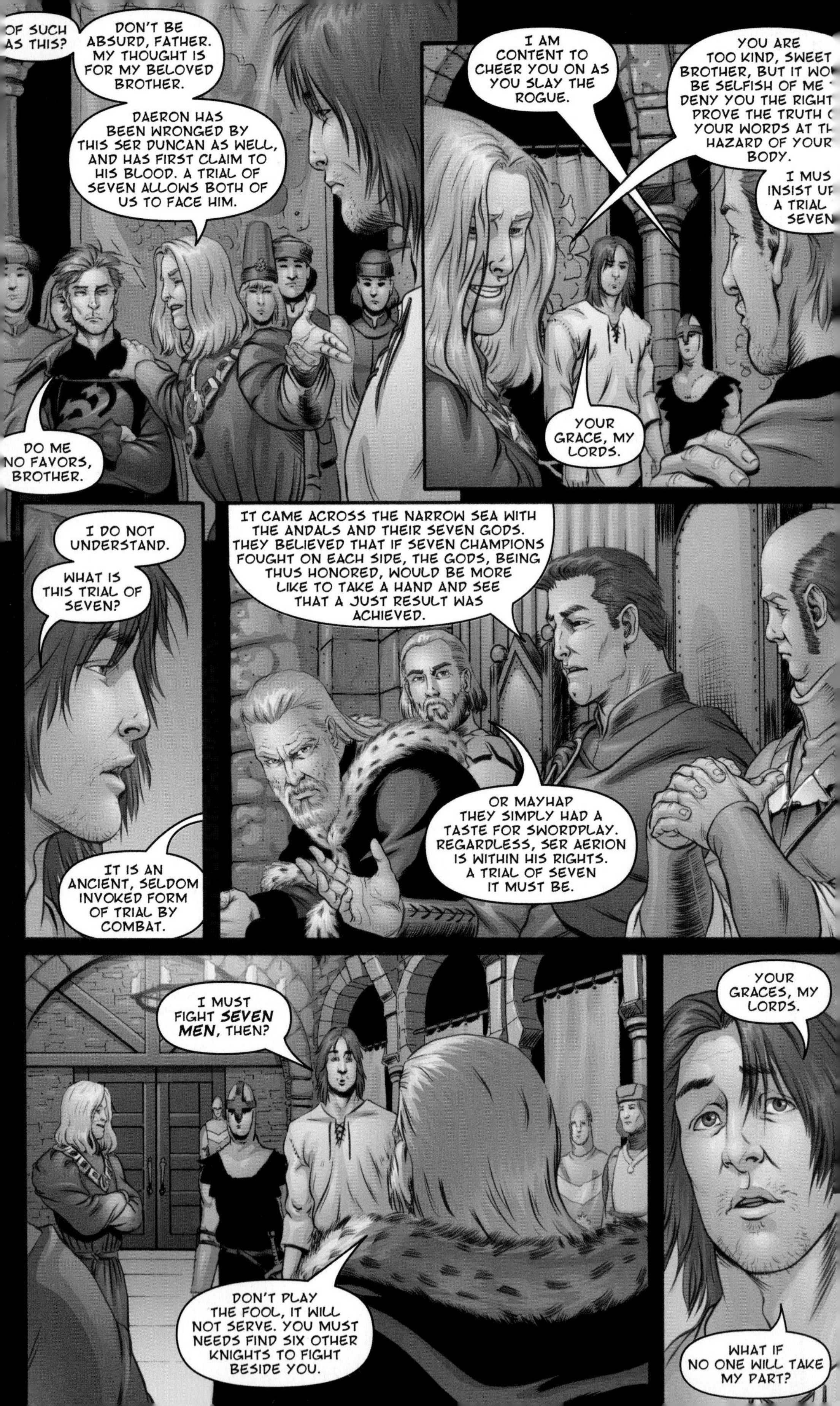
OF SUCH
AS THIS?
DON'T BE ABSURD, FATHER. MY THOUGHT IS FOR MY BELOVED BROTHER.
DAERON HAS BEEN WRONGED BY THIS SER DUNCAN AS WELL, AND HAS FIRST CLAIM TO HIS BLOOD. A TRIAL OF SEVEN ALLOWS BOTH OF US TO FACE HIM.
DO ME NO FAVORS, BROTHER.
I AM CONTENT TO CHEER YOU ON AS YOU SLAY THE ROGUE.
YOU ARE TOO KIND, SWEET BROTHER, BUT IT WO
BE SELFISH OF ME
DENY YOU THE RIGHT
PROVE THE TRUTH
YOUR WORDS AT TH
HAZARD OF YOUR BODY.
I MUS
INSIST U
A TRIAL
SEVEN
YOUR GRACE, MY LORDS.
I DO NOT UNDERSTAND.
WHAT IS THIS TRIAL OF SEVEN?
IT IS AN ANCIENT, SELDOM INVOKED FORM OF TRIAL BY COMBAT.
IT CAME ACROSS THE NARROW SEA WITH THE ANDALS AND THEIR SEVEN GODS. THEY BELIEVED THAT IF SEVEN CHAMPIONS FOUGHT ON EACH SIDE, THE GODS, BEING THUS HONORED, WOULD BE MORE LIKE TO TAKE A HAND AND SEE THAT A JUST RESULT WAS ACHIEVED.
OR MAYHAP THEY SIMPLY HAD A TASTE FOR SWORDPLAY. REGARDLESS, SER AERION IS WITHIN HIS RIGHTS. A TRIAL OF SEVEN IT MUST BE.
I MUST FIGHT **SEVEN MEN**, THEN?
DON'T PLAY THE FOOL, IT WILL NOT SERVE. YOU MUST NEEDS FIND SIX OTHER KNIGHTS TO FIGHT BESIDE YOU.
YOUR GRACES, MY LORDS.
WHAT IF NO ONE WILL TAKE MY PART?

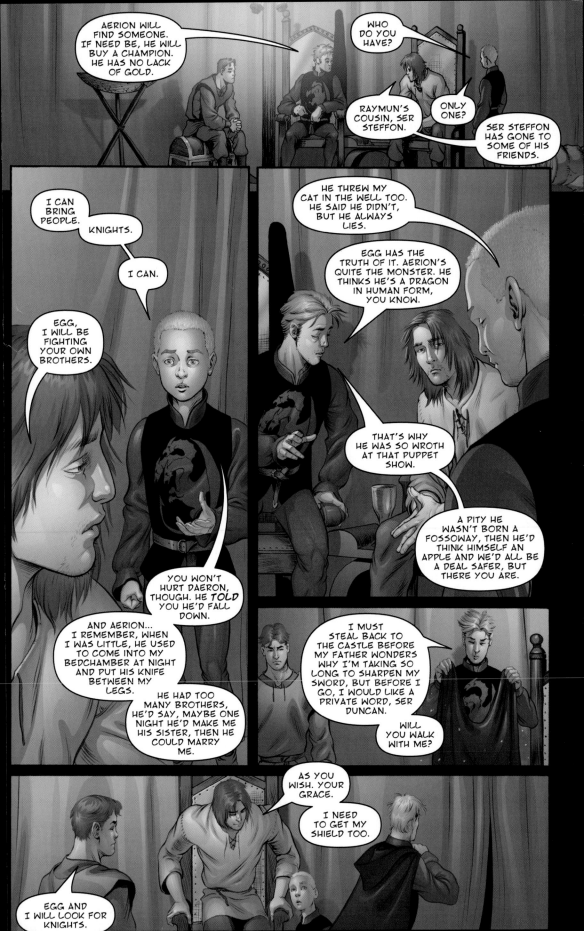

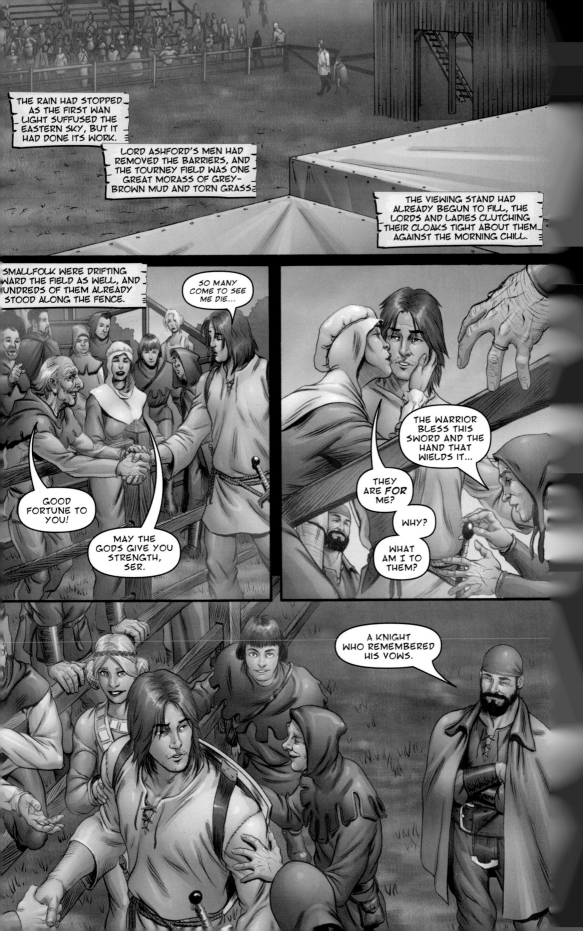

THE RAIN HAD STOPPED AS THE FIRST WAN LIGHT SUFFUSED THE EASTERN SKY, BUT IT HAD DONE ITS WORK.

LORD ASHFORD'S MEN HAD REMOVED THE BARRIERS, AND THE TOURNEY FIELD WAS ONE GREAT MORASS OF GREY-BROWN MUD AND TORN GRASS.

THE VIEWING STAND HAD ALREADY BEGUN TO FILL, THE LORDS AND LADIES CLUTCHING THEIR CLOAKS TIGHT ABOUT THEM AGAINST THE MORNING CHILL.

SMALLFOLK WERE DRIFTING [TO]WARD THE FIELD AS WELL, AND [H]UNDREDS OF THEM ALREADY STOOD ALONG THE FENCE.

SO MANY COME TO SEE ME DIE...

GOOD FORTUNE TO YOU!

MAY THE GODS GIVE YOU STRENGTH, SER.

THE WARRIOR BLESS THIS SWORD AND THE HAND THAT WIELDS IT...

THEY ARE *FOR* ME?

WHY?

WHAT AM I TO THEM?

A KNIGHT WHO REMEMBERED HIS VOWS.

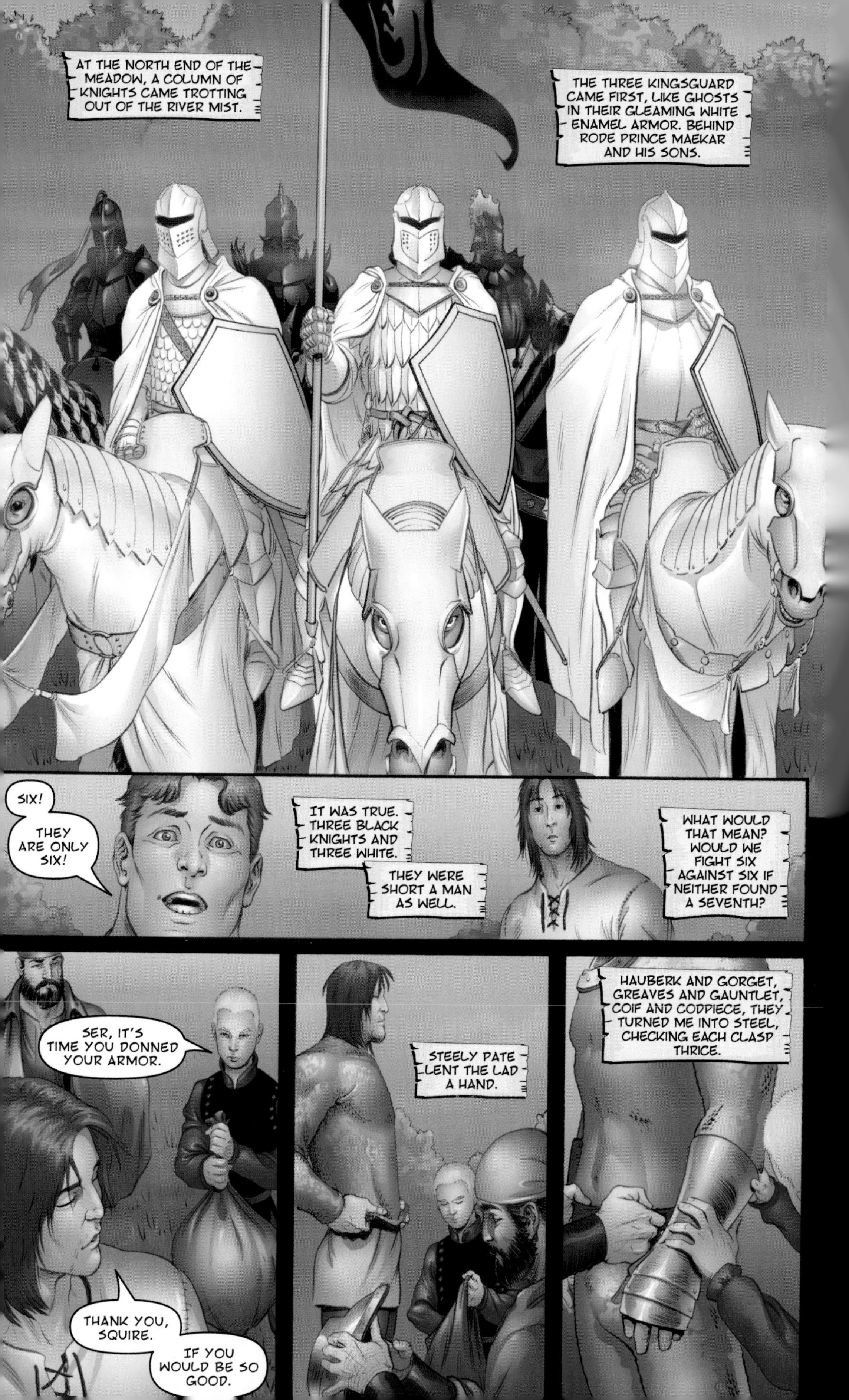
AT THE NORTH END OF THE MEADOW, A COLUMN OF KNIGHTS CAME TROTTING OUT OF THE RIVER MIST.
THE THREE KINGSGUARD CAME FIRST, LIKE GHOSTS IN THEIR GLEAMING WHITE ENAMEL ARMOR. BEHIND RODE PRINCE MAEKAR AND HIS SONS.
SIX!
THEY ARE ONLY SIX!
IT WAS TRUE. THREE BLACK KNIGHTS AND THREE WHITE.
THEY WERE SHORT A MAN AS WELL.
WHAT WOULD THAT MEAN? WOULD WE FIGHT SIX AGAINST SIX IF NEITHER FOUND A SEVENTH?
SER, IT'S TIME YOU DONNED YOUR ARMOR.
THANK YOU, SQUIRE.
IF YOU WOULD BE SO GOOD.
STEELY PATE LENT THE LAD A HAND.
HAUBERK AND GORGET, GREAVES AND GAUNTLET, COIF AND CODPIECE, THEY TURNED ME INTO STEEL, CHECKING EACH CLASP THRICE.

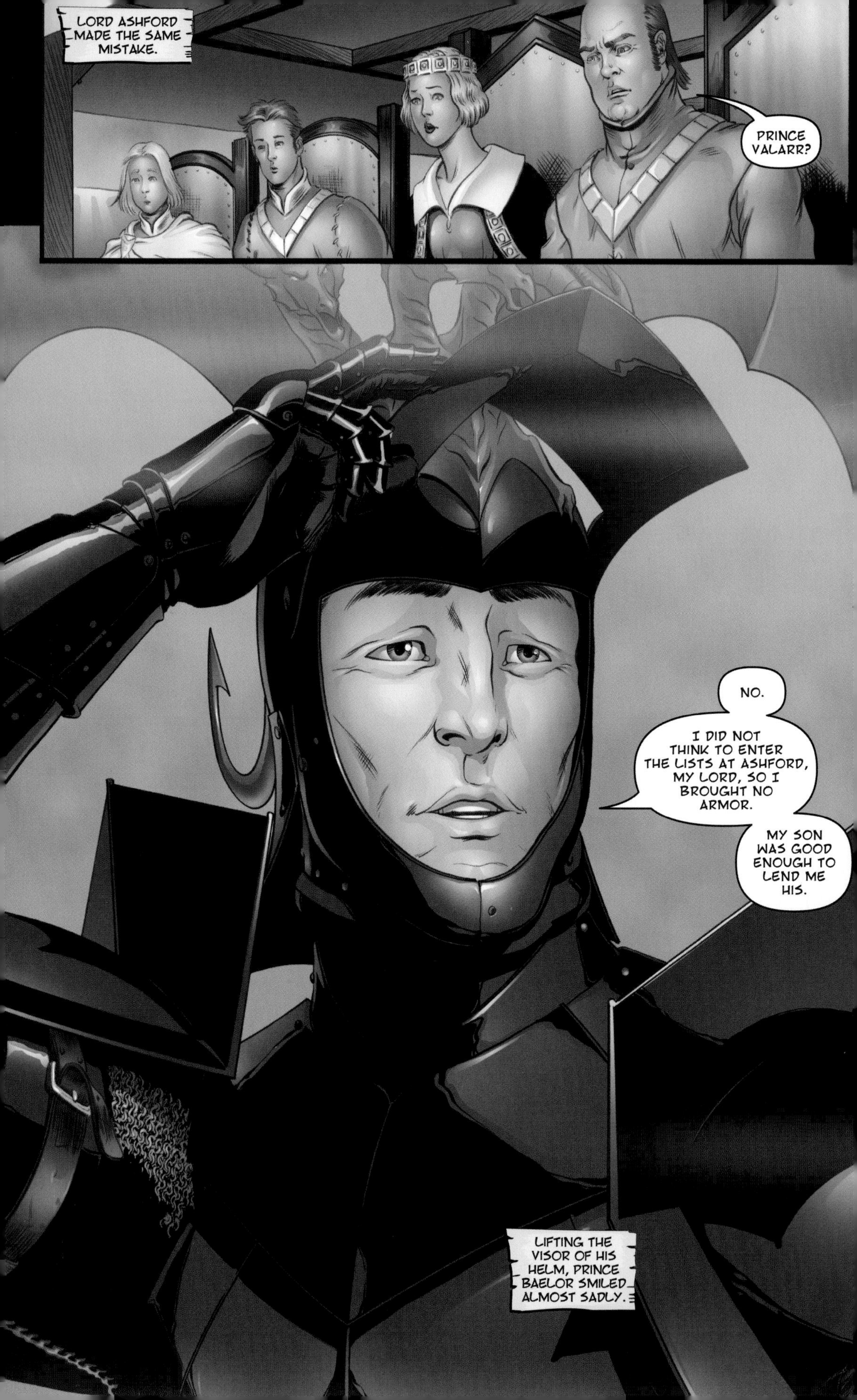
LORD ASHFORD MADE THE SAME MISTAKE.
PRINCE VALARR?
NO.
I DID NOT THINK TO ENTER THE LISTS AT ASHFORD, MY LORD, SO I BROUGHT NO ARMOR.
MY SON WAS GOOD ENOUGH TO LEND ME HIS.
LIFTING THE VISOR OF HIS HELM, PRINCE BAELOR SMILED ALMOST SADLY.

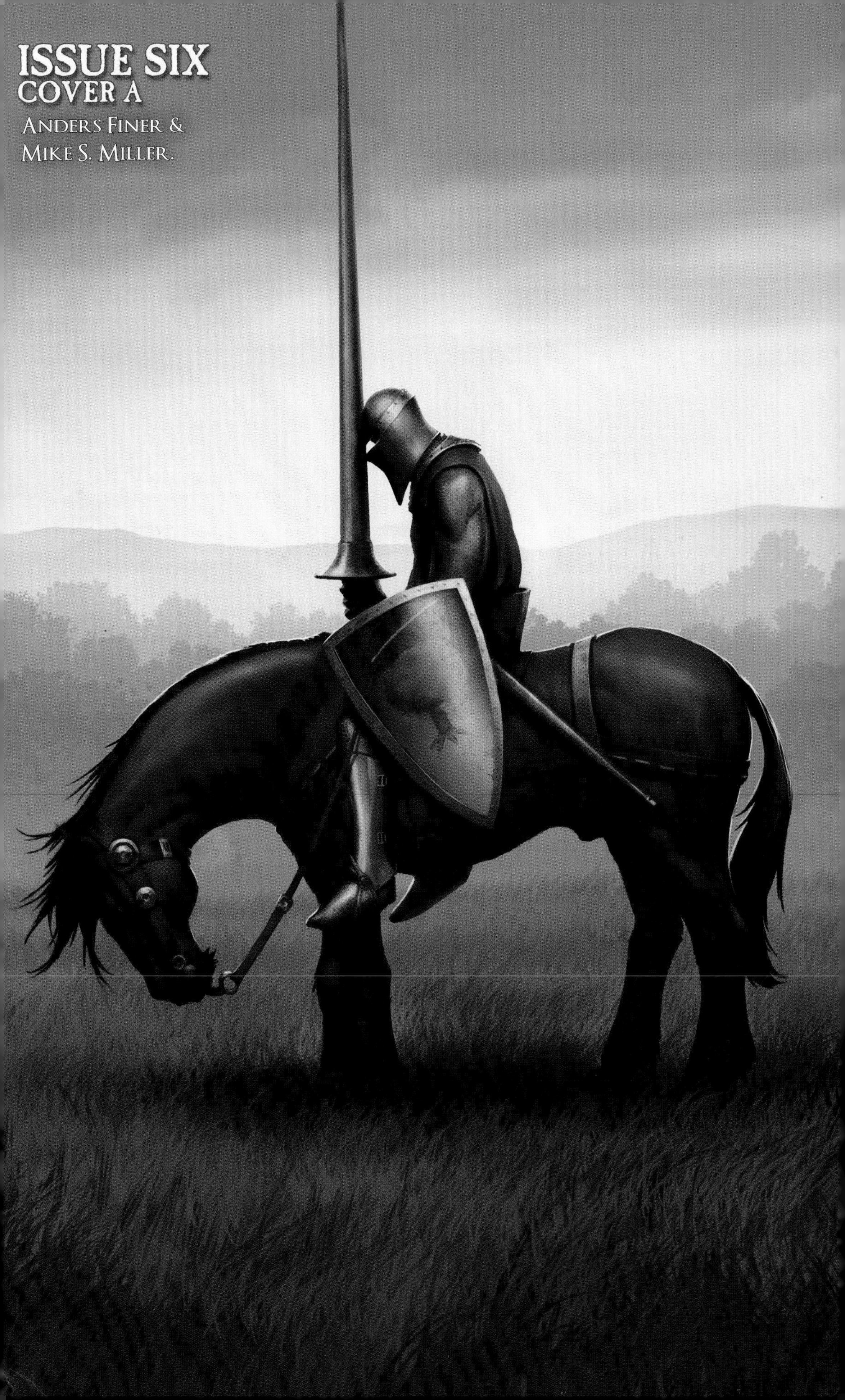
ISSUE SIX
COVER A
ANDERS FINER &
MIKE S. MILLER.

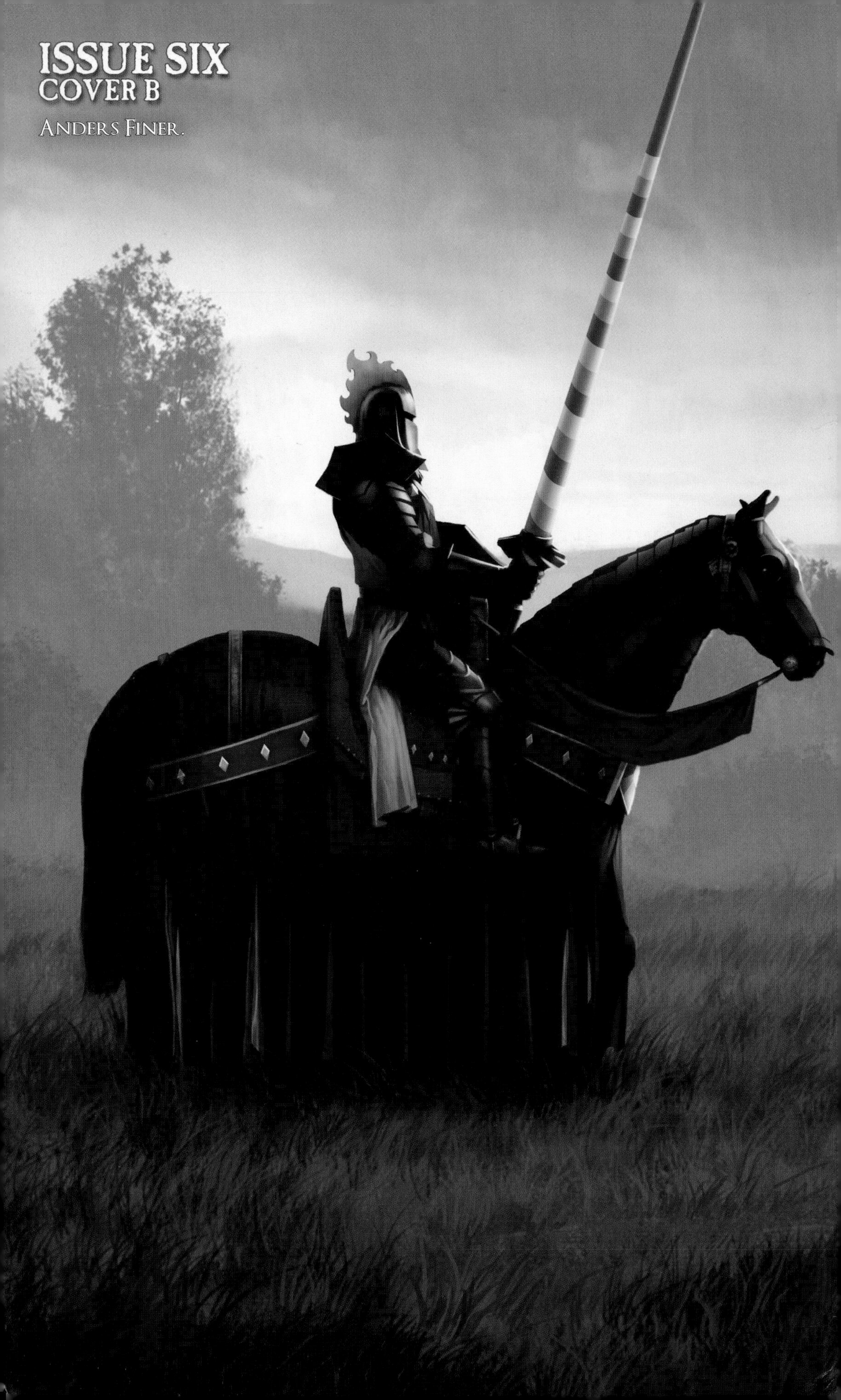

ISSUE SIX
COVER B

Anders Finer.

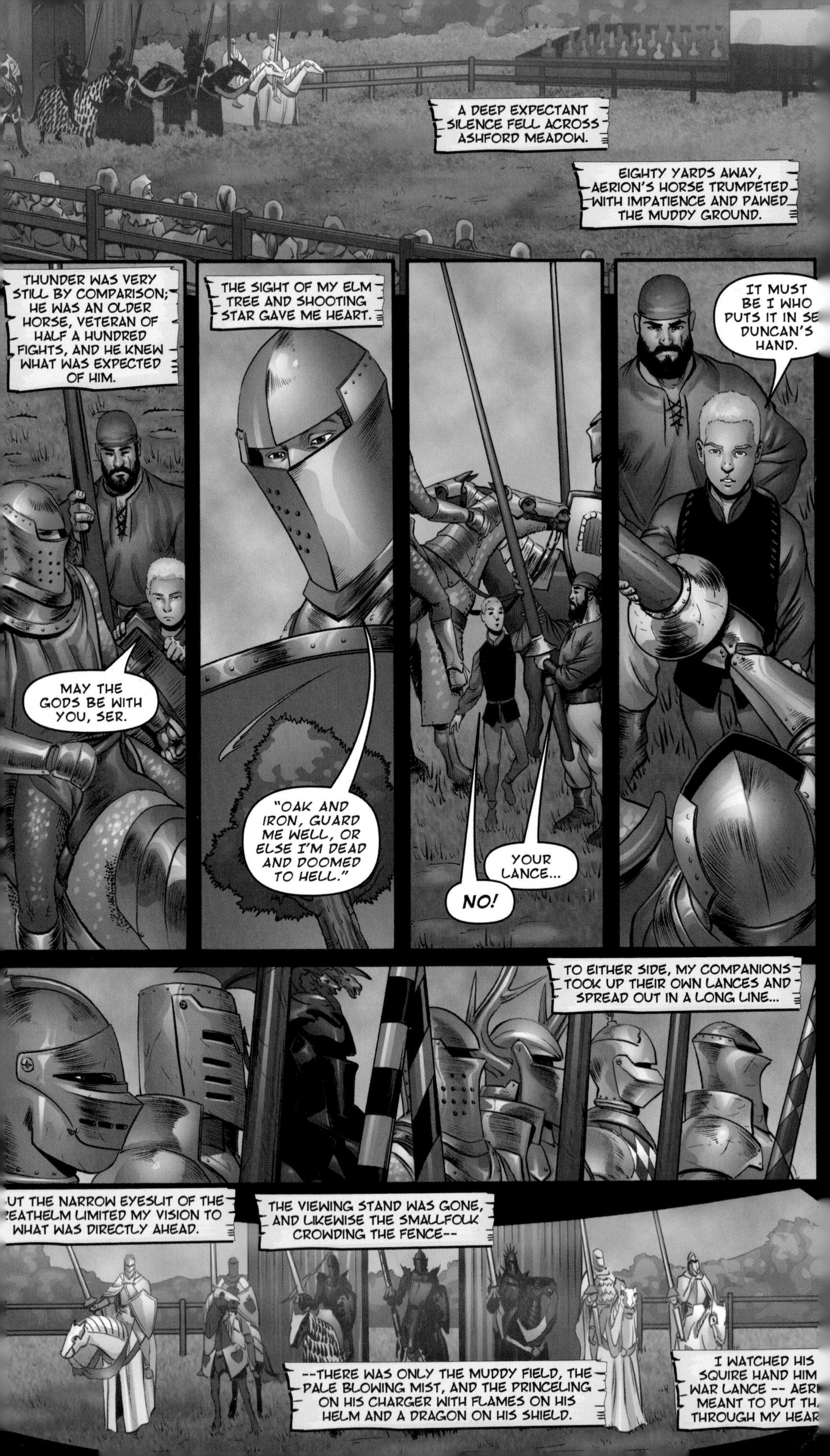
A DEEP EXPECTANT SILENCE FELL ACROSS ASHFORD MEADOW.
EIGHTY YARDS AWAY, AERION'S HORSE TRUMPETED WITH IMPATIENCE AND PAWED THE MUDDY GROUND.
THUNDER WAS VERY STILL BY COMPARISON; HE WAS AN OLDER HORSE, VETERAN OF HALF A HUNDRED FIGHTS, AND HE KNEW WHAT WAS EXPECTED OF HIM.
MAY THE GODS BE WITH YOU, SER.
THE SIGHT OF MY ELM TREE AND SHOOTING STAR GAVE ME HEART.
"OAK AND IRON, GUARD ME WELL, OR ELSE I'M DEAD AND DOOMED TO HELL."
YOUR LANCE...
NO!
IT MUST BE I WHO PUTS IT IN SE DUNCAN'S HAND.
TO EITHER SIDE, MY COMPANIONS TOOK UP THEIR OWN LANCES AND SPREAD OUT IN A LONG LINE...
UT THE NARROW EYESLIT OF THE REATHELM LIMITED MY VISION TO WHAT WAS DIRECTLY AHEAD.
THE VIEWING STAND WAS GONE, AND LIKEWISE THE SMALLFOLK CROWDING THE FENCE--
--THERE WAS ONLY THE MUDDY FIELD, THE PALE BLOWING MIST, AND THE PRINCELING ON HIS CHARGER WITH FLAMES ON HIS HELM AND A DRAGON ON HIS SHIELD.
I WATCHED HIS SQUIRE HAND HIM WAR LANCE -- AER MEANT TO PUT TH THROUGH MY HEAR

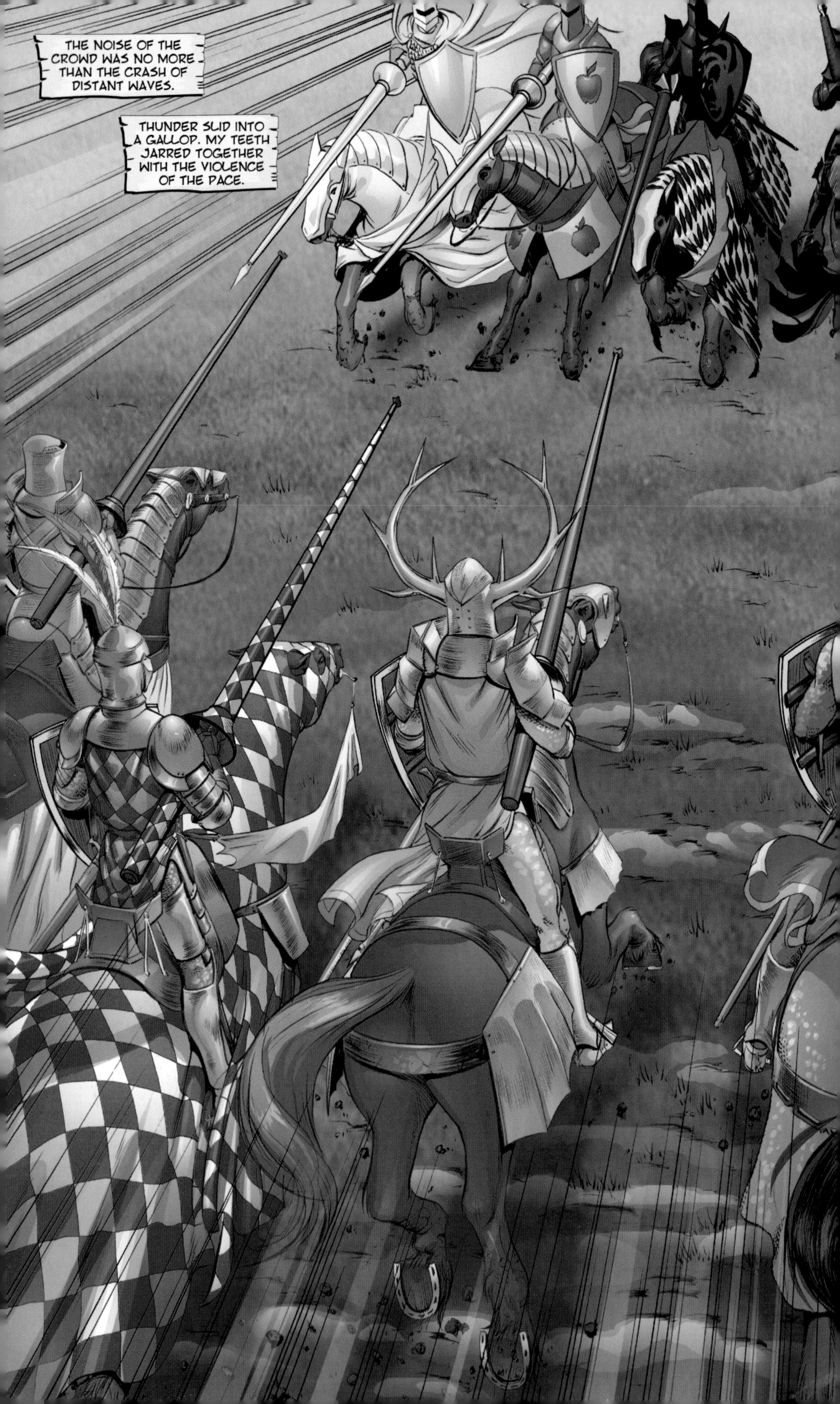
THE NOISE OF THE CROWD WAS NO MORE THAN THE CRASH OF DISTANT WAVES.
THUNDER SLID INTO A GALLOP. MY TEETH JARRED TOGETHER WITH THE VIOLENCE OF THE PACE.

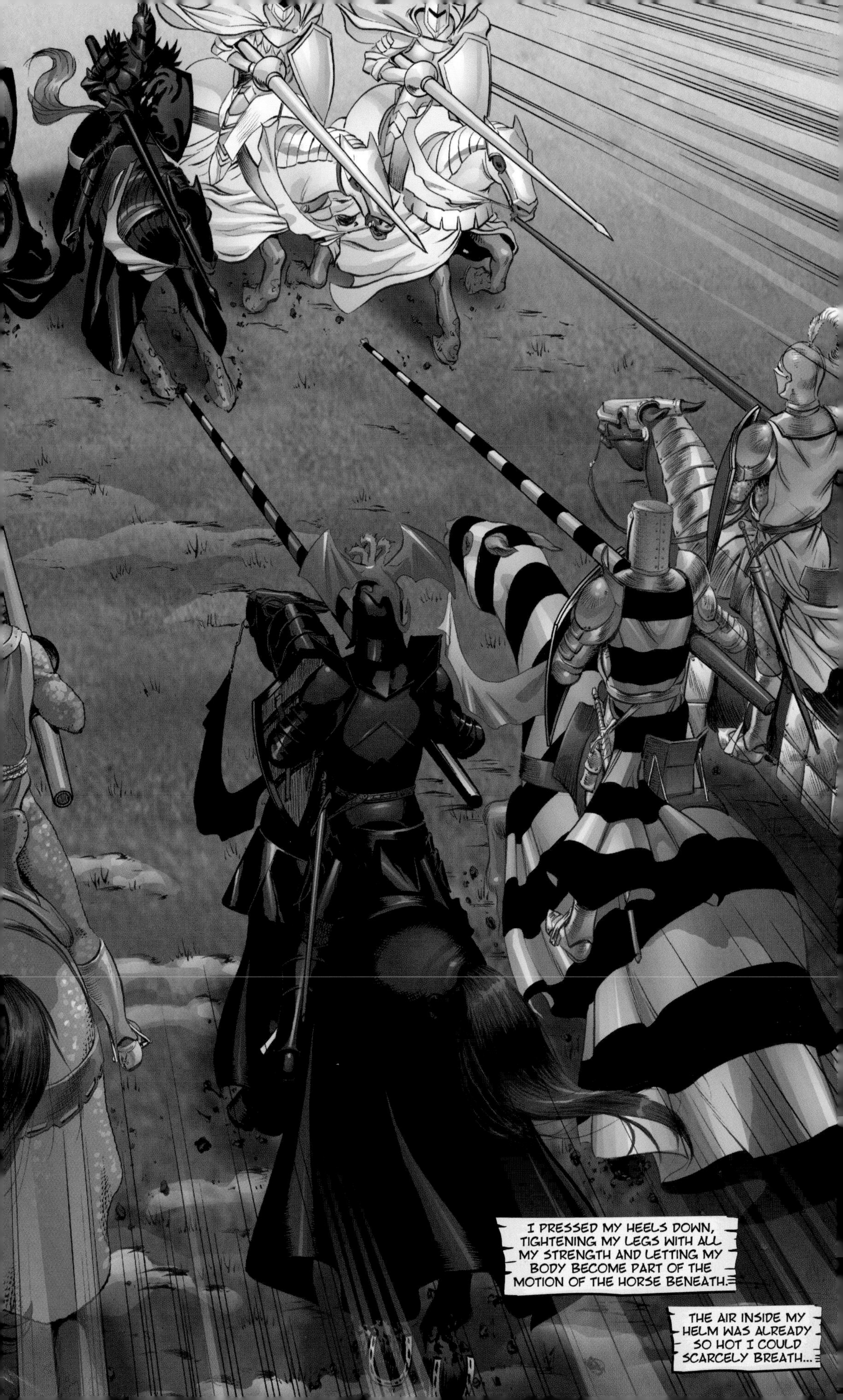
I PRESSED MY HEELS DOWN, TIGHTENING MY LEGS WITH ALL MY STRENGTH AND LETTING MY BODY BECOME PART OF THE MOTION OF THE HORSE BENEATH.
THE AIR INSIDE MY HELM WAS ALREADY SO HOT I COULD SCARCELY BREATH...

AAAARRGH!

THE WORLD SWAM AND I ALMOST FELL.

DIMLY, THROUGH THE PAIN, I COULD HEAR VOICES CALLING MY NAME.

MY BEAUTIFUL SHIELD WAS USELESS NOW.

I TOSSED IT ASIDE, ELM TREE, SHOOTING STAR, BROKEN LANCE AND ALL.

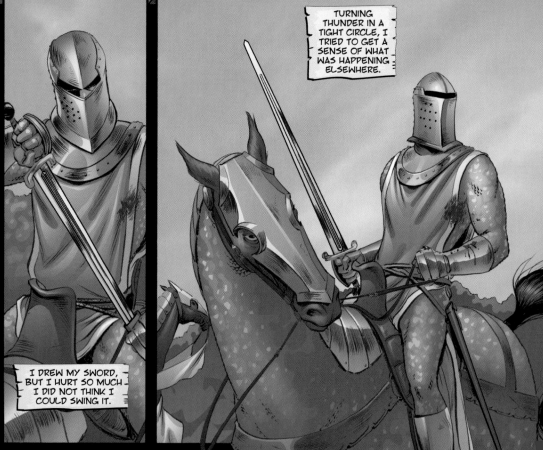

TURNING THUNDER IN A TIGHT CIRCLE, I TRIED TO GET A SENSE OF WHAT WAS HAPPENING ELSEWHERE.

I DREW MY SWORD, BUT I HURT SO MUCH I DID NOT THINK I COULD SWING IT.

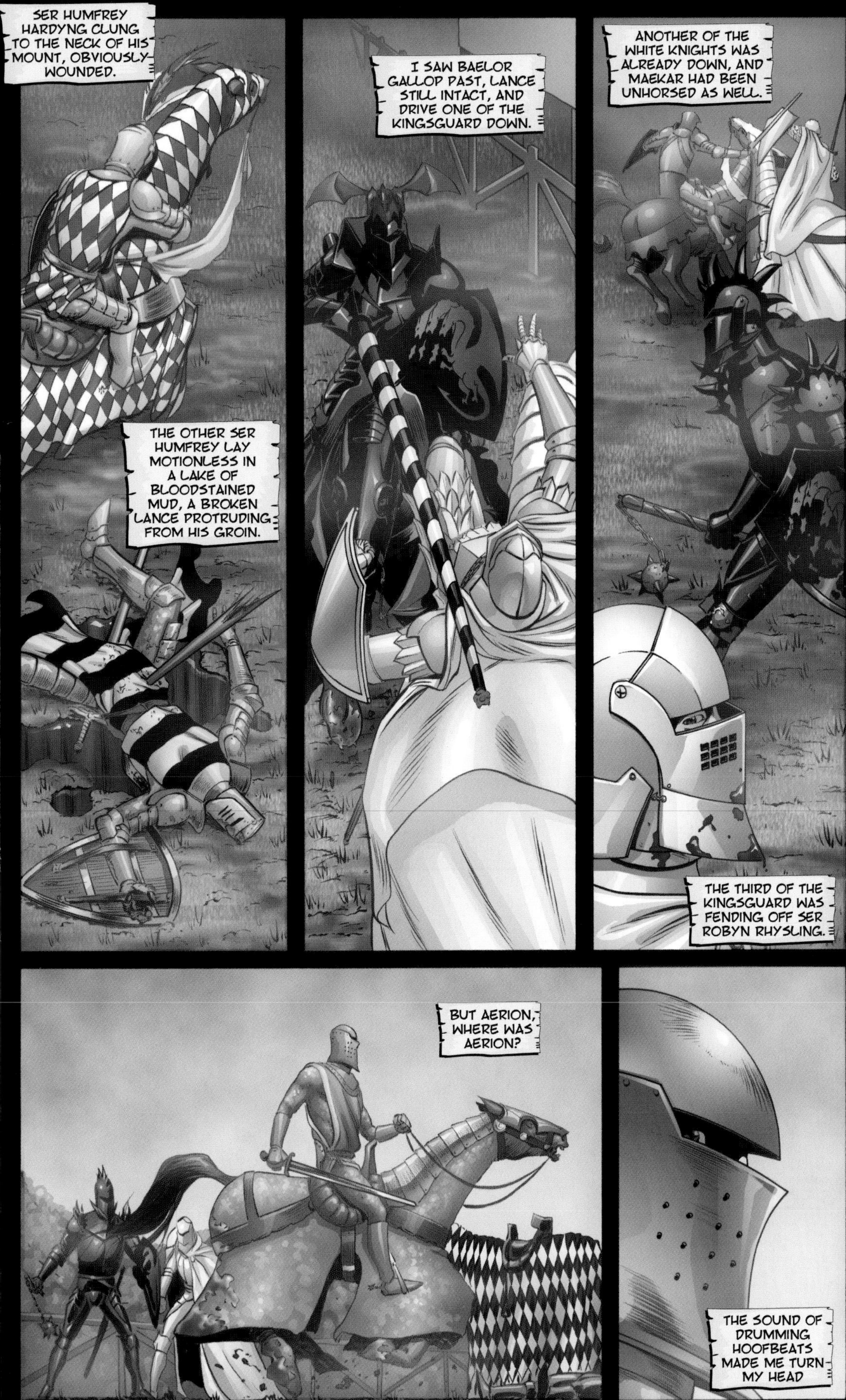
SER HUMFREY HARDYNG CLUNG TO THE NECK OF HIS MOUNT, OBVIOUSLY WOUNDED.
THE OTHER SER HUMFREY LAY MOTIONLESS IN A LAKE OF BLOODSTAINED MUD, A BROKEN LANCE PROTRUDING FROM HIS GROIN.
I SAW BAELOR GALLOP PAST, LANCE STILL INTACT, AND DRIVE ONE OF THE KINGSGUARD DOWN.
ANOTHER OF THE WHITE KNIGHTS WAS ALREADY DOWN, AND MAEKAR HAD BEEN UNHORSED AS WELL.
THE THIRD OF THE KINGSGUARD WAS FENDING OFF SER ROBYN RHYSLING.
BUT AERION, WHERE WAS AERION?
THE SOUND OF DRUMMING HOOFBEATS MADE ME TURN MY HEAD

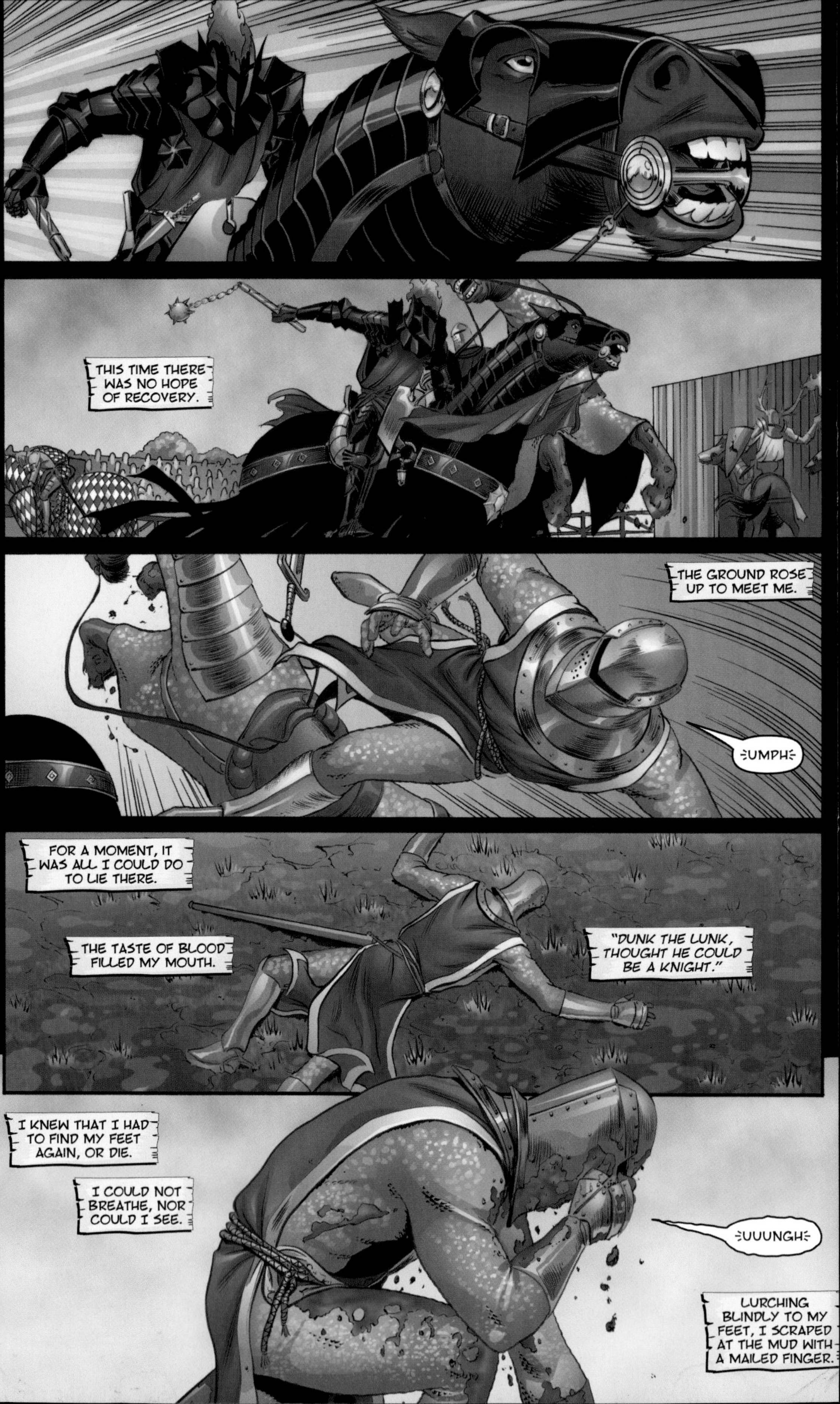
THIS TIME THERE WAS NO HOPE OF RECOVERY.
THE GROUND ROSE UP TO MEET ME.
UMPH
FOR A MOMENT, IT WAS ALL I COULD DO TO LIE THERE.
THE TASTE OF BLOOD FILLED MY MOUTH.
"DUNK THE LUNK, THOUGHT HE COULD BE A KNIGHT."
I KNEW THAT I HAD TO FIND MY FEET AGAIN, OR DIE.
I COULD NOT BREATHE, NOR COULD I SEE.
UUUNGH
LURCHING BLINDLY TO MY FEET, I SCRAPED AT THE MUD WITH A MAILED FINGER.

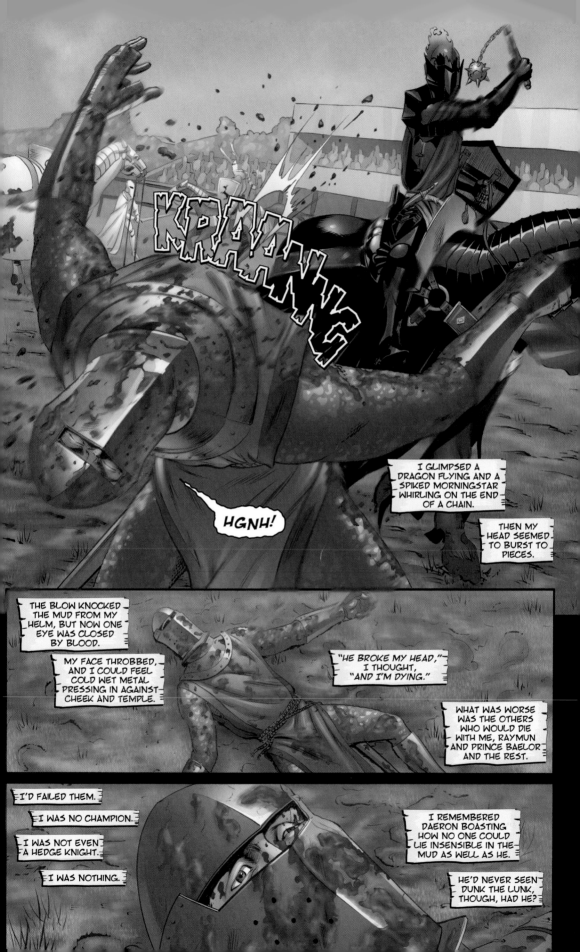

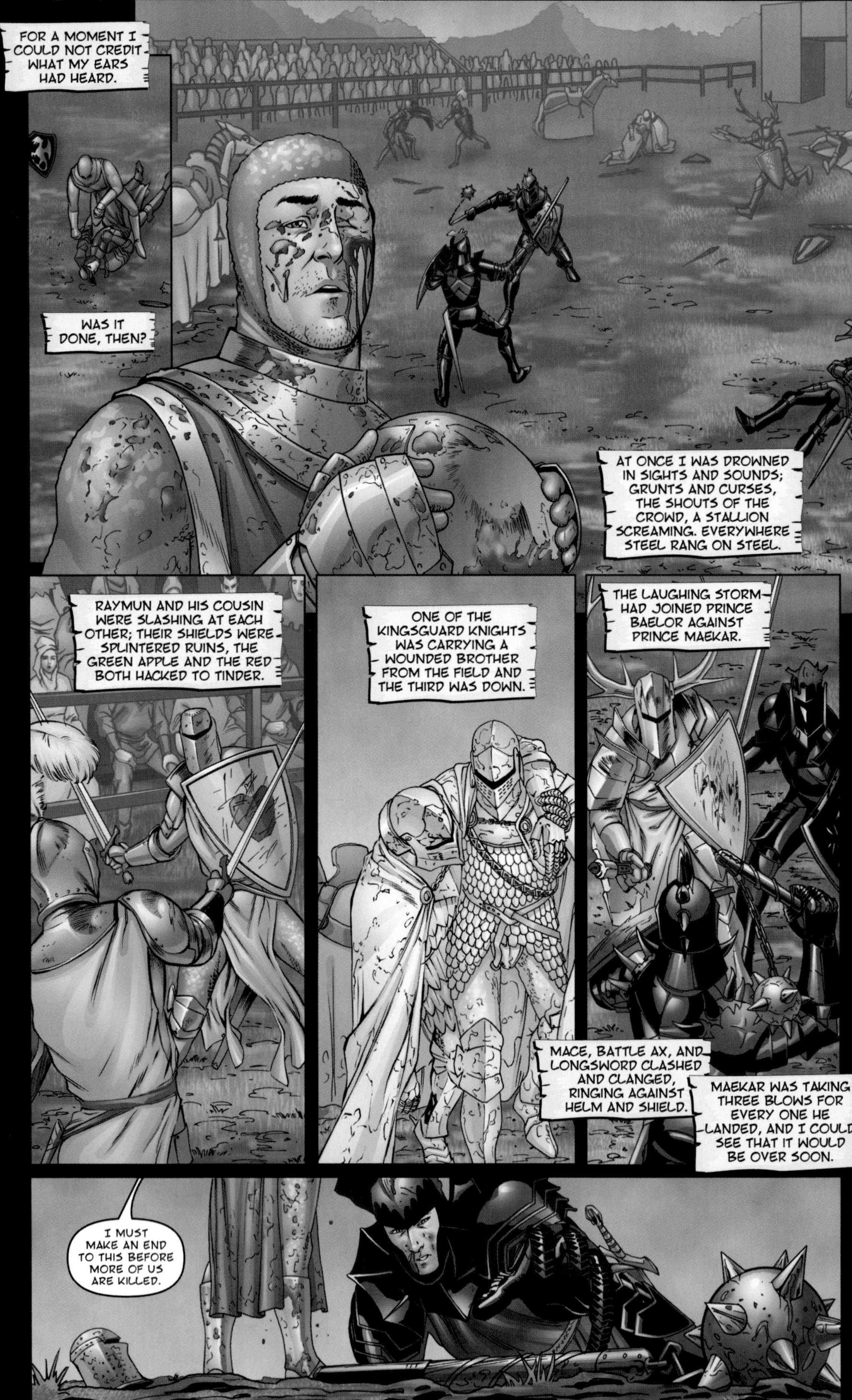
FOR A MOMENT I COULD NOT CREDIT WHAT MY EARS HAD HEARD.
WAS IT DONE, THEN?
AT ONCE I WAS DROWNED IN SIGHTS AND SOUNDS; GRUNTS AND CURSES, THE SHOUTS OF THE CROWD, A STALLION SCREAMING. EVERYWHERE STEEL RANG ON STEEL.
RAYMUN AND HIS COUSIN WERE SLASHING AT EACH OTHER; THEIR SHIELDS WERE SPLINTERED RUINS, THE GREEN APPLE AND THE RED BOTH HACKED TO TINDER.
ONE OF THE KINGSGUARD KNIGHTS WAS CARRYING A WOUNDED BROTHER FROM THE FIELD AND THE THIRD WAS DOWN.
THE LAUGHING STORM HAD JOINED PRINCE BAELOR AGAINST PRINCE MAEKAR.
MACE, BATTLE AX, AND LONGSWORD CLASHED AND CLANGED, RINGING AGAINST HELM AND SHIELD.
MAEKAR WAS TAKING THREE BLOWS FOR EVERY ONE HE LANDED, AND I COULD SEE THAT IT WOULD BE OVER SOON.
I MUST MAKE AN END TO THIS BEFORE MORE OF US ARE KILLED.

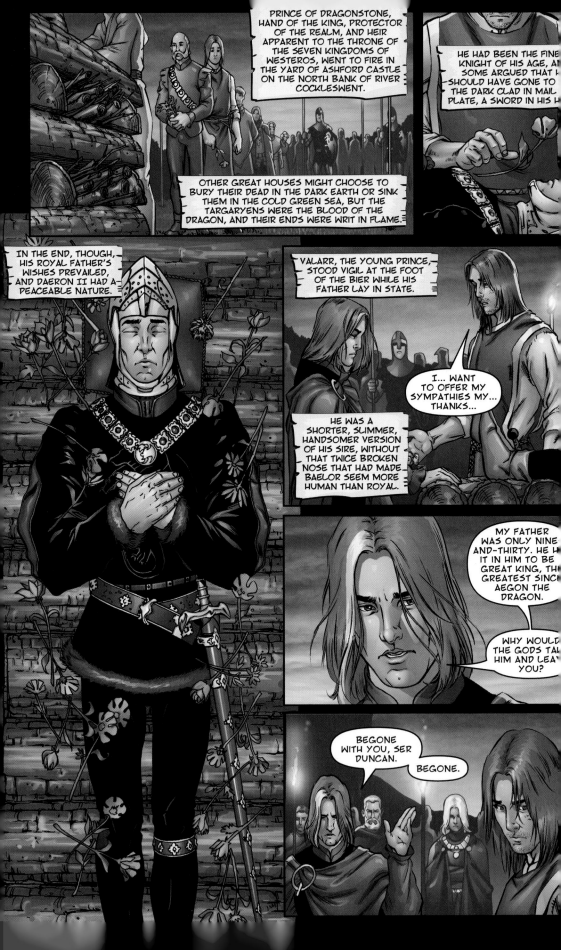

PRINCE OF DRAGONSTONE, HAND OF THE KING, PROTECTOR OF THE REALM, AND HEIR APPARENT TO THE THRONE OF THE SEVEN KINGDOMS OF WESTEROS, WENT TO FIRE IN THE YARD OF ASHFORD CASTLE ON THE NORTH BANK OF RIVER COCKLESWENT.

HE HAD BEEN THE FINE[ST] KNIGHT OF HIS AGE, AN[D] SOME ARGUED THAT H[E] SHOULD HAVE GONE TO THE DARK CLAD IN MAIL [AND] PLATE, A SWORD IN HIS H[AND.]

OTHER GREAT HOUSES MIGHT CHOOSE TO BURY THEIR DEAD IN THE DARK EARTH OR SINK THEM IN THE COLD GREEN SEA, BUT THE TARGARYENS WERE THE BLOOD OF THE DRAGON, AND THEIR ENDS WERE WRIT IN FLAME.

IN THE END, THOUGH, HIS ROYAL FATHER'S WISHES PREVAILED, AND DAERON II HAD A PEACEABLE NATURE.

VALARR, THE YOUNG PRINCE, STOOD VIGIL AT THE FOOT OF THE BIER WHILE HIS FATHER LAY IN STATE.

I... WANT TO OFFER MY SYMPATHIES MY... THANKS...

HE WAS A SHORTER, SLIMMER, HANDSOMER VERSION OF HIS SIRE, WITHOUT THAT TWICE BROKEN NOSE THAT HAD MADE BAELOR SEEM MORE HUMAN THAN ROYAL.

MY FATHER WAS ONLY NINE AND-THIRTY. HE H[AD] IT IN HIM TO BE [A] GREAT KING, TH[E] GREATEST SINC[E] AEGON THE DRAGON.

WHY WOULD[N'T] THE GODS TA[KE] HIM AND LEA[VE] YOU?

BEGONE WITH YOU, SER DUNCAN.

BEGONE.

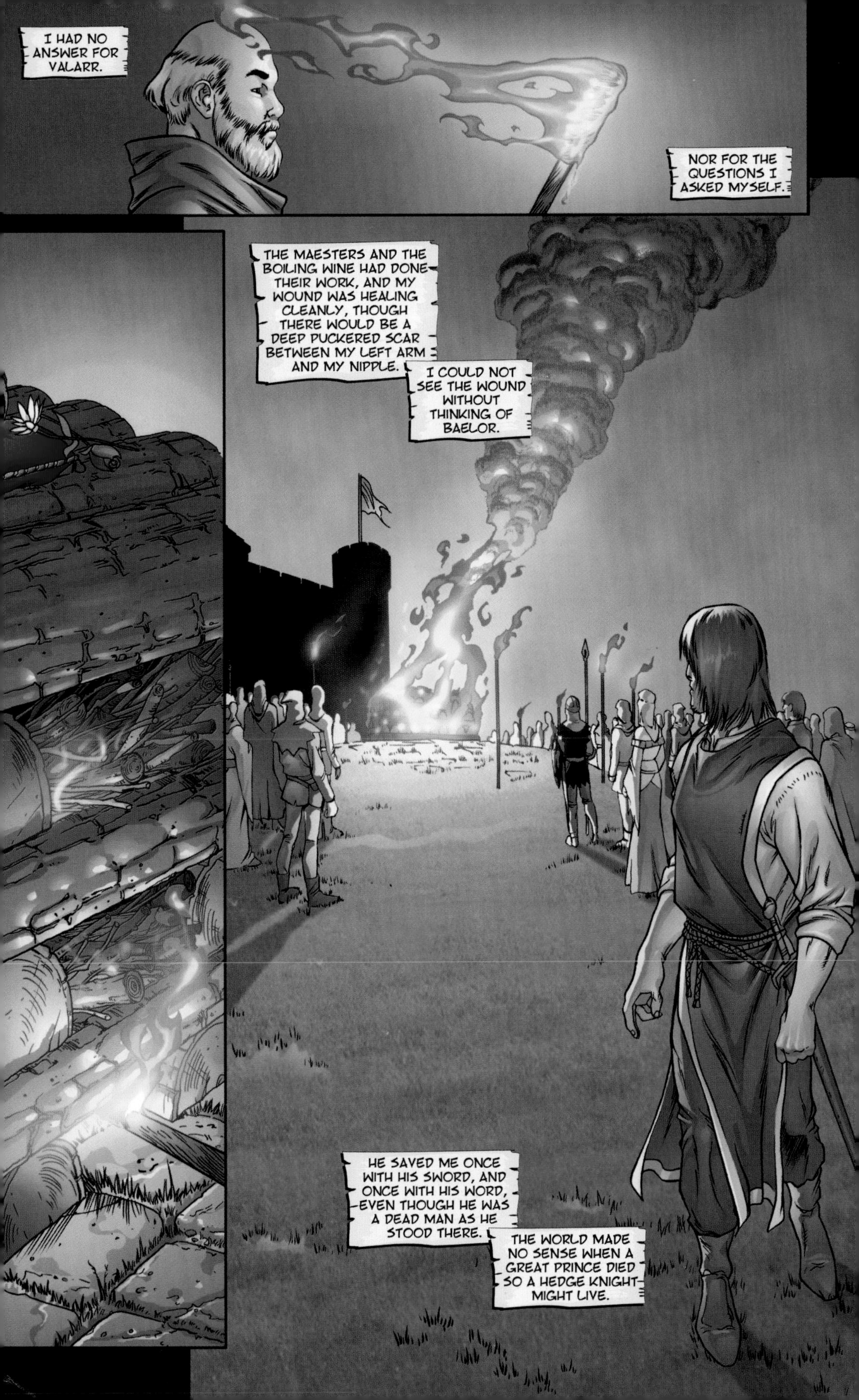
I HAD NO ANSWER FOR VALARR.
NOR FOR THE QUESTIONS I ASKED MYSELF.
THE MAESTERS AND THE BOILING WINE HAD DONE THEIR WORK, AND MY WOUND WAS HEALING CLEANLY, THOUGH THERE WOULD BE A DEEP PUCKERED SCAR BETWEEN MY LEFT ARM AND MY NIPPLE.
I COULD NOT SEE THE WOUND WITHOUT THINKING OF BAELOR.
HE SAVED ME ONCE WITH HIS SWORD, AND ONCE WITH HIS WORD, EVEN THOUGH HE WAS A DEAD MAN AS HE STOOD THERE.
THE WORLD MADE NO SENSE WHEN A GREAT PRINCE DIED SO A HEDGE KNIGHT MIGHT LIVE.

PREVIEW OF FORTHCOMING

the HEDGE KNIGHT
The SWORN SWORD

BATTLE ON REDGRASS FIELD

& VARIANT COVERS AND SKETCHES BY
MIKE S. MILLER FROM THE HEDGE KNIGHT

JETCITY COMICS

the Hedge Knight

The Sworn Sword

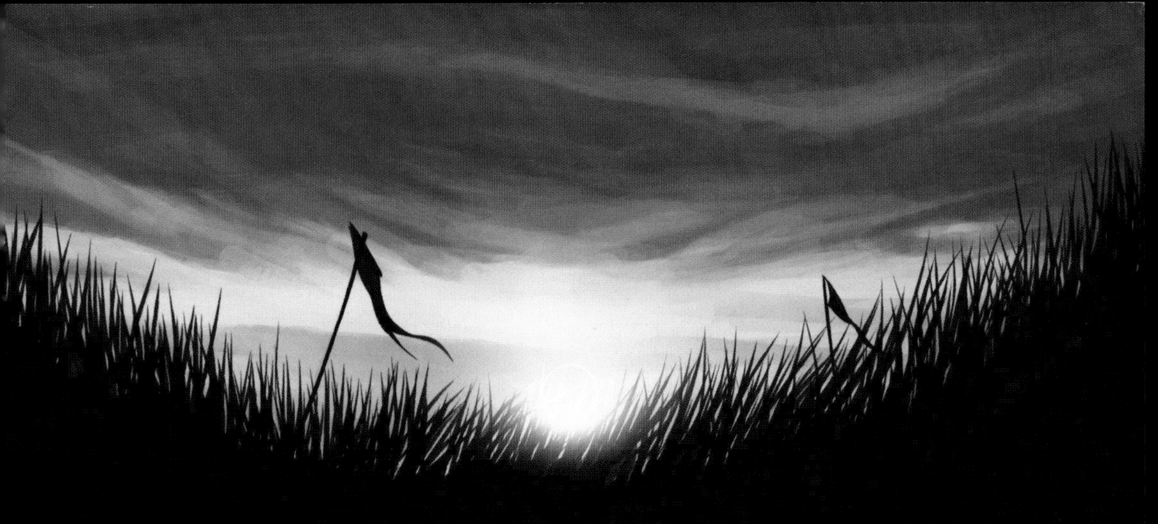

GEORGE RR MARTIN'S BATTLE ON REDGRASS FIELD

(FROM THE SWORN SWORD)

A TALE OF THE SEVEN KINGDOMS
by GEORGE R. R. MARTIN

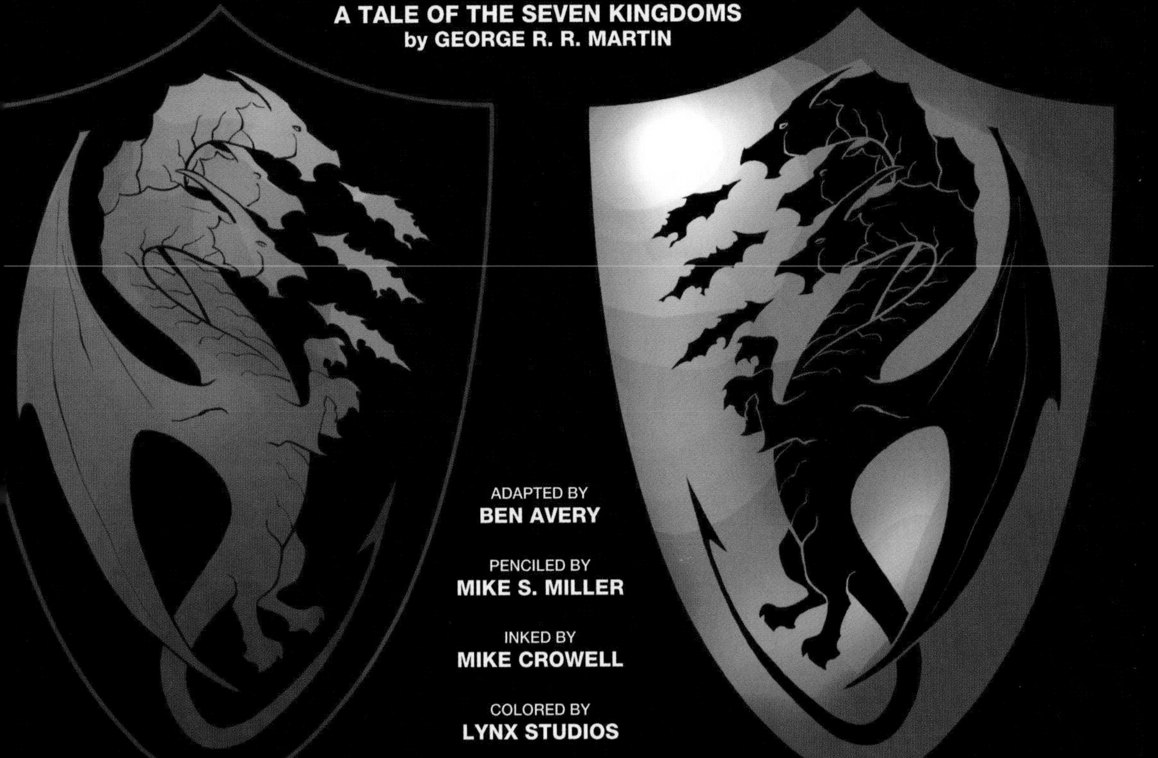

ADAPTED BY
BEN AVERY

PENCILED BY
MIKE S. MILLER

INKED BY
MIKE CROWELL

COLORED BY
LYNX STUDIOS

LETTERS BY
BILL TORTOLINI

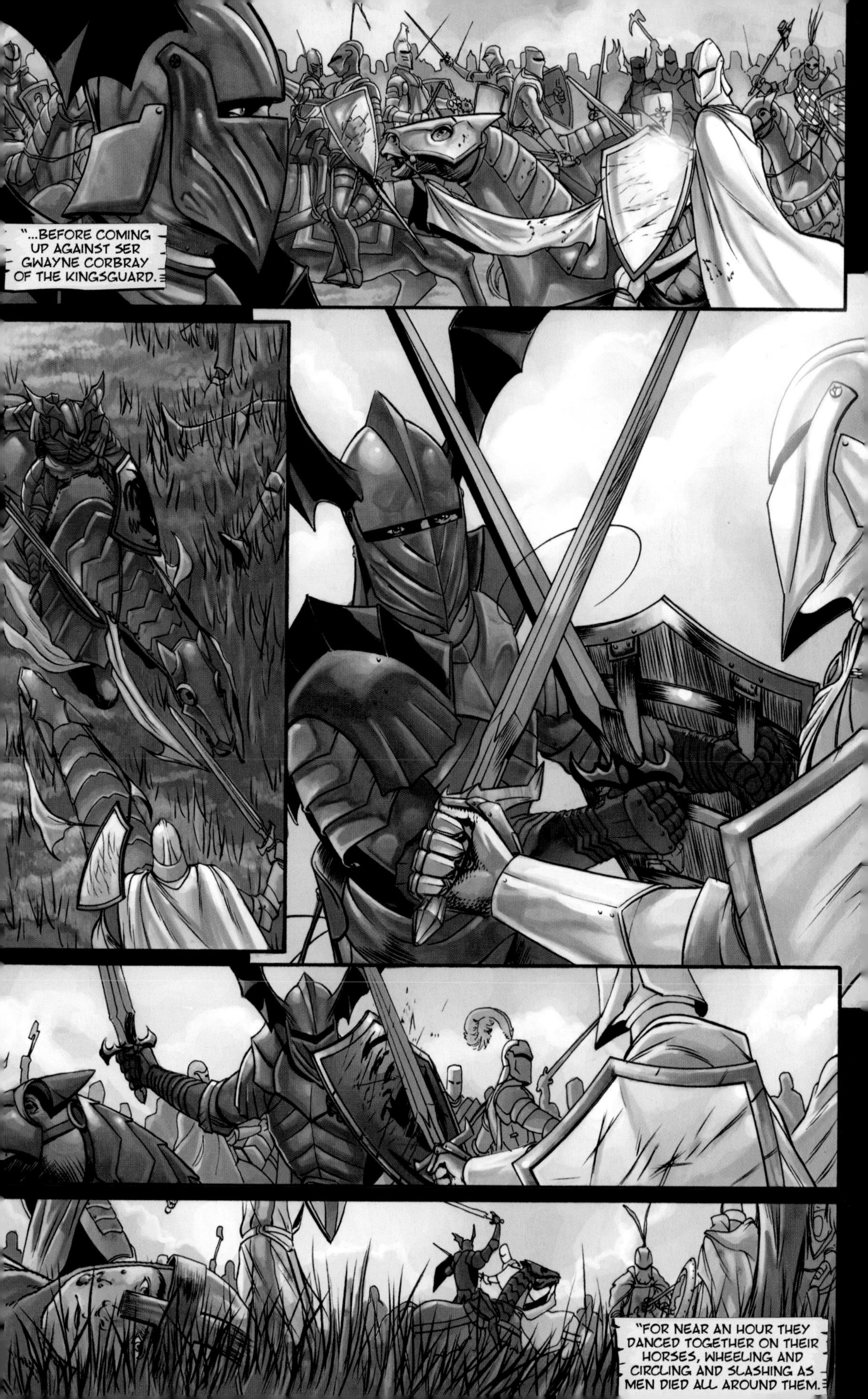
"...BEFORE COMING UP AGAINST SER GWAYNE CORBRAY OF THE KINGSGUARD.
"FOR NEAR AN HOUR THEY DANCED TOGETHER ON THEIR HORSES, WHEELING AND CIRCLING AND SLASHING AS MEN DIED ALL AROUND THEM.

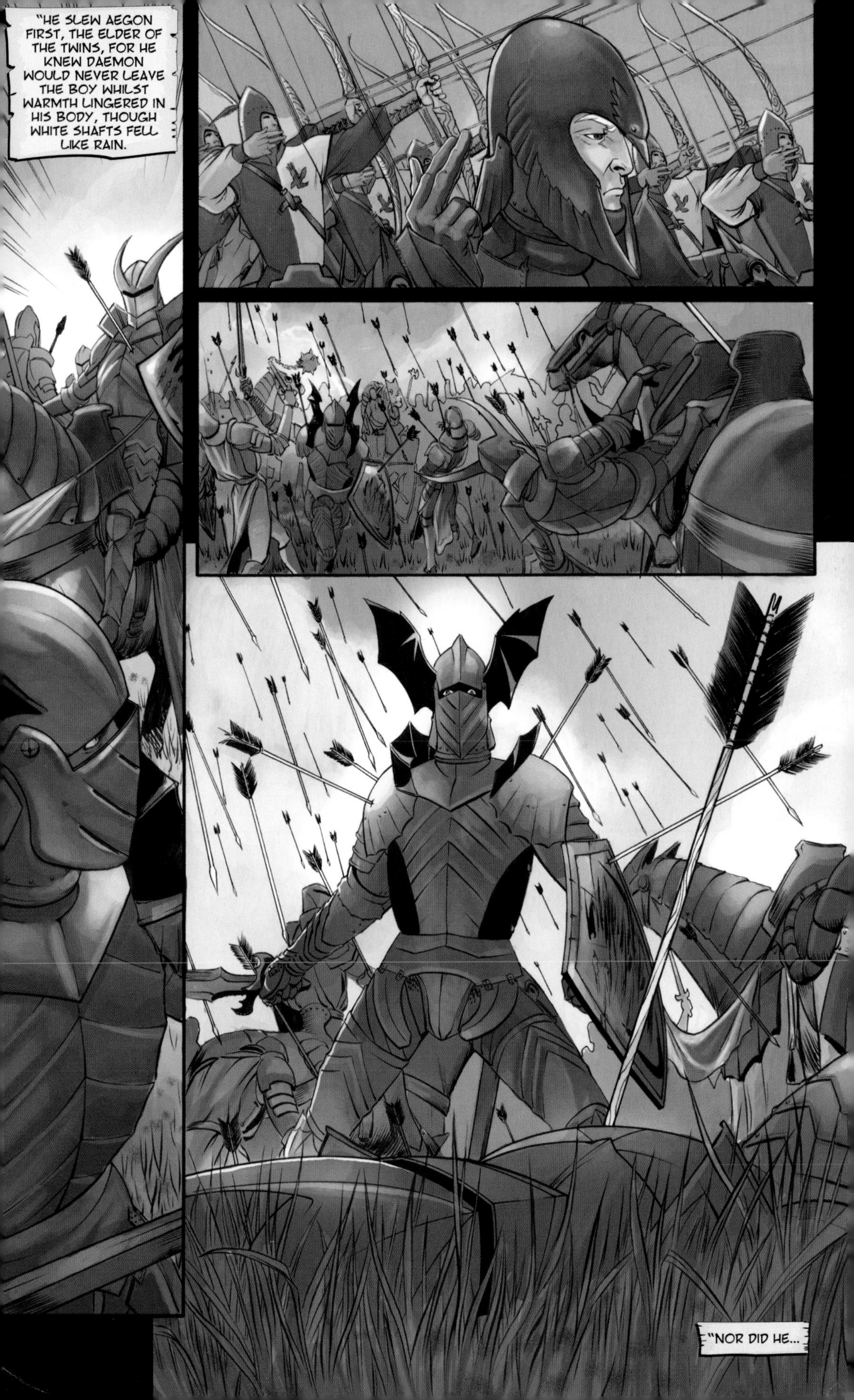
"HE SLEW AEGON FIRST, THE ELDER OF THE TWINS, FOR HE KNEW DAEMON WOULD NEVER LEAVE THE BOY WHILST WARMTH LINGERED IN HIS BODY, THOUGH WHITE SHAFTS FELL LIKE RAIN.
"NOR DID HE...

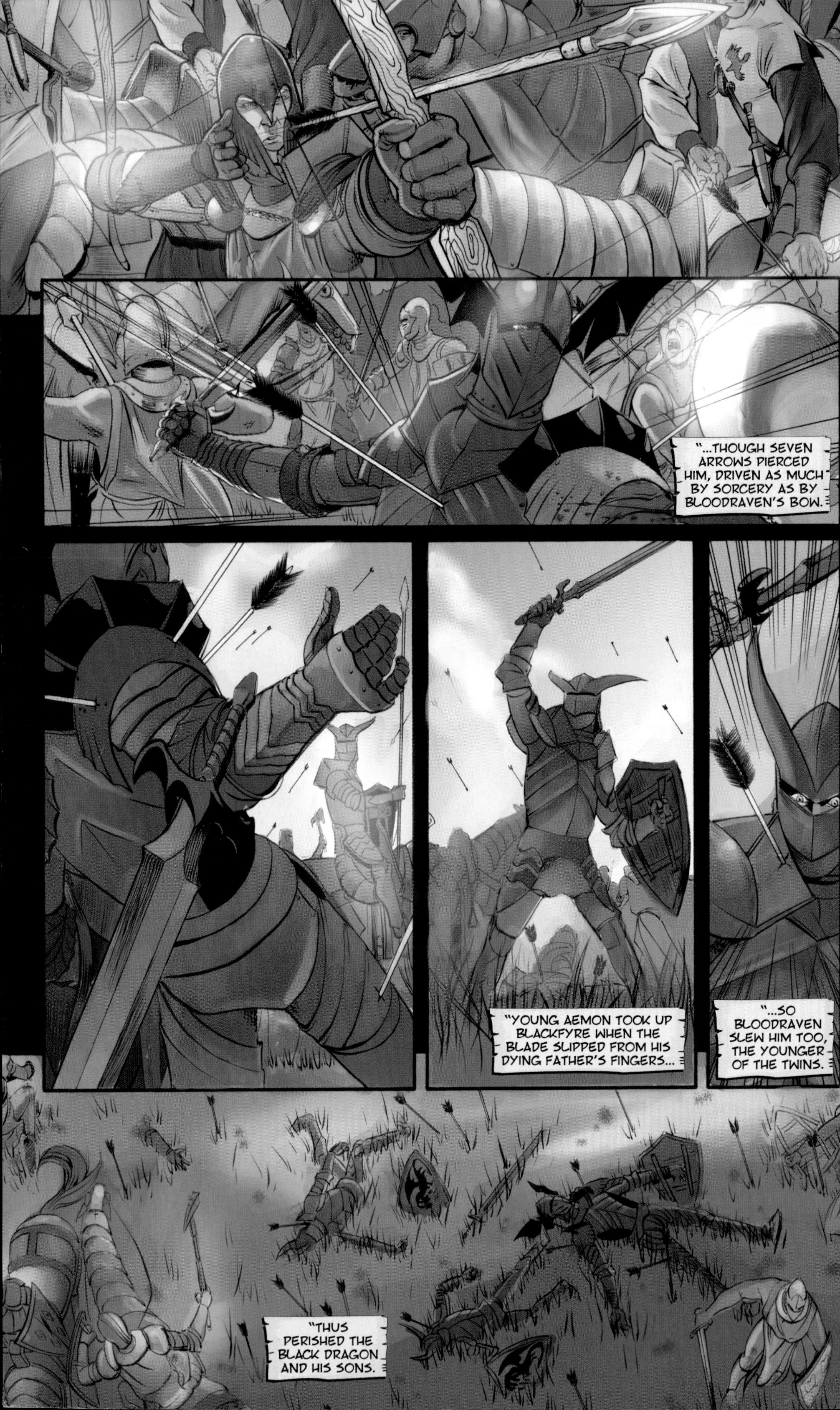
"...THOUGH SEVEN ARROWS PIERCED HIM, DRIVEN AS MUCH BY SORCERY AS BY BLOODRAVEN'S BOW.
"YOUNG AEMON TOOK UP BLACKFYRE WHEN THE BLADE SLIPPED FROM HIS DYING FATHER'S FINGERS...
"...SO BLOODRAVEN SLEW HIM TOO, THE YOUNGER OF THE TWINS.
"THUS PERISHED THE BLACK DRAGON AND HIS SONS.

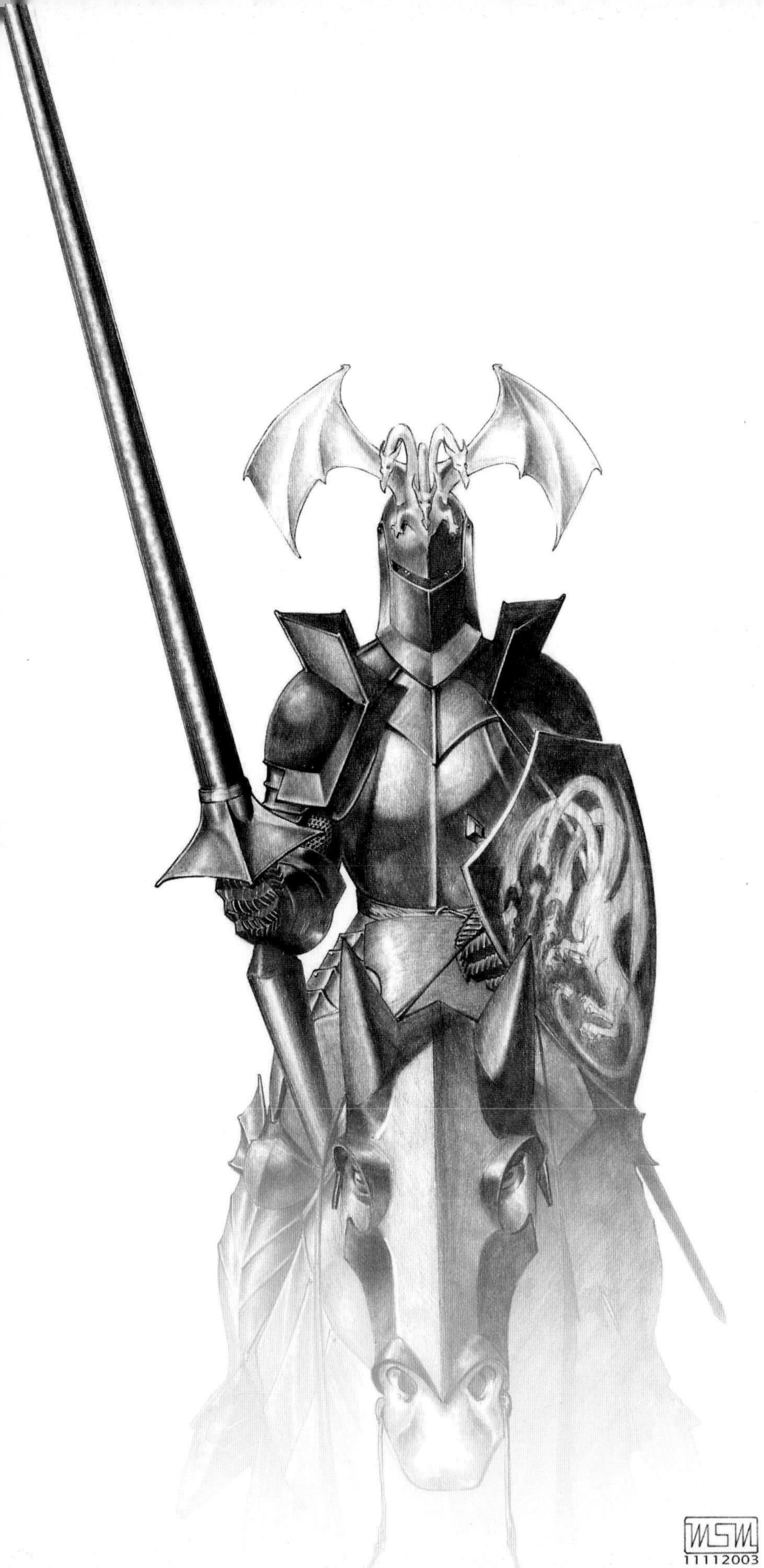
11112003

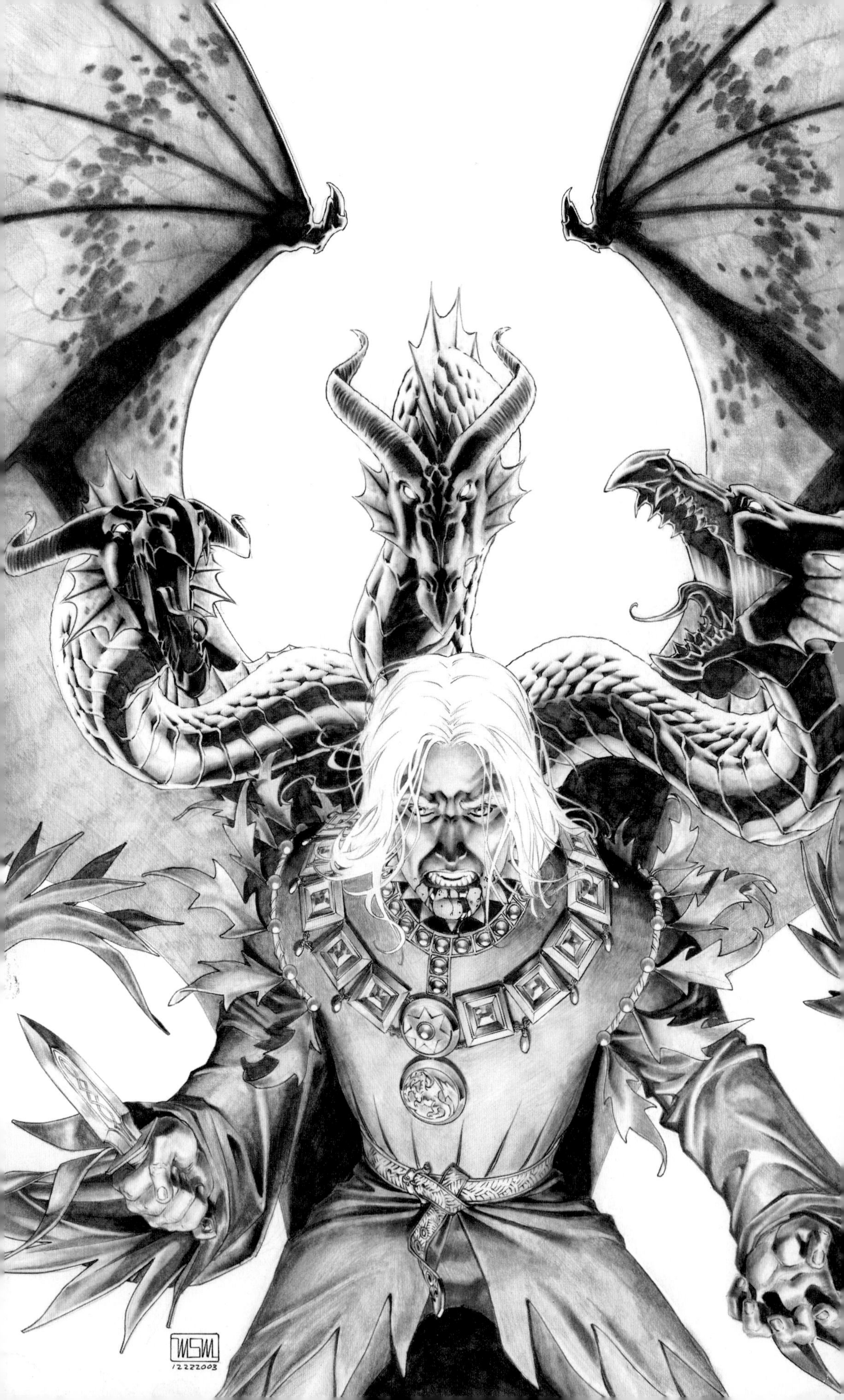
WSM
12222003

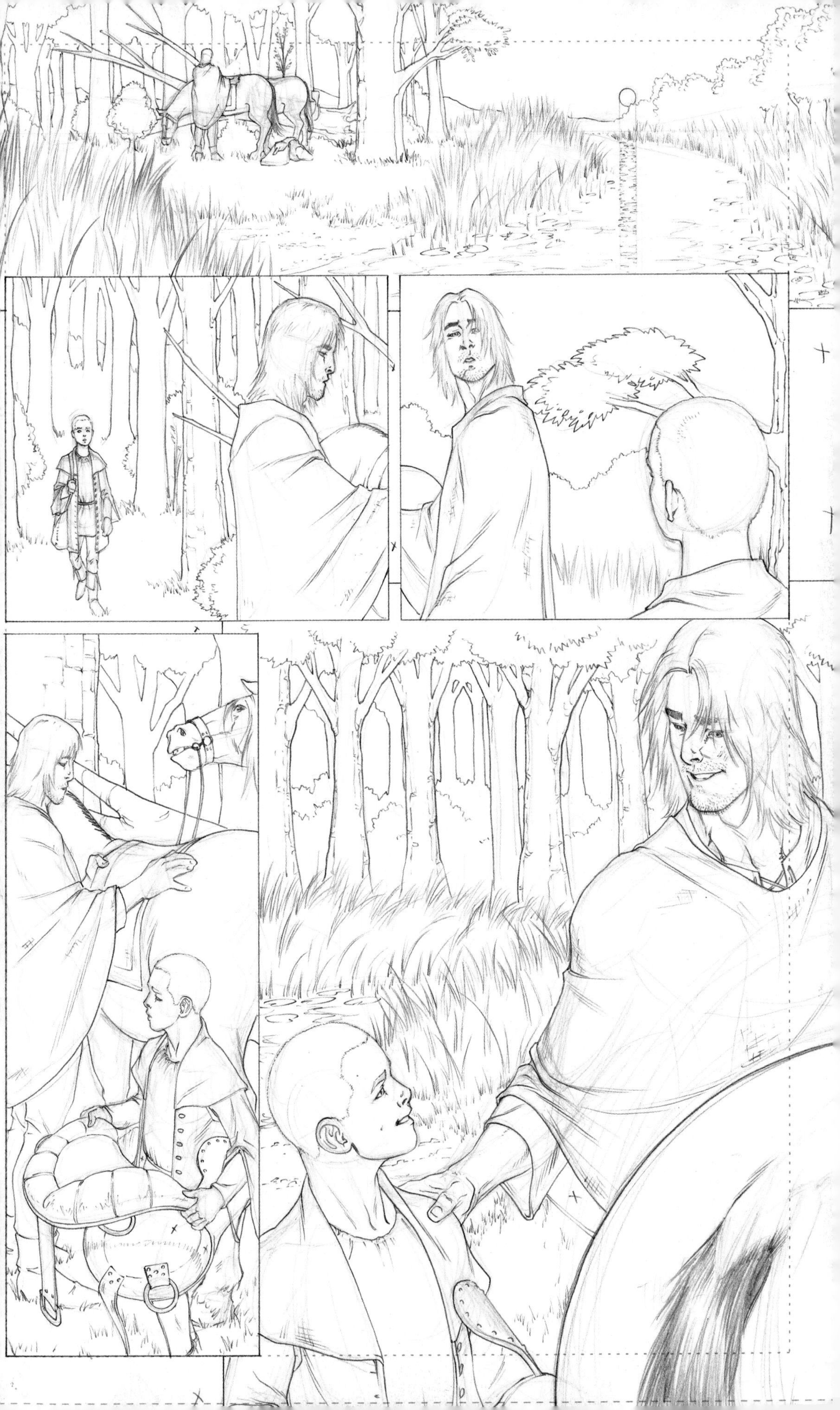

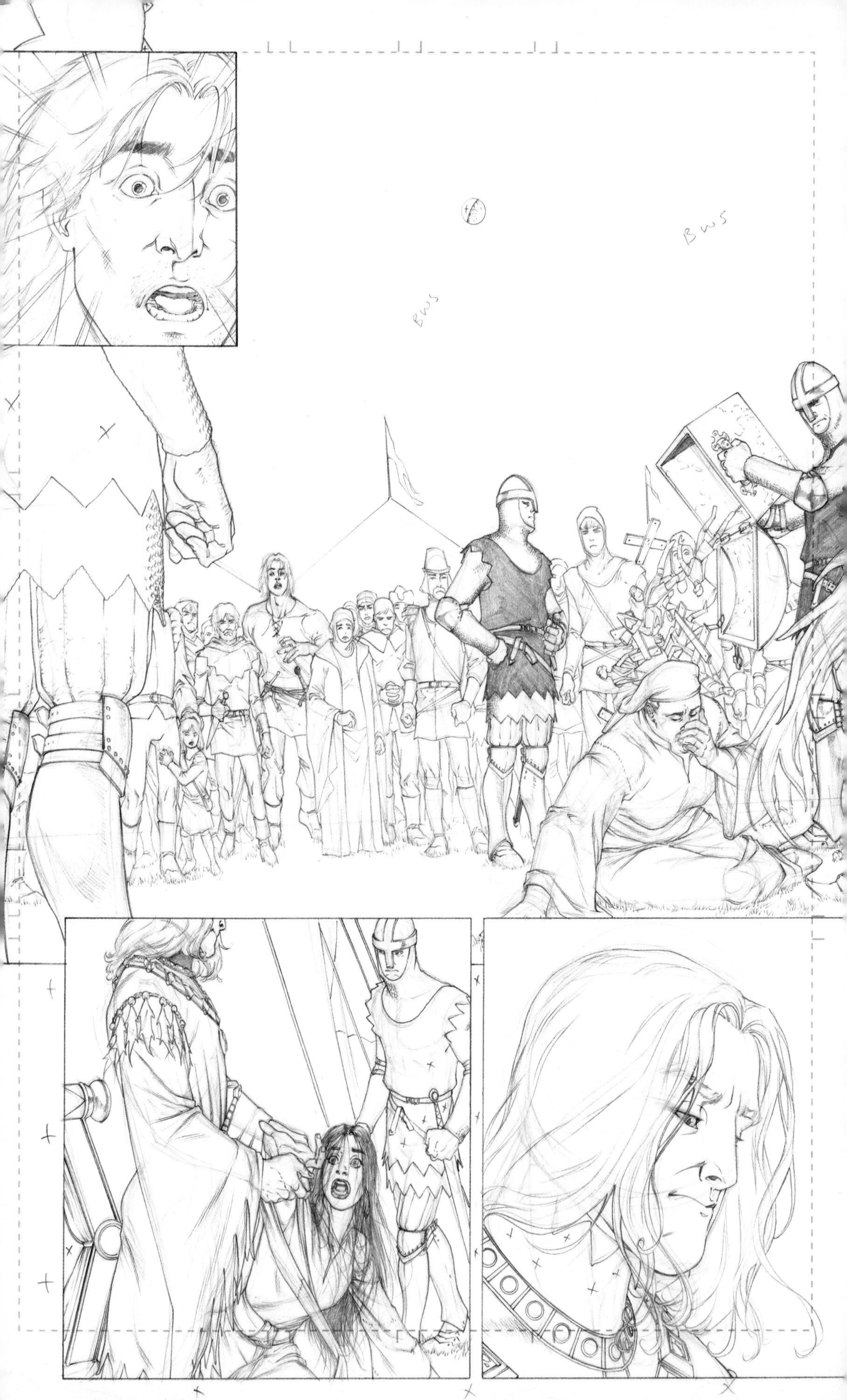
BWS
BWS

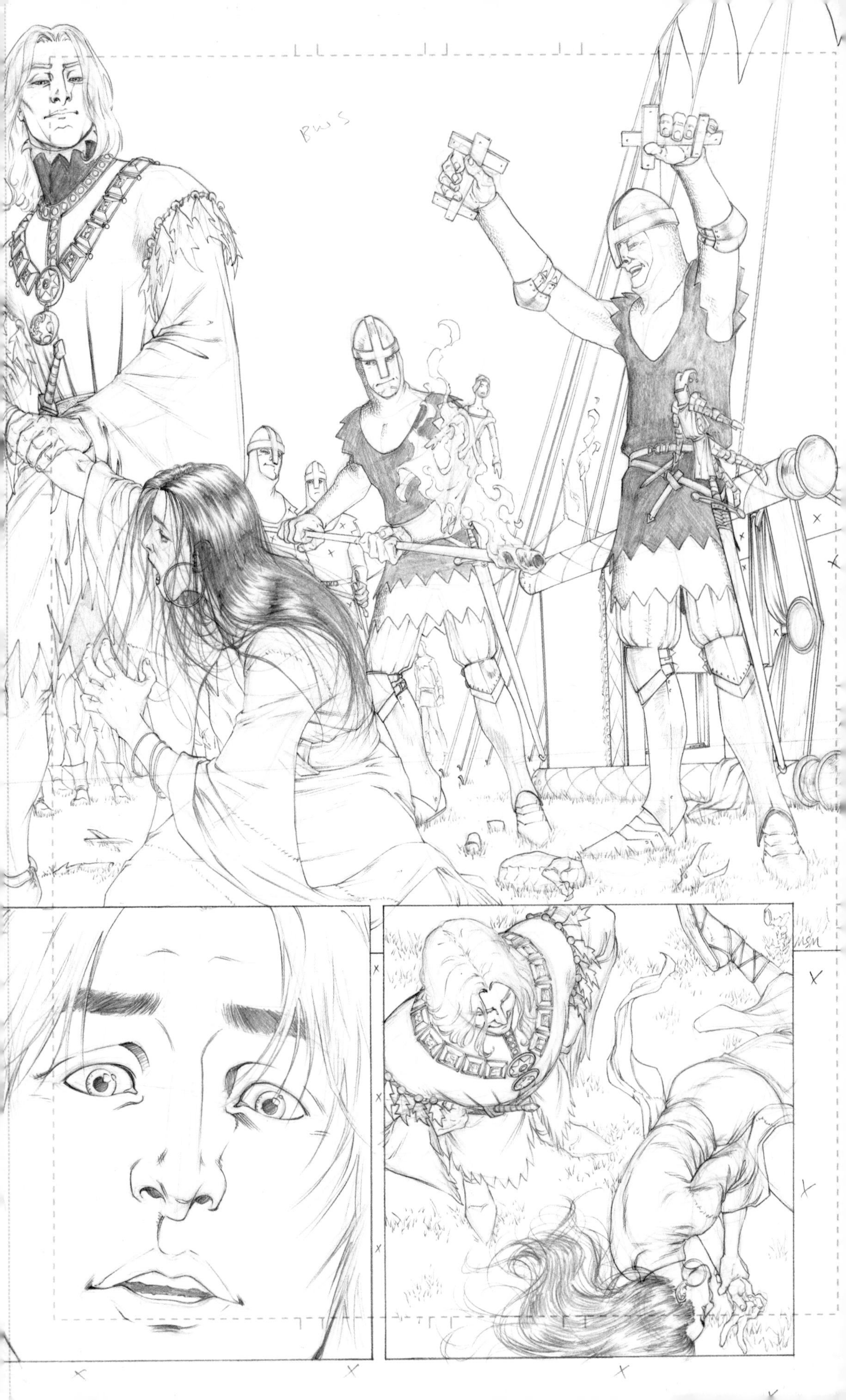

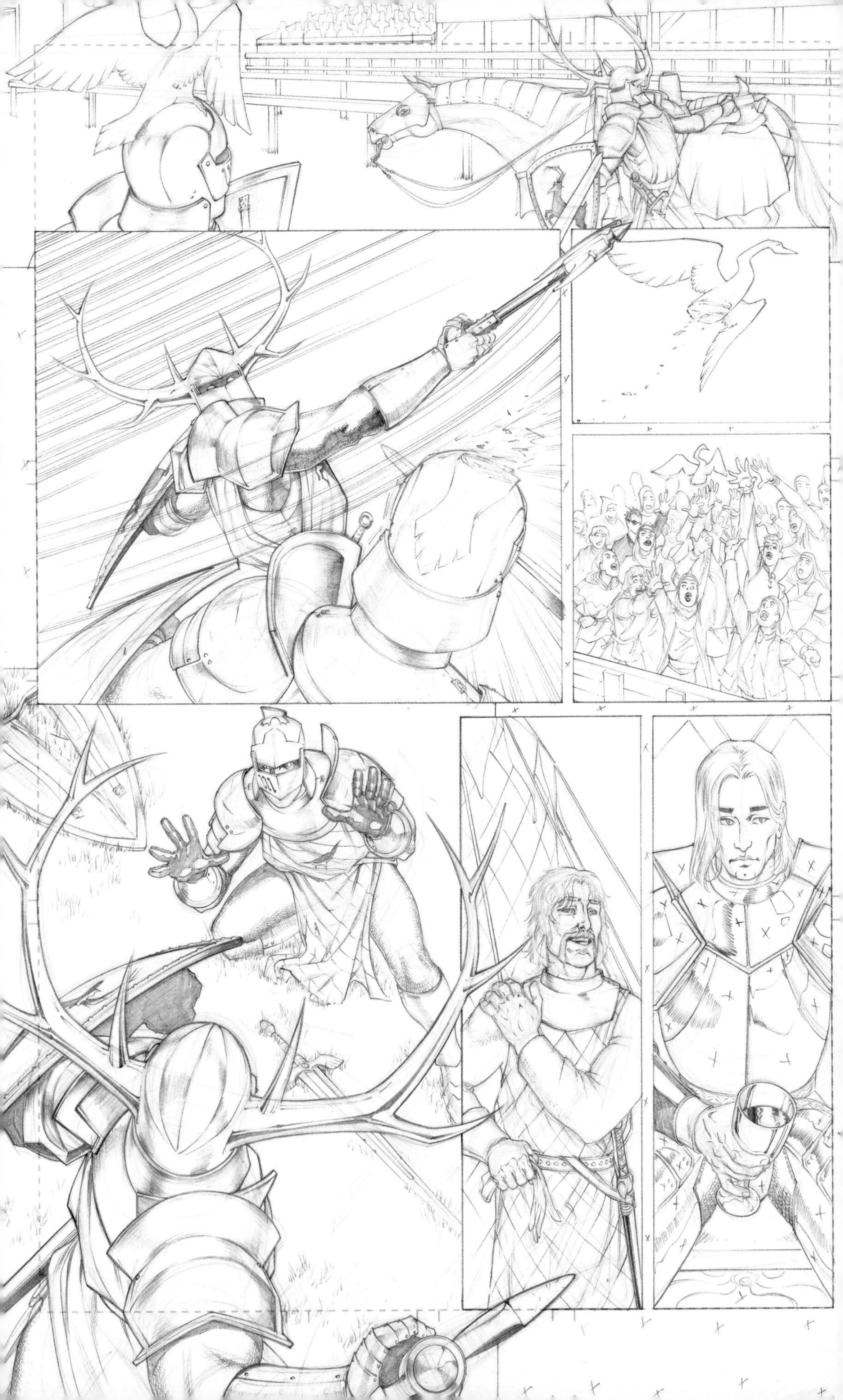

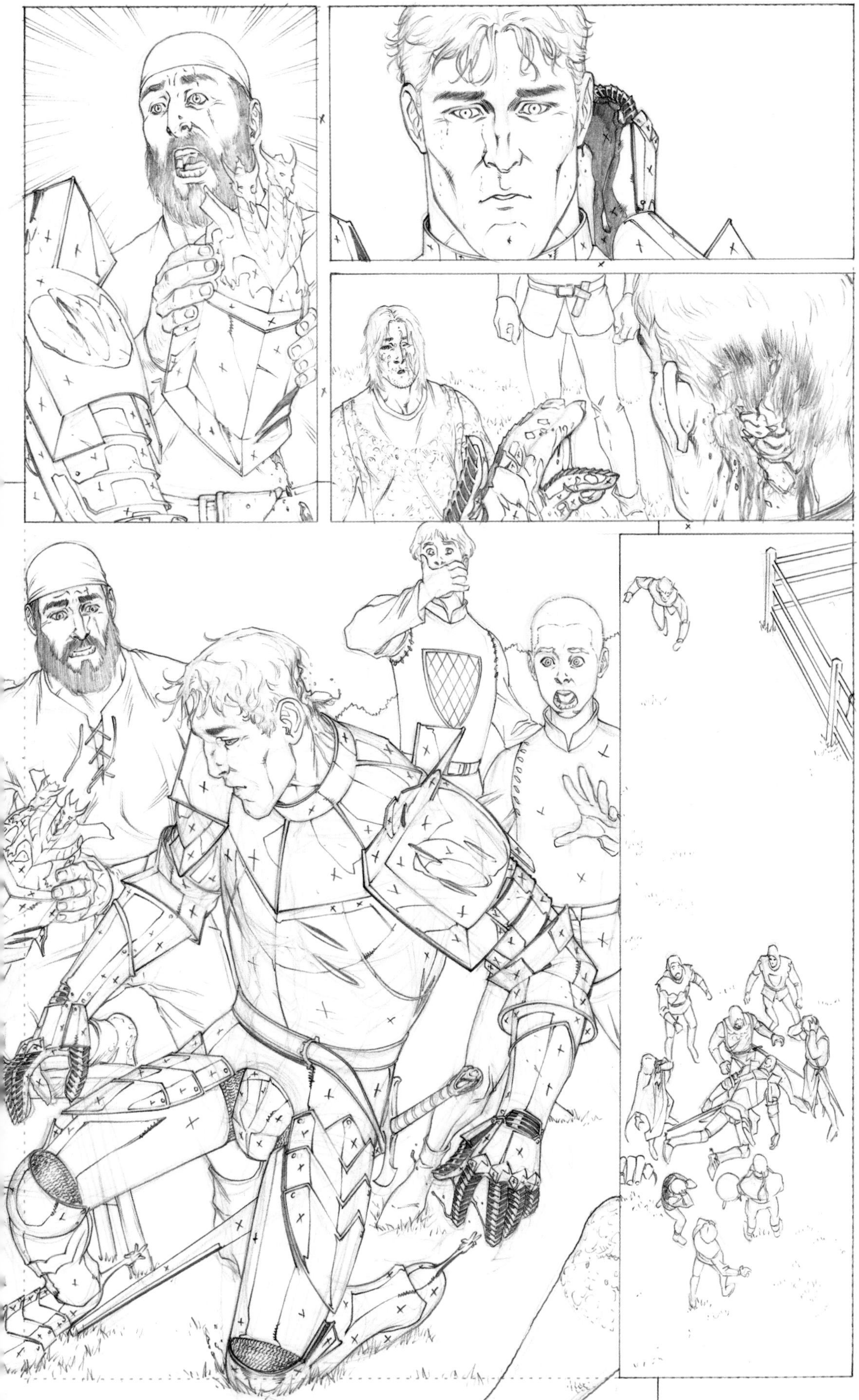

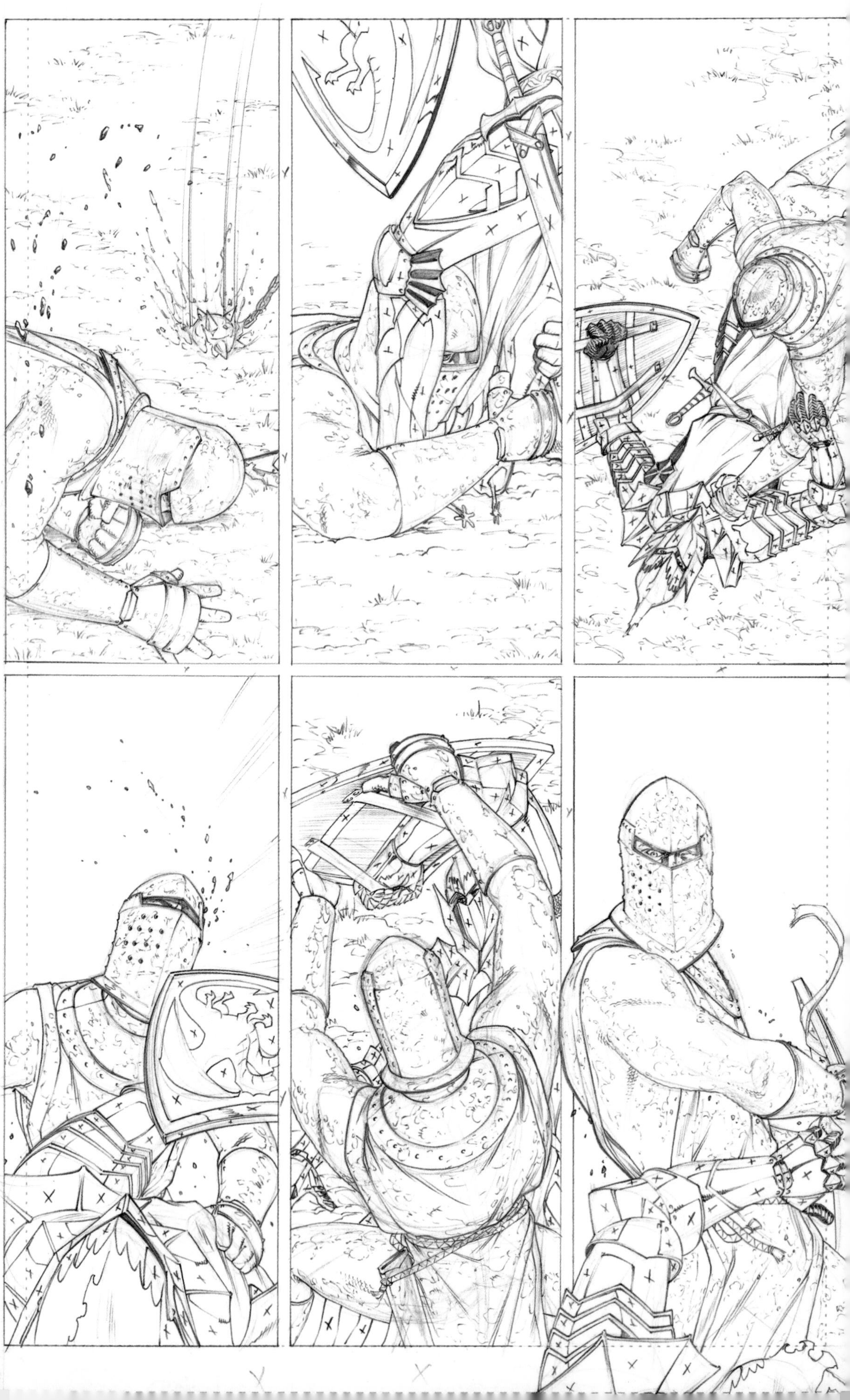

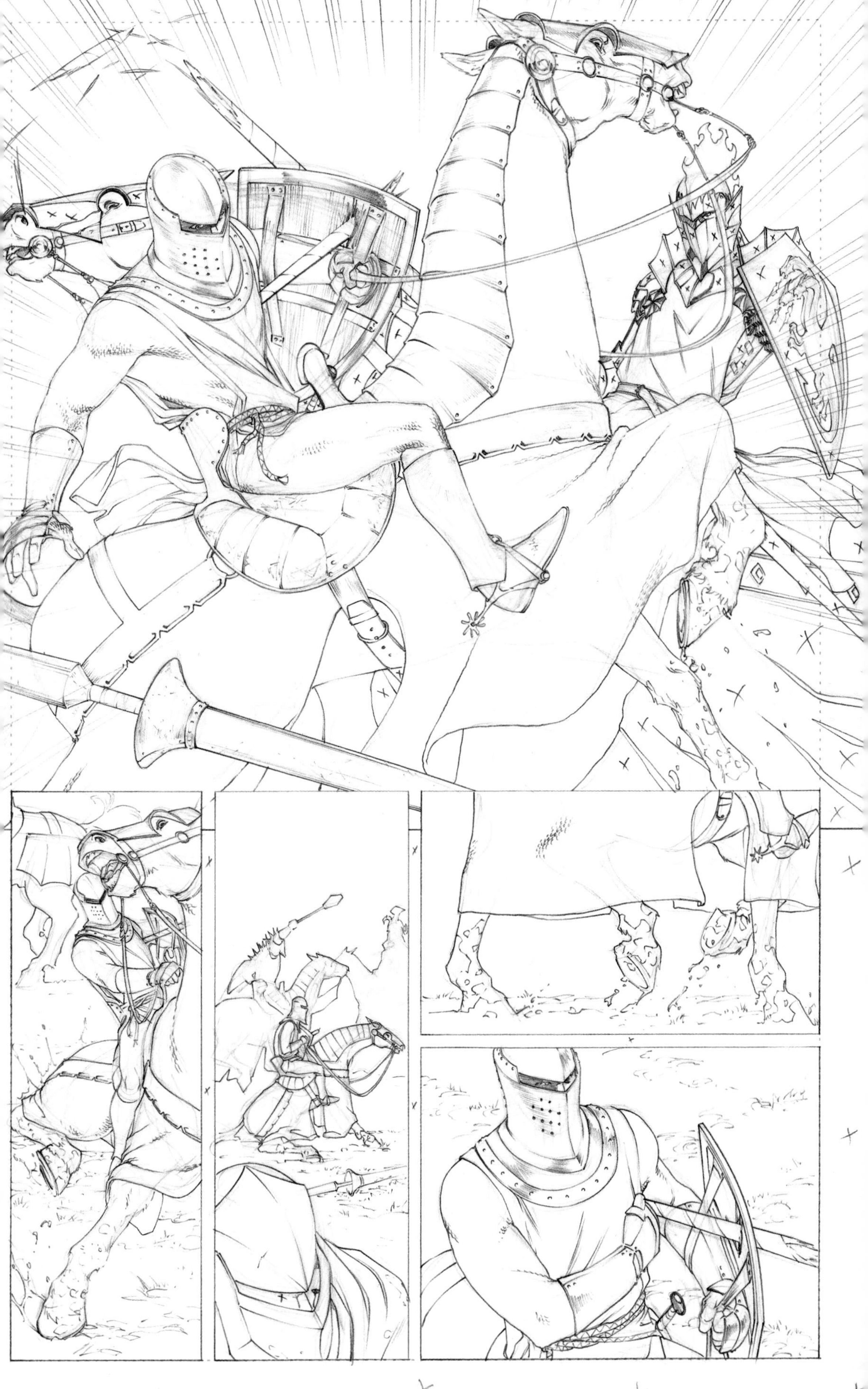

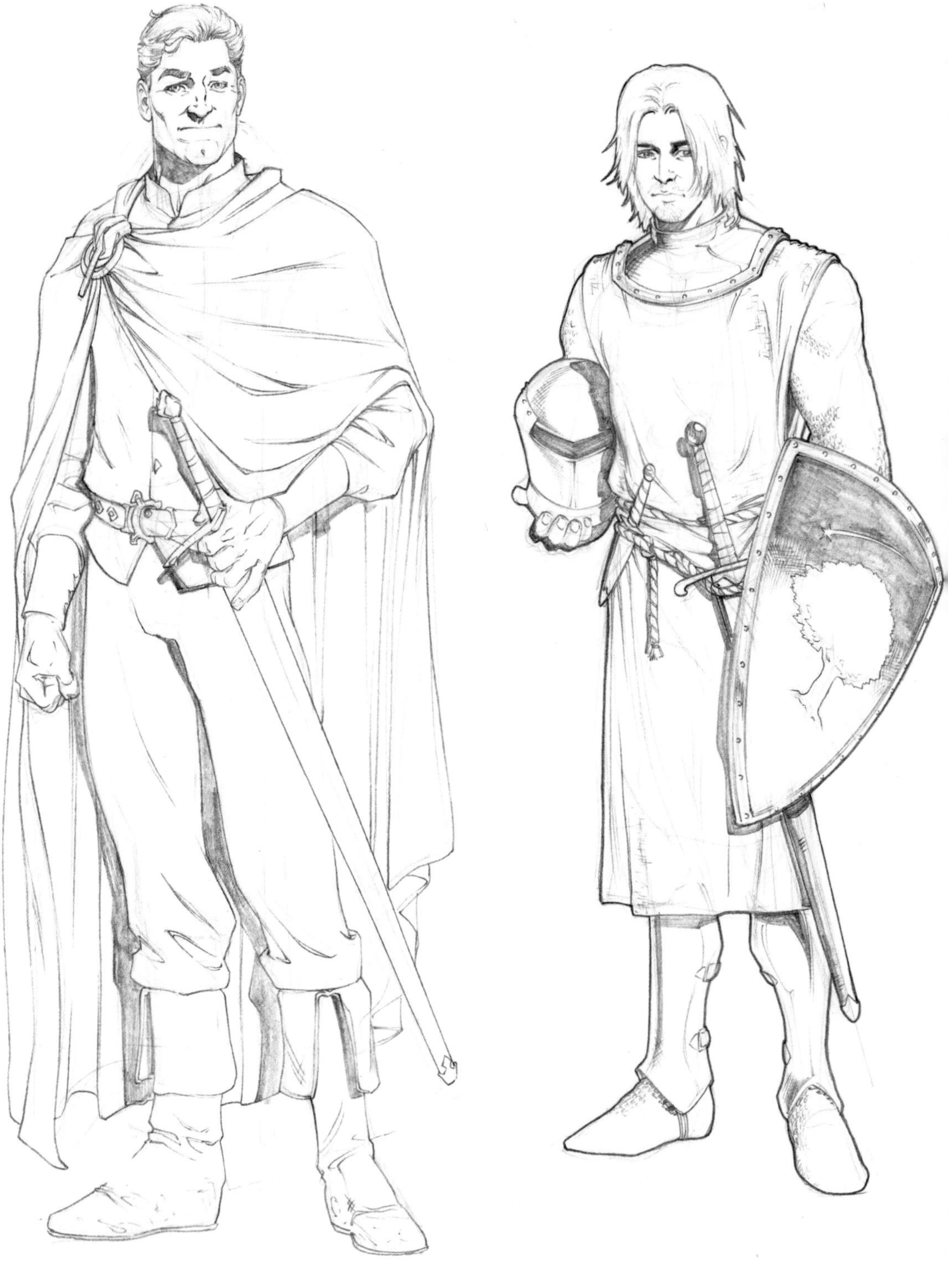

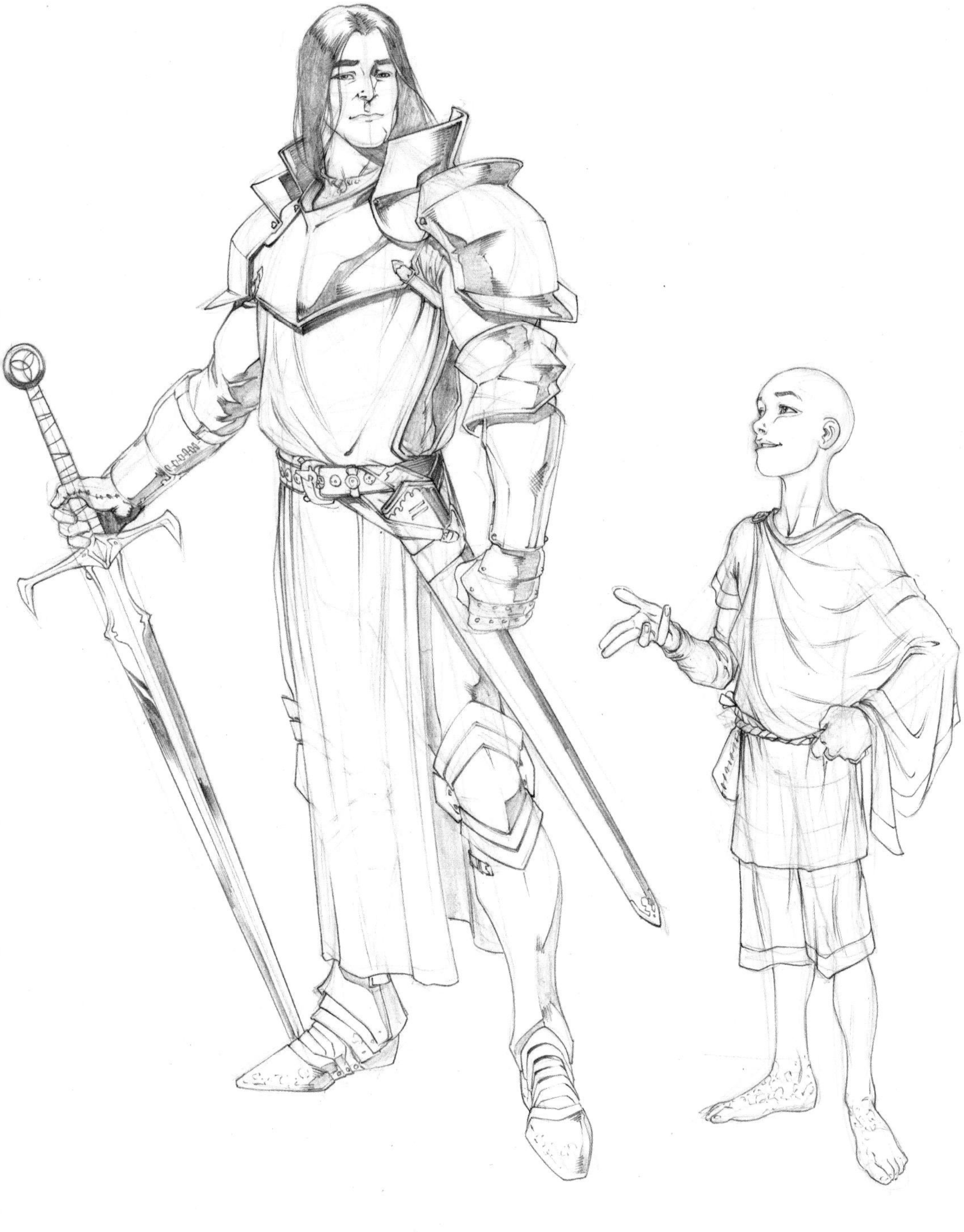

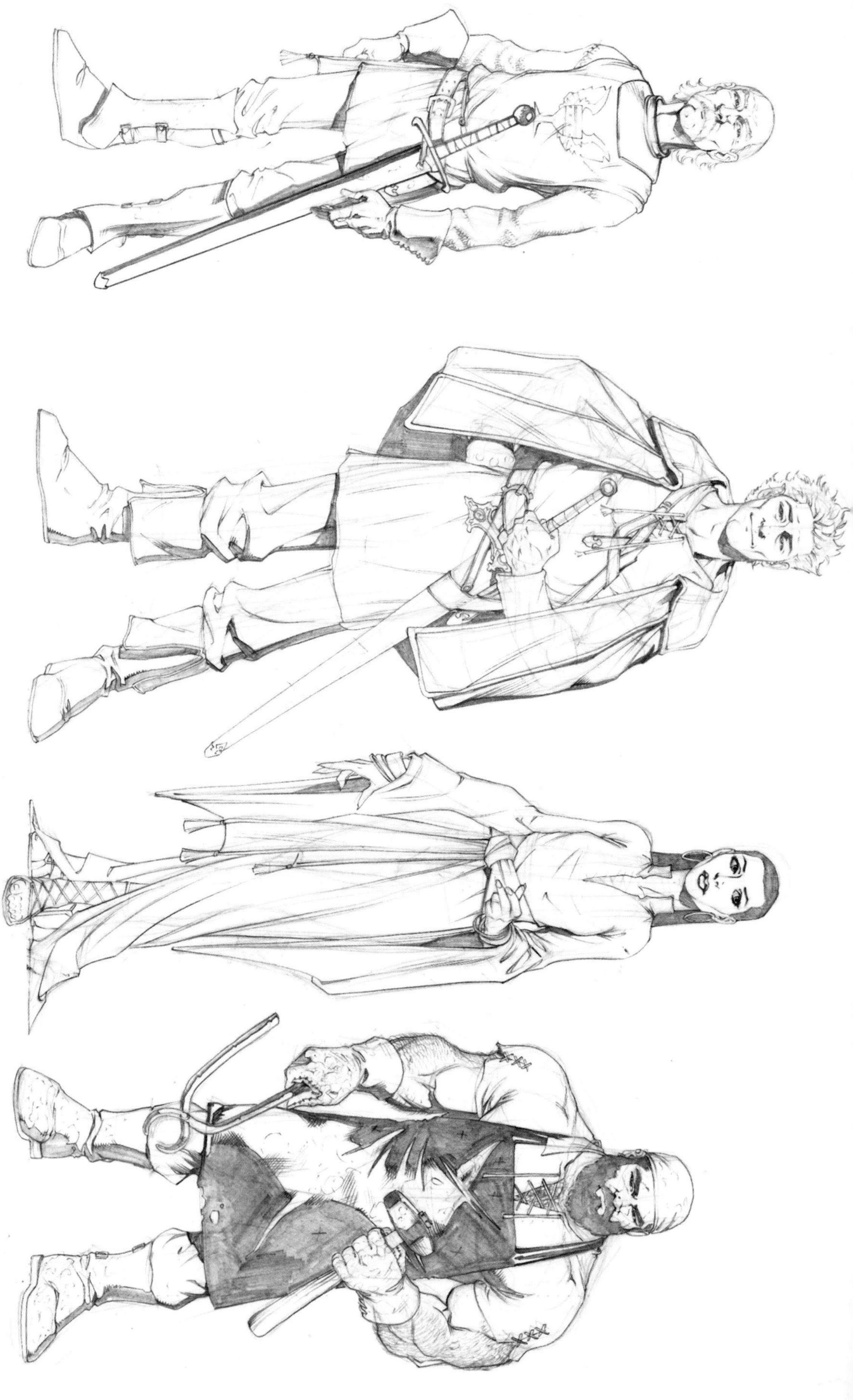

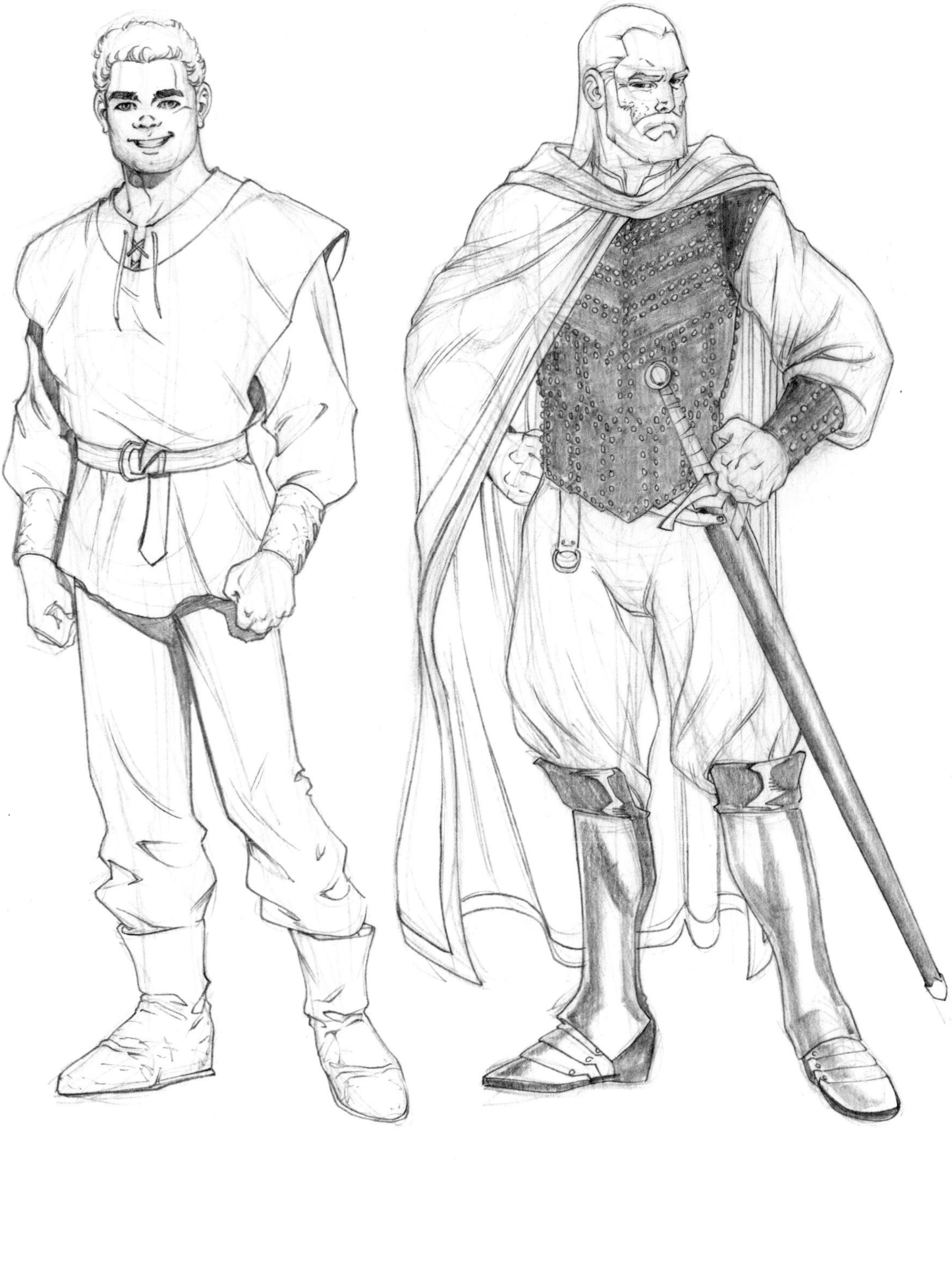

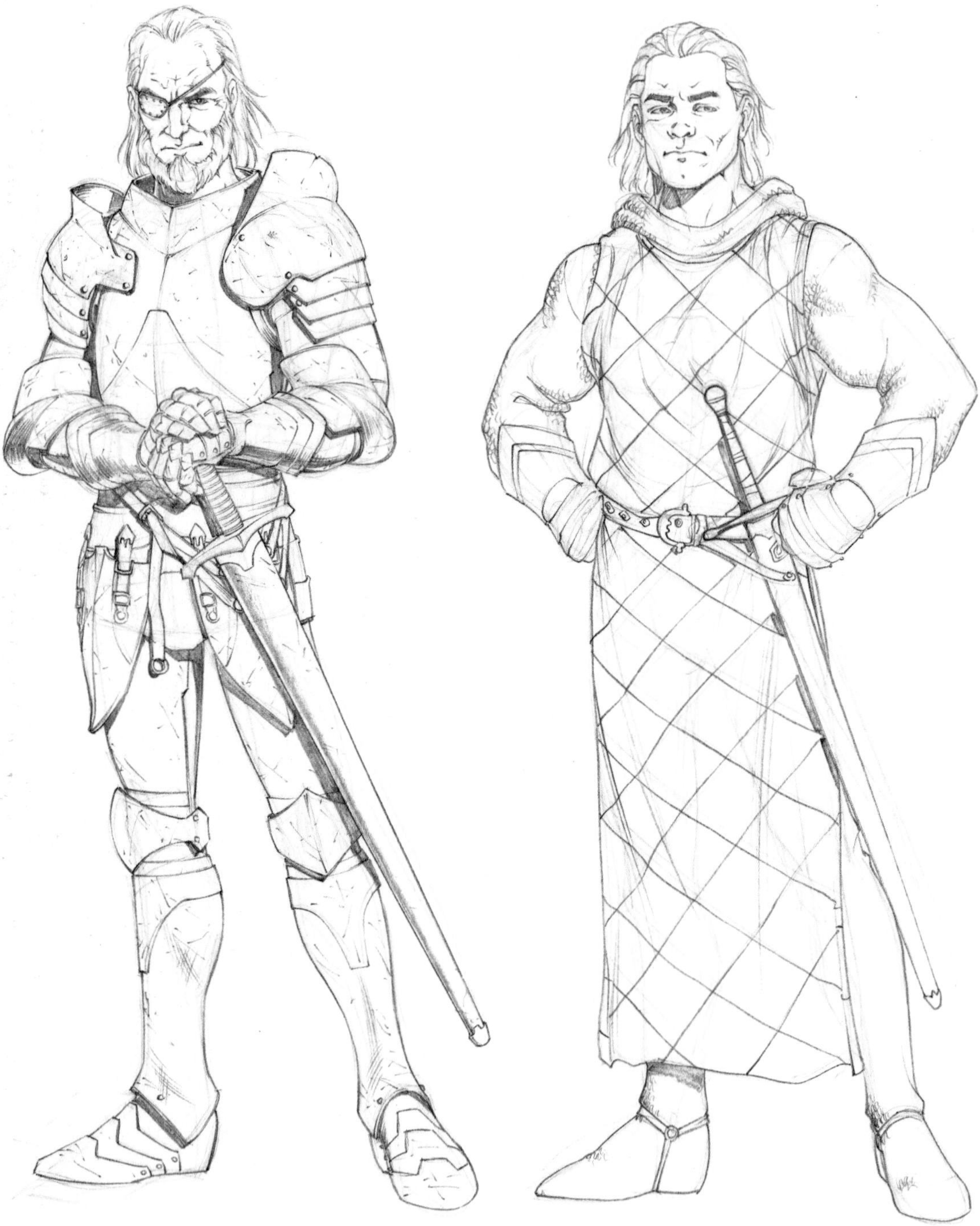

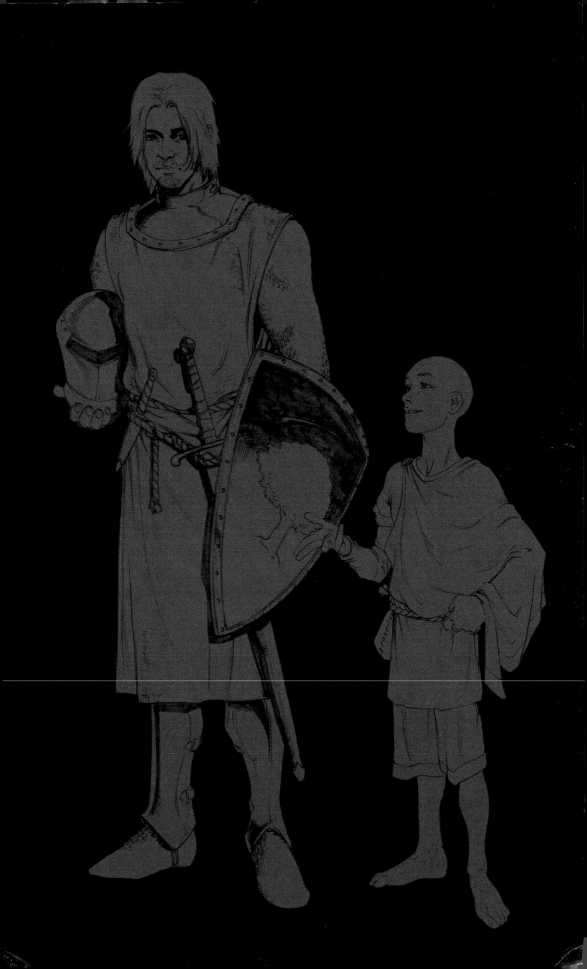

Ser Baelor Targaryen
Prince of Dragonstone

Ser Maekar Targaryen
Prince of Summerhall

Ser Valarr Targaryen
Heir of Dragonstone

Ser Daeron Targaryen
Heir of Summerhall

Ser Willem Wylde

Ser Donnel
of Duskendale

Ser Roland Crakehall

Ser Aerion Targaryen
Prince Royal

Ser Damon Lannister
Lord of Casterly Rock

Ser Leo Tyrell
Lord of Highgarden

Ser Medgar Tully
Lord of Riverrun

Ser Gawen Swann
Lord of Stonehelm

Ser Pearce Caron
Lord of the Marches

Ser Lyonel Baratheon
Heir of Storm's End

Ser Tybolt Lannister
Heir of Casterly Rock

Ser Androw Ashford
Heir of Ashford

Ser Robert Ashford

Ser Humfrey Hardyng